A TEXT BOOK OF
INTERNATIONAL LAW

A TEXT BOOK OF
INTERNATIONAL LAW

Kalinga Kumar Panda

ANMOL PUBLICATIONS PVT. LTD.
NEW DELHI-110 002 (INDIA)

ANMOL PUBLICATIONS PVT. LTD.
4374/4B, Ansari Road, Daryaganj
New Delhi - 110 002

A Text Book of International Law

First Edition, 1998

ISBN 81-261-0107-5

PRINTED IN INDIA

Published by J.L. Kumar for Anmol Publications Pvt. Ltd., New Delhi and Printed at Mehra Offset Press, Delhi.

Dedication

This book is dedicated to the sacred memory of my father, Late Kishore Chandra Panda, as a small token of my gratitude for what he had done for me to make me what I am today.

Kalinga

CONTENTS

Foreword xi

***PART-I* INTERNATIONAL LAW OF PEACE**

1. Definition, Scope, and Nature 1
Is international law, a law?

2. Sources of International Law 9

3. Condification 17

4 Relation between International Law and Municipal Law 23

5. Subjects of International Law 32
Sovereign States—Part-Sovereign States and Non-Sovereign States—International Organisations—Individuals.

6. Rights and Duties of Sovereign States 54
Intervention—Monroe Doctrine—Drago Doctrine.

7. Recognition of State and Government 69
Importance—Theories—Is it a Duty? Types—Withdrawal—Recognition of Government—Recognition of Insurgency and Belligerency Effects.

8. State Succession 87
Types—Consequences—

Government Succession.

9. State Territory 97
Importance—Types—Boundary Lines—
Different Parts—Rivers—
Inter Oceanic Canals—Internal
Waters—Air Space—Acquisition
and Lose of Territory.

10. Law of Seas 125
Historical Background—Geneva
Convention—U.N. Convention—
Territorial Sea and Contiguous Zone—
E.E.Z.—Continental Shelf—High Seas.

11. Outer Space

12. Jurisdiction 150
Meaning—Territorial—Personal—
Protective—Universal—Criminal—
Over Aliens—Principle of Double
Jeopardy—Extorritoriality.

13. Nationality 168
Importance—Acquisition and Loss—
Double Nationality—Statelessness.

14. Aliens 177
Admission—Status after Entry—
Expulsion—Asylum—Extradition.

15. Diplomatic Agents 191
Classification—Appointment—
Termination—Functions—Immunities.

16. Consular Relations 201

17. Treaties 206
Definition—Types—Capacity—Conclusion—Invalidity—Doctrine of Pacta Sunt Servanda—Interpretation—Revision—Suspension—Termination.

18. Settlement of International Disputes 222
Peaceful Settlement—Coersive or Compulsive Settlement.

PART-II **INTERNATIONAL LAWS OF WAR**

19. War 233
Attempts for Renunciation—Legal Nature—Types—Non-war Hostilities—Nature of Modern War—Conduct—Effects.

20. Enemy Character 248
Individuals—Ships—Cargoes—Corporations.

21. Laws of Land Warfare 252
Combatants and Noncombatants—Use of Rues and Weapons—Protection of Civilian Population—Prohibition of Wanton Destruction—Treatment of P.O.Ws—Care of Sick and Wounded—Relationship between Belligerents.

22. Belligerent Occupation 260

23. Laws of Naval Warfare 265
Privateering—Merchant ships—Enemy character—Exemption of Ships—Hospital ships—Naval Bombardment—Giving quarters—Sub-marine Warfare—Use of Mines—Postal Correspondences—Use of Ruses—Post-War Developments.

24. Laws of Aerial Warfare 272

25. Termination of War and Hostilities 275

26. War Crimes 278
Nuremburg Trial—Tokyo trial

PART-III LAWS OF NEUTRALITY

27. Neutrality 284
Meaning—Under League and U.N.O.—
Right and Duties—Unneutral Service.

28. Blockade 293
Meaning—Nature—Types—Requirements—
Violations—Termination.

29 Contraband 298
Meaning—Classification—Laws of
Seizure—Doctrine of Continuous Voyage.

PART-IV INTERNATIONAL ORGANISATIONS

30. International Organisation 303
Historical Background—United Nations
Organisation-General Assembly—Security
Council—ECOSOC—Trusteeship Council—
Secretariat—International Court of Justice.

FOREWORD

This book does not claim to be an original book or a treatise on International Law. This is a text book meant to be of use by the students of Honours and M.A. Classes.

This book is a modest attempt to present the various aspects of International Law and International Institutions so as to make it useful to the students from their examination point of view. I have tried to incorporate the latest developments in the field of International Law in the book.

I will consider my labour worthwhile if the students find the book useful.

I must thank my colleagues for their criticism and constructive suggestions in the preparation of this book. I am also thankful to my brother Kiran Kumar for his kind help in bringing the book to limelight.

K.K. Panda

1

DEFINITION, NATURE AND SCOPE OF INTERNATIONAL LAW

The term Public International Law or Law of Nations denotes all those rules and regulations which modern civilised states follow and which they feel legally bound to follow in their mutual relationships. The term International Law was first coined by Jeremy Bentham in 1780, though even now some writers still prefer to use the term Law of Nations. These rules of International Law not only regulate the mutual dealings of the states, but also maintain peace and order in the world and help in avoiding chaos, conflict and indiscipline in the international sphere.

(A) **Definition:** International Law has been defined by various writers. According to Oppenheim "Law of Nations or International Law is the name of the body of customary law and conventional rules which are considered legally binding by the civilised states in their intercourse with each other." Brierly defined it as "the body of rules and principles of action which are binding upon civilised states in their relation with one another." Lawrence defines it as "the rules which determine the conduct of the general body of civilised states in their mutual dealings." Schwarzenberger says "International law is a body of legal rules which apply between the sovereign states and such entities as have been granted international personality." According to Fenwick "International law may be defined in broad terms as the body of general principles and concrete rules which the states that are members of the community of nations recognise as binding upon themselves in their mutual relations." According to Svarlion "Public International law is that body of customs, rules and principles which are recognised as binding upon all states and other international persons in their mutual relations."

These definitions clearly indicate that international law is applicable only to the states. But states have formed several international organisations, specially since 1945, and these international organisations should also be regulated by a set of laws. Further, the recent trend of integration of states into political and economic unions also require regulation by laws. In the post-war period, the international community has shown increasing concern towards the individual and his rights. These emerging trends and development have necessitated a new definition of international law. Accordingly Prof. C.C. Hyde defines international law as that law concerned with "the conduct of states and of international organisations, and with their relations inter se, as well as some of their relations with persons, whether natural or personal." According to J.G. Starke "International law may be defined as that body of law which is composed for its greater part of the principles and rules of conduct which states feel themselves bound to observe, and therefore, do commonly observe in their relations with each other, and which includes also:

(a) the rules of law relating to the functioning of international institutions or organisations, their relation with each other, and their relation with states and individuals; and

(b) certain rules of law relating individuals and non-state entities so far as the rights and duties of such individuals and non-state entities are the concern of the international community."

(B) **Nature:** An analysis of the definitions show the

following nature of the international law:

(a) International law is a body of customary and conventional rules having legality;
(b) States consider these rules as binding upon them;
(c) these rules govern the relations and dealings between states;
(d) all civilised states follow these rules; and
(e) the basis of these rules is the consent or agreement of states to follow them and be bound by them.

(C) **Scope:** Originally the sovereign states alone were within the scope of international law. But during last five decades its scope has considerably been enlarged due to the following developments:

(a) the establishment of large number of international institutions like UNO, WHO, etc. possessing international legal personality and having power to enter into relation not only with each other but also with states;
(b) since the last war, the protection of human rights and fundamental freedoms of individuals as well as creation of new rules for the punishment of individuals for committing such crimes as crimes against peace, crimes against humanity and the conspiracy to commit these crimes, have brought the individual, who was outside its scope previously, within its purview;
(c) the growing internationalisation and consequent formation of larger political and economic unions among the states as well as the globalisation of economic activities have brought into existence such bodies as European Economic Community, Multinational Corporations etc. which require regulation by international law; and
(d) the increasing activities of states in space, outer space,

in the exploration of other celestial bodies and high seas require strict rules for orderly conduct of these activities for avoiding conflict between states.

Thus the scope of international law is an ever expanding concept and with growth of greater internationalism, its scope is bound to increase further.

(D) **Is International Law a Law?** A great controversy is going on the question whether International Law is a Law in the true sense of the term or just it is a "law by courtsey", "a positive international morality" "a Vanishing point of jurisprudence." While John Austin, Willoughby Holland and others do not consider it to be law, Oppenheim, Wheaton and others consider it to be law.

According to Austin, "The law obtaining between the nations is not a positive law, for, every positive law is set by a given sovereign to a persons or persons in a state of subjection to its author." In other words, a set of rules to regulate human conduct to be considered as positive law, must be given and enforced by a superior sovereign political authority. But International law is neither given nor enforced by a superior political authority over the sovereign States to regulate their conduct. Further, all sovereign States being equal, they would not recognise a common superior over them and if they recognise such a superior authority, they would not be considered as sovereign States. According to Austin the International Law is created by the opinion and consent of States and the duties under these laws are enforced by moral sanctions only, and there is no coersive authority to compel obedience of the states to these laws in case of their violation. Hence these rules can only be called "positive international morality" and not "Laws".

Holland, who supported Austin's proposition, said "Such rules as are voluntarily observed by every state in its dealings with the rest can be called law only by courtsey.... It differs from the ordinary law in being unsupported by the authority of a state. It differs from ordinary morality in being the rules for the states and not for the individuals. It is the vanishing point of jurisprudence, since it lacks the arbiter of a disputed question save public opinion, beyond and above the disputant parties.

So according to Holland, any rule in order to be treated as Law must be supported by coersive authority which, in case of municipal laws, the State possess. Further, in a system of laws, there should be an arbiter or judge to decide the disputes arising from that law whose decision should be binding on the parties to the dispute, and any system of law without such an arbiter cannot be called jurisprudence or law. So in view of such an interpretation of the term 'law' by Holland, International Law which is voluntarily and habitually obeyed by the States, cannot be called as Law in the true sense of the term because there is neither an authority to create the law nor there is an arbiter to decide the disputes, but can be called Law "only by courtesy".

On the other hand several prominent writers have advanced strong arguments not only to rebut the views of Austin and Holland, but also have tried to prove that International Law is a Law in true sense of the term.

The Historical School of Law led by Sir Henry Maine has pointed out that before the State came into being, people in the primitive communities obeyed certain laws eventhough they were created by the community and not by any superior sovereign authority through customs, usages and traditions. Further these customary rules were enforced by the community itself and not by any external sovereign authority exercising coersive authority. So if these customary rules which were neither created nor enforced by any sovereign authority can be called Law, International Law also deserves to be called as Law.

Starke has rightly pointed out that Austin's views however right during his times are not true of the modern international law. During last half century a large portion of international law have been created through international conventions and law-making treaties and the proportion of customary rules of international law has correspondingly decreased. These laws are now created through a well established procedure which may be described as "international legislation".

A system of law is meant for a group of subjects and if the subjects consider a set of rules as laws irrespective of the fact that they are not created by a sovereign authority, it is law for them. States who are subject of international law and their Foreign Offices which conduct their international relations, consider international law as Law.

In case of International disputes, States present their case or try to justify their action by quoting or interpreting international law and not on the grounds of rules of morality. Now a days a large number of disputes are submitted by the states to International Court of Justice or numerous Arbitration Courts who decide these disputes according to international law and these decisions are normally followed by the State parties.

A number of States like India, U.S.A. etc. have made provisions in their constitutions through which international laws are made part of their own municipal laws and as such binding on their governments and officials.

The Charter of the U.N.O. also recognises the legal character of international law and states, in order to become members of the U.N.O., will have to accept not only the Charter but also legal nature of international law and be bound by them.

Till recently, international public opinion was the only

sanction behind the international law and in the absence of a recognised political authority, this public opinion compelled a state violating the laws to obey them. But of late, the U.N.O. in general and the Security Council in particular is gradually emerging as the enforcing authority of international law by applying economic sanctions and if necessary, by using force as in case of Iraq's attack on Kuwait.

Finally, according to Oppenheim, law is "a set of rules of human conduct within a community which by common consent of this community shall be enforced by external power." In other words, there are three essential conditions of law, namely, a community, a body of rules within that community to regulate the human conduct, and common consent of the community that these rules be enforced by an external power. Accordingly, the states of the world have formed an international community and have become interdependent due to close relationship developed among them because of rapid development of science, technology and communication. To regulate their conduct, by common consent, they have created a body of rules either through customs or through treaties, which they all agree to obey and be enforced.

Thus, now there is no doubt that international law is a law, yet, the means available for enforcement of these laws are definitely weaker and this weakness becomes conspicuous during the war when those rules are frequently violated. But Oppenheim argues, "a weak law is nevertheless still law." Though states sometimes violate the international law, particularly during war, yet such states never deny its existence; rather such states try to interprete the law in such a way as to justify their action.

However, international law still suffers from the following defects:

(a) these laws are uncertain and unsettled on many points;

(b) these laws are spread over in innumerable customs, treaties, resolutions of conferences and documents of various foreign offices, that they sometimes become obscure.

(c) the international legislative machinery through which now international laws are made cannot be compared with the state legislative machinery;

(d) there is no central authority comparable to the executive in a state that exists in international sphere to enforce these laws;

(e) though there is International Court of Justice, yet it has no compulsory jurisdiction to settle all inter-state disputes.

2

SOURCES OF INTERNATIONAL LAW

The term 'sources of law' ordinarily means the methods of creation of general and permanent legal rules which are capable of repeated and unlimited application. Both, Lawrence and Oppenheim are of the opinion that, so far international law is concerned, there is only one source, namely, the consent of States. This consent of the States may be either express as in case of treaties or tacit as incase of customs which the states habitually follow without declaring their acceptance in words. But Brierly and Westlake are of the opinion that customs and reason are the two sources of international law.

An authoritative list of sources of international law is given by the Art. 38 (1) of the Statute of International Court of Justice which states:

"The Court whose function is to decide in accordance with international law such disputes as are submitted to it, shall apply:

(i) international conventions, whether general or particular, establishing rules expressly recognised by the contesting States;

(ii) international custom as evidence of general practice accepted as law;

(iii) the general principle of law recognised by civilised nations;

(iv) subject to the provision of Art. 59, judicial decisions and the teachings of the most highly qualified publicists of the various nations, as a subsidiary means for determination of rules of law."

Some writers have criticised the above list on the ground that it does not include all the sources of international law, while others criticised it that it includes things which are not genuine sources. Since none of the alternative lists suggested has won general approval, the sources mentioned in Art. 38 (1) should be treated as the authentic list of sources of international law.

(i) Treaties

The Statute directs the Court to apply international conventions or treaties, whether general or particular, recognised by the State parties to a dispute. The International Law Commission has defined a treaty as "any international agreement which is entered into by two or more states or other international persons and is governed by international law." Treaties may be bilateral or multilateral as well as law-making and treaty contracts. All treaties are binding on the state parties because of the principle "pacta sunt servanda," which means that treaties are binding and must be observed. Today, the relation of a state with other states cover a wide variety of situations such as political, economic, military, commercial, financial, technical, cultural etc. Thus the international relations in these fields are now conducted through treaties which may be bilateral or multilateral. But majority of these treaties are called "treaty contracts" and they are not treated as a source of international law. Only the law-making treaties are treated as a source. According to Brierly, the law-making treaties are "those which a large number of states have concluded for the purpose of either declaring their understanding of what the law is on a particular subject, or of laying down a general rule for future conduct, or of creating some international institutions." A law-making treaty according to Brownlie, is one which "creates general norms for future conduct of the parties... and the obligations are basically same for all parties." Though all law-making treaties are multilateral, all multilateral treaties are not making treaties and are not sources of international law.

Some multilateral or even bilateral treaties can become a source of international law in course of time when these are accepted by other states either expressly or tacitly. Further, some multilateral treaties to which Big Powers are signatories can become a source of international law if the Big Powers exert their influence and pull their weight on less powerful states in favour of accepting the treaty.

(ii) International Customs

Custom is an ancient and original source of law in general and international law in particular. Until recently, international law consisted mostly of customary rules. The customary rules had been evolved after a historical process and ultimately accepted by the states. The importance of the customary rules in international law was reduced due to the conclusion of large number of treaties and the various attempts for their codification. Inspite of these attempts, custom still occupies a very important position in International Law.

A custom is described as a practice which has grown up among states and which is followed by the states habitually and continuously, so that after some times it becomes obligatory and binding on them. Thus "Custom is that line of conduct which the society has consented to regard as obligatory."

Sometimes the terms "custom" and "usage" are used interchangeably. But many eminent writers are of the opinion that there is a clear technical distinction between them. According to Oppenheim a custom is "a clear and continuous habit of doing certain actions" which "has grown up under the aegis of the conviction that these actions are, according to international law, obligatory or right." On the other hand, according to him, a usage is "a habit of doing certain actions" which "has grown up without there being the conviction that these actions are, according to international law, obligatory or right." According to Brownlie "A usage is a general practice which does not reflect a legal obligation." Starke who has made a clear technical distinction between the two, says "Usage represents the twilight stage of custom. Custom begins where usage ends. Usage is an international habit of action that has not yet received full legal attestation. Usages may be conflicting, custom must be unified and self-consistent."

Customary law is essentially fluid. It has a built-in mechanism for change and states create or destroy a customary law by observing or violating it. A customary law need not take much time to evolve and can be created as and when required. Sir G.G. Fitzmaurice rightly remarks "a new rule of customary international law based on the practice of states can emerge very quickly and even suddenly." Thus the law relating to outer space could be developed very quickly after the first satellite was sent up.

Sometimes a distinction is made between General customs and Local or Regional customs. According to Michel Virally, "General customs are those which apply to the totality of states in the international community. They arise from practice which are also general in the sense that they are followed by a great number of states." On the other hand Regional or local customs are those which are followed only by a group of states, such as Latin American customs and customs that prevail among Commonwealth of nations.

When in a case before International Court of Justice a State party invokes a customary rule of international law, it has to prove that the other state party has also followed the same rule. The evidence of the proof can be found in papers relating to diplomatic relations with other states, declaration of Statesmen, opinion of legal advisor to government, bilateral treaties signed with other states, newspaper reports, official statements in legislature, and in international conferences, in the municipal laws and judicial decisions, and in official books and documents of the other state party.

(iii) General Principle of Law

It is a fact that the treaties and customs do not cover all cases that may arise under the international law. So in order to provide solution to cases where treaties and customs provide no rules, and for the fear that the Court might not be able decide some cases because of gaps in treaty and customary laws, the Statute has provided the source of "General principle of law recognised by the civilised nations".

Since the international law is developed much later than the municipal law, it is obvious that such "general principles" can only be borrowed from the municipal legal systems of the civilised world. In order to locate such general principles, it would be necessary to have a comparative study of all municipal legal systems. In practice, however, the judges of the International Court of Justice, who, according to Art. 9 of the Statute, are elected so as to ensure "the representation of the main forms of civilisation and the principal legal systems of the world", can find such "general principles" among themselves. In other words, anything which all the Judges of the Court are prepared to accept as a "general principle" must have been "recognised by civilised nations".

In fact several general principles like res judicata, estoppel, no one may be a judge in his case etc. have been incorporated into international law by borrowing them from municipal legal systems of the civilised nations.

(iv) Judicial Decisions

Art. 38 (1) recommends the judicial decisions and teachings of the most qualified publicists of various countries as a subsidiary means "for determination of rules of law". In other words, the judicial decisions of international courts in previous cases and the juristic works by eminent writers in international law are not the principal but subsidiary sources in order to find out what the relevant rules of international law are for a particular case before the international court.

But Art. 59 of the Statute states that the decisions of international court shall have "no binding force except between parties and in respect of that particular case." This provision appears to be contradictory to Art. 38 (1). Since, every judgement contains (a) rules of law relating to the case, (b) analysis of the evidence and reasoning by the judge, and (c) decision, which is the operative part of the judgement, the intention of Art. 59 is to prohibit the Court not to apply the "decision" part of the judgement to other similar cases. But the international court is free to refer to the previous judgements in order to find out the relevant rules of international law as well as the reasoning and analysis while dealing with a similar case.

The decisions of international arbitral courts such as Permanent Court of Arbitration and the various Mixed Claims Tribunals etc. have contributed to the development of international law relating to territorial sovereignty, neutrality, jurisdiction of states, state servitude etc. However, some writers do not accept the arbitral decisions as a source of law because according to them, these decisions are based more on 'compromise' than on strict following of judicial procedure. But judge J.B. Moore has rightly observed, "I have failed to discover for the supposition that international arbitrators have shown a special tendency to compromise, or that they have failed to apply legal principles, or give weight to legal precedents."

During war, the belligerent states set up Prize Courts to determine the status and validity of the capture of various ships and their cargoes by their own war ships. The Prize Courts, which are set up by the law of the legislature of the belligerent state, decide the cases according to the international law, though they are also bound by the laws of their own state. So such Prize Courts cannot strictly administer international law in deciding cases before them. But decisions of certain Prize Courts, presided by judges whose knowledge, impartiality and integrity is not in doubt, contributed to the development of international law. Thus Lord Stowell, who presided over the British Prize Court during the Napoleonic war, established certain important doctrines such as blockade to be binding must be effective, and the doctrine of continuous voyage etc. which now have become part of international law.

The second subsidiary source prescribed by Art. 38 (1) is the teaching of most highly qualified juristic writers like Victoria, Grotius, Vattel, Gentilis, Kent and others. For a long time, it was difficult to know international law because of their uncertainty and ineffectualness. Further, the people who knew them were also limited. So for a long time, the works of those writers who had devoted to this branch of law become not only important but also the only source of law.

Even today, international law still remains difficult to discover and interprete in many matters. So the writings of eminent jurists not only provide evidentiary value of existence of rules of international law but also help in its development through their considered suggestions where no law exists. The importance of writings of juristic writers is summed up by justice Gray of U.S. Supreme Court; "where there is no treaty, and no controlling executive or legislative act or judicial decision, resort must be had to be customs and usages of the civilised nations, and as evidence of these, to the works of jurists and commentators who by years of labour, research and experience have made themselves peculiarly well acquainted with the subjects of which they treat. Such works are resorted to by the judicial tribunals, not for the speculations of their authors concerning what the law ought to be, but for trustworthy evidence of what the law really is."

The Order of the Sources

The International Court of Justice in order to ascertain the law on a given matter has to follow the order of sources mentioned in Art. 38 (1). Normally, the Court give priority to treaties and conventions expressly recognised by the concerned states; if there is no treaty or convention applicable, laws derived from customary rules will be applied and if there is also no customary rules, the general principle of law recognised by the civilised states will have to be applied. If none of the three principal sources provide the law, the judicial and arbitral decisions, and opinion of eminent jurists shall have to be considered, of course, giving more weight to the judicial decisions than to the juristic opinions.

In addition to the list of sources included in Art. 38 (1) of the Statute, some writers suggest other sources of international law. Oppenheim is of the opinion that international comity also produce binding rules. International comity is defined as the rules of politeness, convenience, and goodwill. Many of the earlier rules of international comity has now become parts of international law. Some writers consider the international organisation, particularly, U.N.O. and its various organs indirectly contribute to the development of international law by interpreting the existing rules and by encouraging better understanding through debates in the General Assembly which may lead to a possible agreement in future. Similarly, some writers suggest that the expert opinions stored in the archives of foreign affairs department of every state, the proceedings of various international conferences, declaration of statesmen, opinion of legal advisors to government of states, and instructions given by the government of States to their officials regarding conduct of international relations etc. can be possible sources of international law.

3

CODIFICATION

Codification is a process in which the statutes, conventions, customary laws and rules created through judicial pronouncements are created and arranged in order to avoid inconsistency and overlapping. The importance of codification of International Law is greater because bulk of customary rules are in the form of customary law causing inconsistency and controversy.

According to Oppenheim the codification of International Law has two meanings: "(1) the act or process of translating into statutes or conventions, customary law and rules arising from the decisions of tribunals with little or no alternation; (2) the process of securing agreement among states by reconciling their conflicting views on certain conventional or customary laws by modifying them." According to Fenwick it means: (1) an attempt to state in a systematic form the rules actually in force between the states; (2) compilation of the rules in force modified by such amendments according to the need of the times, and (3) complete reconstruction of the existing law according to the new principles.

Advantages: The following are the advantages of codification of International Law:

(1) International Law being uncertain and obscure, codification will make them definite, clear, and help the states to refer them without much difficulty.

(2) It will bring unity and uniformity in the absence of which different opinions may be held on the same question.

(3) It wil' help the judges of international courts and tribunals to refer the concerned law while deciding cases before them.

(4) The number of gaps that are found in the law can be bridged by the judges through their pronouncements and by the eminent jurists through their commentaries and writings, there by making the law full and complete.

(5) The disagreement, controversy, and confusion that prevails on many matters of law would disappear once laws on them are codified.

(6) The customary laws being by nature very time consuming, cannot keep pace with the changing times and needs. On the other hand, codified laws can easily be amended according to the needs of time and situations.

(7) Codification will increase the binding force of International Law and will enable the states either to follow them or submit the matter to the International Court for their interpretation.

Disadvantages: The following are the disadvantages of codification:

(1) The natural growth of customary law is based on the wisdom and rich experience of ages is obstructed if the laws are codified.

(2) Codification makes the laws rigid and inadoptable, thereby creating new and fresh controversies.

(3) States usually prefer a solution based on their political necessity, national interest, and compromise. But a judicial decision according to the codified law do not always confirm

to the political realities.

(4) Codification leads to strict adherence to the letter than to the spirit of law and leads to hair splitting interpretation of these codified laws, creating more controversies.

(5) Codification makes the law not only rigid but also inadaptible as a result of which many cases may not be covered by the codified laws.

On the whole, the advantages of codification outweighs the disadvantages which can be rectified by systematic and planned arrangement of the laws.

History of Codification

The idea of codification of International Law was first conceived by Jeremy Bentham in the late 18th century. The first effort for codification was made by the National Convention of France in 1792 to proclaim the Rights of Nations, which was unfortunately rejected by the convention. But real codification was started with the Declaration of Paris, 1856, which was signed by several European states at the end of Crimean War.

The Declaration laid down the following principles:

(a) Privateering is and remains abolished;
(b) Neutral flags covers enemy goods with the exception of contraband;
(c) Neutral goods under enemy flag are not liable for capture except the contrabands of war;
(d) Blockade in order to be real and binding must be effective.

Several writers like Prof. Francis, Liber, Bluntschli, Dudley Field and Duplexis and others attempted to codify the International Law.

At the initiative of Emperor Nicholas II of Russia, the Hauge Conference of 1899, produced two codes namely, the Convention for Pacific settlement of International Disputes, and the Convention with Respect to the Laws and Customs of War on Land. The Second Hague Conference in 1907 not only revised the rules of War on Land, but also produced a number of codes, relating to neutrality in war on land and sea, the status of merchantman at the outbreak of hostilities, conversion of merchantmen into men of war, bombardment by naval forces and laying of automatic submarine contact mines etc.

Codification Under League

After League of Nations came into existance it appointed a committee of 16 jurists in 1924 to report on codification. The committee submitted its report in 1927 in which it listed the topics ripe for codification. After considering the report of the committee, the League convened a conference at the Hague in 1930 to codify three topics, namely Nationality, Territorial Waters, and Responsibility of States for damages done on its territory to the person or property of foreigners. The Conference produced three codes namely, (1) Convention of certain questions relating to conflict of Nationality Laws, (2) A Protocol relating to military obligations in certain cases of Double Nationality and relating to certain cases of statelessness. In addition, a number of codes were also produced under the auspices of League namely, a code of Air Warfare rules, a protocol prohibiting the use in War of asphyxiating, poisonous or other gases, a convention on the treatment of the sick and wounded prisoners of war, a convention concerning air navigation etc.

Codification Under UNO: The process of codification received a fillip after establishment of UNO, Art 13 (1) of the UN Charter directs the General Assembly to initiate studies and make recommendation for the purpose of "encouraging the progressive development of International law and its codification". Accordingly, the General Assembly through a resolution in 1947 decided to setup the International Law Commission and entrust it with the task of selecting topics of International Law ripe for codification and making recommendation on them. The Commission was constituted in 1949 and since then it is engaged in the task of codification. The commission while submitting its recommendation to General Assembly for codification of a topic in the draft form must also submit a commentary containing:

(a) all available precedents including treaties, judicial decisions and doctrines relating to the topic, and
(b) a conclusion relating to the extent of agreement as well as points of disagreements in the practices of states.

To start with, the General Assembly referred to the commission the following topics for codification:

(a) the rights and duties of the state,
(b) the laws as established by Nuremburg Trial,
(c) the International criminal jurisdiction.

In addition, the commission in its first session also prepared a list of following 14 topics which were ripe for codification, namely (1) Recognition of states (2) Succession of states (3) Immunities of the states and their properties (4) Jurisdiction of states over crimes committed abroad (5) Regime of High Seas (6) Regime of Territorial Waters (7) Nationality (8) Treatment of aliens (9) Right of Asylum (10) Law of Treaties (11) Arbitral Procedure (12) State responsibility (13) Diplomatic Immunities and (14) Consular Immunities.

Since its inception in 1949, the Commission has succeeded in the codification of a number of laws, the important of which are:

(1) Rights and duties of states
(2) International Penal Law as per Nuremburg Trial
(3) Offence against Peace and Security of Mankind
(4) Nationality including statelessness
(5) Right of Refugees
(6) Definition of agression
(7) Regime of High Sea
(8) Regime of Laws relating to Outer Space
(9) Vienna Convention on Diplomatic Relation
(10) Vienna Convention on Consular Relation
(11) Vienna Convention Law of Treaties.

Even today the codification of several topics are in progress and it is hoped that the declared purpose of UN Charter regarding codification and progressive development of International Law will be achieved in near future.

4

RELATION OF INTERNATIONAL LAW WITH MUNICIPAL LAW

Many a times the courts of various states have to deal with cases under international law. Very often these municipal courts find their own municipal law coming in conflict with the international law or a treaty. In such cases of conflict the primacy of one law over the other may arise. So it is very essential to understand the status of international law in relation to the municipal law. Starke has rightly said," Nothing is more essential to a proper grasp of the subject of international law than a clear understanding of its relation with sate law."

The relationship between the two laws can be explained through theories as well as practices of various states. There are two principal theories, namely, Monism and Dualism. While the Monistic theory states that both international and municipal laws are parts of a single legal system, Dualists argue that they represent two entirely different and distinct legal systems.

Monistic Theory

Monists argue that all laws being binding rules, these rules are binding either on states or on individuals. Though international laws are applicable to states, the states, after all, are groups of individuals organised for law. While municipal laws are applicable to individuals, the international law is applicable to individuals in their corporate capacity. In other words, both the laws are same.

Secondly, they argue that both the laws are derived from the same source, namely, the principle of right and wrong. Thus many legal principles like the principle of equality, the principles of succession etc. are common to both the laws. Since the source of both these laws is same, the Monists argue that both the laws can be treated as parts of the same system.

Thirdly, they argue that the nature of both the laws is same, as they are binding on their subjects independently of their will.

Lastly, they point out that normally conflict between the two laws do not occur and whenever such conflicts arise, the states are always willing to change their laws in accordance with the international law.

So they conclude that both the laws may be treated as two phases of a single legal system binding on all human beings either collectively or individually.

Dualistic Theory

The chief exponent of dualism are Triepel and Anzilotti, who are also positivist writers. According to Triepel there are two fundamental differences between the two legal systems, namely, the subjects are different and the origin of both the laws are different. Schwazenberger says," in the dualist view the systems of international law and municipal law are separate and self contained to the extent to which rules of one cannot expressly or tacitly received into the other system."

According to the dualists, the sources of both the laws are different. While the source of municipal law is the constitution, statutes passed by their legislature and the customs grown up with in their boundaries, the sources of international law are treaties and customs grown up among the states.

Secondly, they argue that the nature of both the laws is different. While municipal law regulates the relation between the individual and state as well as among the individuals, the international law regulates the relation between the states.

Thirdly, both the laws differ in their substance. The municipal law is sovereign over the individuals and all individuals are bound to obey them. By the coersive power, the state can compel the individuals to obey its laws and also can punish them for the disobedience of the laws. On the other hand, international law is a law between the states. It is neither above them nor it has the coersive power to compel the states to obey them.

Lastly, they point out that the subjects of both the laws are different. While the states are the subject of international law, individuals are the subjects of municipal law. They point out that international law cannot be applied to the individuals without being adopted by the state.

In addition to these two theories, Starke has referred to the following two theories:

Transformation or Specific Adoption Theory

According to this theory, no international law can be applied by the municipal court of a state unless it is specifically adopted by the state and incorporated into the municipal law of the state. In case of treaties, these have to be transformed into state laws by approving them by their legislatures. Since treaties are in the nature of promises and municipal laws are in the nature of commands, the moment the treaty is transformed into municipal law, the promises become commands and as such binding on the individuals and courts.

But this theory is only an extension of dualistic theory

and it explains only the procedure of changing treaties into binding instruments.

Delegation Theory

According to this theory, international law delegates to each state the right to determine when and how the rules or provisions of a treaty are to be adopted into the state law. The procedure and method adopted for the purpose by a state is only a continuation of the procedure of treaty making. By this process there is no need of transformation or specific adoption or passing new laws by the state. Thus the entire procedure of conclusion of treaty by states is a single process. So this theory is only a supplement to the Monistic Theory.

Practices of States

1. British Practice

In England, while dealing with a case under international law the Courts make a distinction between the customary rules and the rules laid down by treaties.

In case of customary rules of international law the British Courts followed different principles in different period of history. In the 18th century, the Blackstonian doctrine of incorporation was followed according to which all customary international laws were automatically made part of the British Common law and were enforced by the British Courts.

But in 1876, in the Franconia Case the court refused to apply the customary international law on the ground that there was no Parliamentary approval. But in 1905, in the West Rand Gold Mining Case, the court again adopted the doctrine of incorporation and applied the customary international law even without the approval of Parliament.

From 1939 onwards, the British courts have accepted all customary laws as part of British Common Law subject to the condition "it is not inconsistent with rules enacted by

Statutes or finally declared by their tribunals." So today, the British courts consider all universally accepted customary international laws as part of British law subject to the following conditions:

(a) These rules should not be in conflict with any existing Statutes;

(b) Once a customary law is determined by the highest British court, all British courts must follow it evenif such a law comes in conflict with a new customary law developed at a later date;

(c) The Acts of State by the executive such as war, aggression etc., even if are against the customary international law, cannot be questioned by the Court;

(d) A certificate from the executive in regard to certain matters such as recognition of a state or government or diplomatic status of a person cannot be questioned by the court, even if such a certificate go against the existing customary international law.

On the other hand, treaties, to be part of the British municipal law and to be enforced by the British courts must fulfill the following conditions:

(a) All treaties requiring ratification must be placed before both the Houses of Parliament for a period of 21 days before granting of ratification by the government;

(b) An enabling law passed by the Parliament is required in case a treaty:

    (i) affect the private rights of the citizens,

    (ii) require changes in the existing common or statute laws,

    (iii) require vesting of additional power on the Crown,

    (iv) impose direct or indirect financial obligations on the government.

(c) Those treaties which specifically require the approval

of the legislature, must be approved by the Parliament in order to become a part of British law.

(d) Treaties granting cession of British territory require approval of Parliament in order to be legally binding.

But all other treaties which either do not require ratification or which do not require change of any statute such as administrative agreements, are treated as part of British law.

If an old treaty comes in conflict with a present statute, the statute will prevail; while if an old statute comes in conflict with a recent treaty , the treaty will prevail.

2. *Practice of U.S.A.*

In case of customary laws, the U.S.A. follows the same practice as in England. Accordingly, if there is a conflict between a law passed by the Congress and a customary law, the U.S. courts will pressume that it is not the intention of the Congress to oppose the customary international law. But if a later statute is very clear over an earlier customary law or such customary law comes in conflict with the provisions of the Constitution of U.S.A., then the later law or Constitution will prevail over the customary international law.

So far the treaties are concerned, the U.S.A. practice is different than the British practice. According to Art. VI (2), all treaties to which the USA is a party are to be treated as "supreme law of the land" provided they are ratified by the Senate and all courts are bound to enforce them. In other words, all treaties which are ratified by the Senate as well as the Executive Agreements which President signs but do not require Senatorial ratification, are treated as part of the municipal law of U.S.A.

However, the U.S. courts make a distinction between a self-executing and a non-self executing treaties. A self-executing treaty becomes a part of U.S. laws automatically, provided, it is not against the constitution. But in case of a non-self-executing treaty, an enabling law by the Congress is required in order to make it a part of U.S. laws. Further, if a law passed by the Congress clearly modifies or abrogates an earlier treaty, the Congressional law will be valid.

3. *Practice of India*

Art. 51 of the Indian Constitution directs the government to respect international law, to maintain good relations with the neighbouring countries, and to resort to arbitration to solve international disputes. But this article being a part of the Directive Principle of State Policy, it is not binding on the government. But Art. 253 of the Constitution gives power to the Parliament to make law for the whole country or any part of the country on any subject included in any of the three lists, in order to implement the treaties. So from this it is clear that treaties, in order to be a part of Indian law and binding on the courts, must be approved by the Parliament.

So far the customary international laws are concerned, Indian courts follow the British practice.

Conclusion

From the practices of the states it is clear that many states such as Britain, U.S.A., India and some countries of Western Europe treat the customary international law as the part of their municipal law and this amounts to the acceptance of Monistic Theory so far as the customary international laws are concerned.

In respect of treaties, some states like Britain and India hold the view that treaties must be changed into municipal law by the legislature before they are applied by their municipal courts, and in this regard they follow the Dualistic Theory. On the other hand, in states like U.S.A. the treaties concluded by the state become automatically part of their municipal laws and as such are binding on their courts. Of course, in some of these states certain constitutional formalities like publication of the treaty in the official gazette or ratification by one of the houses of the legislature etc. have to be completed before it becomes the part of municipal law and such states follow Monistic theory.

Conflicts between the international and municipal laws may arise under various circumstances, such as a new municipal law may come in conflict with an old customary or treaty law. Or a newly created customary or treaty law may come in conflict with an old or existing statutory law.

In general, the courts of most states avoid conflicts by interpreting municipal law on the assumption that it is not the intention of the legislature to pass a law which goes against the international law. But this is not always possible. So different solutions have been adopted by different municipal legal systems to solve the problem.

The states where the legislature is supreme such as Britain, the courts must apply the laws passed by the legislature, even if they go against the international law. In other words, in such states the municipal law prevails over the international law.

In states where a treaty is part of municipal law, like U.S.A., a new treaty will prevail over an old statute; and a new statute will prevail over and old treaty in case of conflict.

In states where there is a written constitution, like USA and India, if an international law comes in conflict with any provision of the constitution, the constitutional provision will prevail over the international law.

5

SUBJECTS OF INTERNATIONAL LAW

Every system of law has its own 'subjects' to whom the laws are applicable. A subject of law is also known as 'legal Person'. To be a subject of law or a legal person, three essential elements are required, namely, the subject:

(a) has to perform duties and responsibilities prescribed by that law;
(b) has to the capability to claim the benefits of rights granted by that law;
(c) has to the capacity to enter into contractual and other legal relations with other legal persons recognised by that system of law.

Under a particular system of law, there may be different types of subjects such as, under the municipal law the subjects are citizens, residents, minors and aliens etc., and all the subjects do not possess exactly the same nature and characteristics. The International Court of Justice in its Advisory Opinion on the Reparation for Injuries case, 1949, also confirmed this differentiation of subjects when it said," The subject of law in any legal system are not necessarily identical in their nature or in the extent of their rights...." In other words, under a system of law, different subjects enjoy different rights and perform different duties.

According to the classical definition of international law, it is a body of rules which govern the conduct of states in their mutual dealings and as such the states alone are the subjects of international law. But in recent years, particularly after the First World War, the role of international law expanded considerably and consequently, the definition of international law too has undergone a change. Today, international law not only regulates the mutual dealings of states, but also is concerned with non-state entities, international organisations, and individuals. Thus Nkambo Mugerewa rightly pointed out, "We may say that states are the primary concern of international law but not its sole concern." The states are still considered as primary subjects of international law because the law itself owes its origin to the existence of the states, and while states alone possess all the characteristics required for a subject of international law, other subjects possess them to a limited extent.

Thus today the following are considered as the subjects of international law, enjoying rights and performing duties in varying degrees namely;

(a) Sovereign States
(b) Part-Sovereign or Non-Sovereign States
(c) International Organisations
(d) Individuals.

A. Sovereign States as Subjects of International Law

The Sovereign States enjoy a distinct position in the international law and whatever rights are conferred by the law were enjoyed by them in full, as well whatever duties imposed were performed by them. A Sovereign State is one which excercises undivided authority over all persons and property within its territory and is independent of direct control by any other person.

Though there is no unanimity among writers about an

exact definition of a sovereign state, yet, the essential characteristics of it are well settled. The Montevideo Convention, 1933, enumerates these characteristics in its Art. 1: "The State as a person of international law should possess the following qualifications:

(a) a permanent population (b) a defined territory (c) a government and (d) a capacity to enter into relation with other States."

Though all the modern states are formed with in the defined territory, yet, sometimes a state can be formed legally without a defined territory, as was in case of Israel in 1949, when it was admitted as a member of the U.N.O., even when its boundary was not defined and demarcated. The geographical contiguity is also not necessary as a state may consist of territories lacking contiguity and widely separated from each other as was in case of Pakistan before 1971. If there is a change in the territory due to either increase or decrease in size, it does not effect the international personality of the state.

As regards the government, it must be capable of maintaining effective control over its territory and of conducting its relations with other states. But a state does not loose its international personality if it is temporarily deprived of its effective government as a result of civil war or temporary exile of the government due to occupation of the territory by an aggresor state.

So far international law is concerned, the qualification that a state must have recognised capacity to maintain its external relations with other states is important. This qualification distinguish a state proper from other state-like entities like protectorates or units of a federation etc.

A Sovereign State may be a Simple or Composite Sovereign State. A Simple Sovereign State is one which has got one ruler, one government, and one territory, while a Composite Sovereign State may take any of the following forms:

(a) Personal Union

When two sovereign states link themselves together in the person of same monarch or ruler, a personal union is created. Between 1714 and 1837, the crowns of Great Britain and Hanover and between 1885 and 1908 the crowns of Congo and Belgium were linked up with one monarch. In such cases, the sovereign states who make up the personal union, remain separate international persons and treaties signed or wars declared by one did not effect the other. Theoritically, both the states may also enter into war. Today Personal Unions are only of historical importance because they do not exist any more.

(b) Real Union

When two sovereign states, through a treaty, link together to become one unit, a Real Union is formed. Norway and Sweden from 1814 to 1905 and Austria and Hungary from 1867 to 1918 were the Real Unions. When a Real Union is formed, it is treated as a single international person and single subject of international law. So neither of the two units can declare war separately nor can they fight a war between them and all international agreements are binding upon them. At present there is no Real Union in existence.

(c) Confederation

When a number of full sovereign states, through a treaty, link together and create certain organ or organs vested with certain powers, a confederation is formed. A confederation is not a state under international law and the member states retain their own international personality. It is described as a loose association of sovereign states, formed for certain specific purposes like common defence and mutual cooperation. Germany, Switzerland and the U.S.A. were examples of confederations which later became federations. In a confederation, the member states maintain their separate international personality, remain sovereign, get out of the confederation at any time, and can even declare war against another member. International actions of one member state such as declaration of war, conclusion of peace or treaties are not binding on other member states.

(d) Federation

A federal state is a union of several sovereign states with a central organ vested with independent powers over the member states and their citizens. In most federations, the external sovereignity being vested in the central government, it is responsible for conducting international relationship, concluding treaties and declaring war. The units of the federation normally do not possess international personality. But there has been certain exceptions to this rule, such as the units of the erstwhile U.S.S.R. federation enjoyed separate membership in the U.N.O., and the Swiss Cantons can enter into treaties with other states and cantons. In these exceptional cases, the units of such federations enjoy only limited international personality.

In a federation, the constitution divides the powers of the state between the central and the unit governments and each government is not only independent of the other in its own sphere of powers but also supreme authority over them. But by virtue of power to conduct external relations and conclude treaties, when the central government conclude a treaty which falls with in sphere of powers of the unit governments such as human rights, labour and health etc., their enforcement power is vested in the unit governments. If the unit governments fail to implement such treaties, the central government is held responsible internationally for the failure. So modern federations have made a provision in their constitutions to implement the treaties concluded by the central government obligatory on the part of the unit governments.

B. Part—Sovereign States or Dependent States as Subjects

The position of states at international law varies according to the extent of sovereignty enjoyed by them. Apart from full sovereign states, there are many other types of states whose sovereignty is either restricted or who are sovereign but have limited capacity or those which are part or non sovereign states. Such states are treated as limited subjects, and their position, rights and duties are different than the full sovereign states under the international law.

1. Holy See

Since the medieval period, the Pope has been recognised as an international legal personality because of position as the head of Roman Catholic Church as well as the ruler of certain Italian states known as Papal states. Thus Pope occupied a distinct but anomalous position and was treated as a sovereign monarch. This position continued even after annexation of Papal states to Italy in 1870. Though the Pope lost the Papal states, yet he still continued to be an international personality by virtue of his being the Spiritual Head and enjoyed the sovereign rights of legation and treaty making. The Italian Parliament granted him personal immunities and privileges of a head of state. Still the Pope's position, without a state and a territorial base, continued to be anamolous.

This anamoly was rectified by the Treaty of Lateran, 1929, by which the Vatican City, with an area of 100 acres, was created as a state, thereby making the Pope a head of state. Under the Lateran Treaty, Italy recognised:

(a) the Sovereignty of Holy See;
(b) Sovereignty of Pope over Vatican City;
(c) Pope's right to active and passive legation; and
(d) the neutrality of Holy See.

Thus the Treaty of Lateran created a new international personality of unique and exceptional character.

However, it is still not clear whether the Treaty of Lateran vested sovereign statehood upon the Holy See or Vatican City, as some writers consider Holy See and Vatican City as two distinct legal persons. But according to Oppenheim, "The accurate view is probably that the Lateran Treaty has created a new State of Vatican City with the incumbant of the Holy See as its Head." This view is also supported by Svarlien. So far the international law is concerned, Pope maintains diplomatic relations with other states through diplomatic agents known as Nuncioes, sign treaties known as Concordats, and become member of certain international organisations and attend international conferences which do not affect his neutrality.

2. *Diminutive or Micro States*

As a result of the adoption of the principle of national self determination, a number of very small sovereign states came into existence who are described as "Liliputian", "Diminutive," "Mini" and at present "Micro States". These states may properly claim to full international personality, yet due to their small size and population, have never taken their formal position in the family of nations. The Secretary General of the U.N.O. in his annual report for 1966-67 defined a micro state as an entity "exceptionally small in area, population, and human and economic resources", yet independent. Such states at present are, Andorra, Monaco, Lichtenste in, San Marino and Nauru etc.

While possessing defined territory, a government, and population, these states are all dependent to a greater or lesser extent on a third state, specially for conduct of their foreign affairs; as such they cannot be treated as full sovereign states. Though they are 'states' according to the International law, yet they are not admitted as members of the U.N.O., because the criterion for the admission being the "ability" to carry out the obligations contained in the Art. 4 of the Charter, these states cannot fulfil these obligations due to their meagre population and resources. So Starke has suggested that these states can enjoy the following privileges:

(a) participate in the regional economic commissions of U.N.O.,
(b) approach the International Court of Justice,
(c) participate in the Specialised agencies of the UNO and in the diplomatic conferences convened for the purpose of adopting international conventions; and
(d) send permanent observer mission to UNO. They can also be made Associate Members of UNO by amending Art. 4 suitably.

3. Condominium

When over a particular territory, two or more external powers excercise the sovereignty and jurisdiction jointly, a Condominium is created. Sudan was subjected to an Anglo-Egyptian condominium until 1953. The Anglo-French condominium over New Hebrides exists since 1914. The French—Algerian condominium over Sahara deserts exists since 1962 "with in the frame work of Algerian sovereignty".

A condominium is not a full subject of the international law and the Powers excercising the sovereignty over it are internationally responsible for its conduct.

4. Vassal States

'Vassal' is a relic of feudalism. A Vassal State is one which is completely under the suzerainty of another state. Suzerainty is not sovereignty; it is a kind of international guardianship. A Vassal state can excercise its internal and external sovereignty under the direction of the Suzerain State and other states can have dealings with the Vassal state only through the Suzerain state. A Vassal state can neither enter into a treaty relation with another state nor can it declare war. Tibet upto 1949, Egypt upto 1951, and Indian States upto 1947 were Vassal states. At present there are no vassal states.

All treaties concluded by the Suzerain State were automatically binding on the Vassal state unless exception is made. The war declared by the Suzerain State was also automatically became the war of the Vassal state. The Suzerain State was internationally responsible for the actions of the Vassal state. Thus internationally the independence of the Vassal states were restricted so much that they were not at all considered even as partial subjects of international law.

5. *Protectorates*

When a weak state puts it self under the protection of a strong and powerful state through a treaty, a Protectorate is created. Normally, by the treaty agreement, the Protector state undertakes to conduct the foreign relation and defence of the protected state. While, in general, the protected state retains large measure of control over its domestic affairs, the extent of authority of the protector state over the external and internal affairs of the protected state are not based on uniform pattern and each case depend upon:

(a) the particular terms of the treaty creating the protectorate,

(b) the condition under which the protectorate is recognised by the third states.

Although not completely independent, a protected state may enjoy sufficient measure of independence, either at the time of creation of the protectorate, or subsequently, in the management of its internal matters and to some extent, in the external matters also; and this aspect of protectorate distinguishes it from a Vassal state. As decided in the Duff Development Co., V. the Kelantan Government, a protected state may claim jurisdictional immunity in the territory of another state. But when a third state wants to enter into treaty or other relations with the protected state, it can do so only through the protector state. The treaties or international agreements to which the protector state is a party, are not automatically binding on the protected state, unless specifically adopted by it. Similarly, the war declared by the protector state is not binding on the protected state. Thus protected state is a part subject of international law.

6. *Colonies or Non-Self Governing Territories*

Colonies or non-self governing territories are now only of academic interest, because their number has been considerably reduced. The internal and external sovereignty of the colonies were vested in the metropolitan states under whose control they were. The colony along with the metropolitan country was treated as one unit under international law. But the rights of the people of the colonies were protected under the international law and the metropolitan country was responsible internationally for them.

At one time almost all European states had colonies at different parts of world and the extent of internal and external autonomy granted to them varied from one metropolitan country to another. The British colonies like Canada, India, Australia and New Zealand etc. enjoyed certain amount of internal autonomy and external freedom and they even signed treaties such as the Treaty of Versailles and the Charter of U.N.O. in their individual capacity.

But the process of decolonisation was started immediately after the Second World War and the establishment of the U.N.O. expedited the process. The Chapters of XI and XII of the Charter gave a legal status to these colonies and non-self governing territories and made their metropolitan countries internationally accountable for their administration. The Charter also provided for the right of self determination of all people of colonies.

The General Assembly of the U.N.O., in a resolution of 14th December, 1960, adopted a Declaration and urged the metropolitan states to bring about a speedy end to the colonialism in all forms and grant full independence to the colonial countries and their people by transfering power. The U.N.O. also established an ad hoc committee, which later became semi-permanent, to supervise the process of decolonisation. Thus the principles of the Charter, supplemented by the Declaration of the General Assembly, provided for a framework which helped the colonial countries to achieve independent statehood.

7. Mandated and Trust Territories

At the end of the First World War, the League of Nations experimented with Mandate System in order to govern certain territories recovered from Germany and Turkey which were placed under it. According to their preparedness for independence, these territories were classified into A, B, and C territories and the League handed over the administration of them as Mandate to more advanced member states. The category A mandated states included mainly the former states of Turkish Empire which were fairly advanced in civilisation, such as Iraq, Palestine, Syria and Lebanon. Their mandatory states, England and France, were only to tender administrative advices until they were able to look after themselves. These mandatory states enjoyed considerable measure of independence both in their internal and external affairs and possessed partial international personality even before their independence. Category B states included Tanganyika, Ruanda-Urundi etc. for which mandatory state was responsible for internal administration as well as external relation. Mandate C states included South-West Africa (Namibia) and South Pacific Islands. These were administered as integral part by the mandatory states with certain safeguards of the interest of the local population.

When the United Nations came into existence in 1945, it created a new system of 'Trust Territories' as a logical extension of the Mandate System. According to Art. 77 of the Charter, the trusteeship system was applicable to (a) former Mandated territories, (b) the territories recovered from the enemy during the Second World War, and (c) territories voluntarily placed under the system by States responsible for their administration. The object of the system was to entrust these territories to certain members of the UNO as a 'sacred trust of civilisation' and the Trustee States were to promote social, economical and political development of the people of these territories, progressively leading them towards their independence.

The terms under which each trustee state administered the territory were decided by a treaty between the UNO and the trustee state. The treaty was to be approved, in case of Strategic Areas, by the Security Council, and in case of other areas, by the General Assembly. The Trustee states were accountable and subject to the supervision of General Assembly in general and its specialised agency, the Trusteeship Council in particular. The Trusteeship Council was to consist of such members of the Security Council who were not trustees and equal number of members to be elected by the General Assembly for a term of three years. The responsibilities of General Assembly and the Trusteeship Council were (a) to consider the annual reports submitted by the trustee states, (b) to accept petitions from the people of these territories and consider them, (c) to arrange periodic visits to these territories, (d) to prepare questionnaire for collecting informations on social, economical and political development of the people on the basis of the annual report submitted by the Trustee, and (e) to take such other actions as per the Trusteeship Treaty.

The sovereignty of these territories were vested on the trustee states, subject to accountability to and supervision of the UNO. Thus the trustee states enjoyed only delegated sovereignty and the trust territories enjoyed the status of partial subjects of international law. The people of these territories did not acquire the nationality of the Trustee state nor the treaties of the Trustee states were automatically binding on them.

8. Neutralised States

When a weak state is threatened by strong states or when it is necessary to maintain balance of power or to create a buffer state between two powerful states, a state is neutralised. According to Starke, "A neutralised state is one whose independence and political and territorial integrity are guaranteed permanently by a collective agreement of Great Powers subject to the condition that the particular state concerned will never take up arms against another state—except to defend itself—and will never enter into treaties of alliances, etc., which may compromise its impartiality or lead it to war." Oppenheim defines it as "a state whose independence and integrity are for all future time guaranteed by an international convention" on the condition that such a state shall never take up arms except in case of self defence and shall not enter into any international obligation which could directly or indirectly involve it in a war.

Thus a state is neutralised permanently through a treaty entered collectively by Great Powers with the concerned state. The neutralised state undertakes not to involve itself in a war, except in case of self defence, in return of the guarantee by Great Powers to maintain its independence and political and territorial integrity, even by coming to its rescue in case of necessity.

A state cannot unilaterally declare itself neutralised without the approval and support of other concerned states and the Great Powers. The neutralised state undertake to obey the laws of neutrality in case of war and must not allow any foreign interference in its internal affairs. Some times, a state is neutralised with its consent, while in many cases it is imposed on it by Great Powers. The status of neutralisation can be ended only with the consent of all guarantor states. Today, the neutralised states are Switzerland since 1648, Laos since 1962, and probably Austria since 1955.

Neutralisation differs from 'neutrality', which according to Starke, "is a voluntary policy assumed temporarily in regard to a state of war affecting the Powers and terminable at any time by the state declaring neutrality." Thus while neutralisation is permanent, collectively guaranteed through a treaty, and many a times imposed by other states, the status of neutrality is temporary, voluntary, unilaterally declared during a state of war, and can be ended unilaterally at any time at the will of the concerned state. Neutralisation also differs from 'Non Allignment' which "is a policy of a state not to involve itself in any conflicts or defensive alliances."

Very often it is argued that a neutralised state is a part-sovereign state because of its incapacity in war or in concluding certain treaties due to the restrictions undertaken by it. But this opinion has no basis when the facts and conditions of neutralisation are considered. Oppenheim has rightly said "If sovereignty is nothing else than supreme authority, a neutralised state is as fully sovereign as any non-neutralised state. It is entirely independent outside as well as inside its borders." The neutralised states can become members of international organisations, conclude certain types of treaties, excercise right of legations, and fight a war for self defence etc., like any full sovereign state subject to two conditions, namely, it cannot declare war and cannot conclude treaties which may directly or indirectly involve it in a war.

9. Commonwealth of Nations

It is a unique organisation of sovereign states, consisting of multi-racial people from across all the five continents of the world. The organisation in its present form came into existance in 1949. All the member states of this organisation have one thing in common that they possess a common heritage and that they all, at one time or another, formed a part of British Empire.

Commonwealth defies any known classification of states as it is neither a state, nor a super state, nor a federation, nor a confederation, nor a personal union. It is, in the words of Svarlien, "a community held together by bonds of common origin, sentimental traditions, and solidarity of interests." It is a free association of sovereign states in which members are equal to one another and not subordinate to any other either in their internal or external matters. Though the British Queen is the head of this organisation, her role is simply symbolic and member states do not owe any allegiance to her. The Heads of Government Meeting at Singapore in 1971 defined it as "a voluntary association of independent sovereign states, each responsible for its policies, a consulting and cooperating in common interests of their peoples and in promotion of international understanding and peace." Thus the emphasis is placed by this organisation on "consultation, discussion and cooperation" among the member states. Since 1965, its activities are coordinated by a Secretariat with a Secretary General with its headquarters at London.

The position of Commonwealth under international law is not very clear. On one hand, there are commonwealth citizenship, government to government diplomatic relationship, and annual or periodic conferences of heads of governments, parliamentarians, Speakers, and jurists etc., on the other hand, the member states are separate members of UNO and other international organisations, conclude separate treaties, declare ware separately, and can even go to war against another member state such as Indo-Pak war of 1948, and can leave the organisation voluntarily at any time they like. Though the common features make it appear as a state, yet it is not a state and not an international person; rather its members states are separate international persons and subjects of international law. Thus Starke has concluded "In ultimate analysis, the Commonwealth is held together by a web of mixed tangible and intangible advantages, that have evolved pragmatically, and are difficult to express in terms of legal relationships. Had the ties between member states of the Commonwealth been more formalised, it might have been appropriate to describe the Commonwealth as an international organisation, but it is at least correctly labelled as an 'association' of states."

10. Belligerents

Usually, when a part of the people of a state rise in revolt against their parent government, it is treated as an internal matter of that state by the third states. The parent government is competent to take any action against these rebels as per its own municipal laws. The parent state must also have the capacity to control the situation as well as pay compensation for the damages which the rebels might cause to the interests of the third states. But when the conflict become wide spread and the parent government is not in a position to control and take responsibility for the actions of the rebels, the third states recognise these rebels and establish relations with them to protect their own interests, thereby raising their status to the international level by granting them certain belligerent rights.

But to be considered as belligerents, the rebels must fulfil the following conditions:

(a) there must exist a state of general armed conflict;
(b) the rebels must be in occupation of substantial portion of national territory and excercise control over the population on that territory;
(c) the hostilities are conducted as per the international laws of war and neutrality;
(d) the rebels should be organised under responsible leadership.

Once the rebels are recognised as belligerents, by the third states, they become subject of international law, eventhough to a limited extent, and become entitled to certain rights and discharge certain duties and thus become partial subjects of international law.

11. Insurgents

Sometimes, in a civil revolt, the conditions required for belligerency may be absent, such as the rebels might not have effective control over a portion of the national territory, or they might not be under an organised leadership. In such cases, the rebels may be treated as robbers or pirates and as such hostis humanis generis or public enemy by other states. But in practice, when the actions of these rebels harm the interests of the third states and the parent government is unable to control them, the third states will have to enter into relations with these rebels by recognising them as insurgents on the condition that the rebels conduct their activities as per the laws of war and neutrality, and to that extent they are made subjects of international law. But Insurgency, like Belligerency, is not a status and as such do not give rise to the problem of definite rights and duties. The nature of rights and duties of the insurgents are normally decided between the Insurgents and recognising third states.

C. International Institutions as Subjects

For a long time a controversy was going on whether the international institutions are subjects of international law. The traditional definitions of international law considered the States alone as the subjects. But due to the development of international law, specially after the First World War, a new trend emerged according to which the international institutions were granted a certain degree of international personality by the international law. The Conventions, Charters and the constituent instruments creating these international institutions have vested them with certain rights and duties, which are recognised by their member states. Thus these international institutions have a limited degree of international personality. Oppenheim while discussing the status of the League of Nations, grudgingly agreed by saying "The League appears to be a subject of international law and an international person side by side with the several states." This trend of confering limited degree of international personality to the international institutions also continued after the Second World War and was confirmed by the Advisory Opinion of International Court of Justice on Reparations for Injuries Suffered in the Services of the UNO (1949), in which the Court considered the UNO as an International Person and said, "That is not the same thing as saying that it is a state, which it certainly is not, nor that its legal personality and rights and duties are the same as those of a state. Still less is it the same thing as saying that it is a 'Super State'.... What it does mean is that it is a subject of international law and capable of possessing rights and duties, and that it has capacity to maintain its rights by bringing international claims."

Thus Art. 104 of the Charter of UNO directs each of its member states to grant the organisation with in their territory "such legal capacity as may be necessary for the excercise of its functions." The UNO, which has a juridical personality shall have the capacity:

(a) to contract,
(b) to acquire and dispose movable and immovable property,
(c) to institute legal proceedings.

These above capacities are also acquired by its Specialised Agencies and other regional organisations like NATO etc. Several states like U.S.A. and Switzerland etc., have recognised the legal capacity of the international organisations through their municipal laws.

Though the Charters and Conventions etc., establishing the international organisations do not give general authorisation to conclude treaties, yet many of them authorise them to conclude certain types treaties such as Art. 43 of the UNO Charter gives it the power to conclude agreements relating military matter, with the member states, Art. 63 authorises it to conclude treaties with the Specialised Agencies in order to establish relationship with them. Irrespective of these provisions, the UNO has concluded a large number of treaties both with the states and other international institutions.

The opinion of several jurists, the practices of international organisations and the opinion of International Court of Justice supports the view that the international institutions derive their treaty making power not only from their Charter, Convention or constituent instruments, but also by implications. They derive their powers from the application of doctrines of Implied or Inherent Powers. In the Advisory Opinion in the Reparation Case, the Court said, "Under International law, the Organisation must be deemed to have those powers which, though not expressly provided in the Charter, are conferred upon it by necessary implication as being essential to the performance of its duties." Several writers agree to extend this doctrine of implied powers, specially to their capacity for treaty making, to the other institutions, by analogy. But Prof. Brierly says "the inherent treaty making capacity of international organisations...is confined to the capacity to make treaties compatible with letter and spirit of their several constitution."

In the Advisory Opinion in the Reparation Case, the International Court of Justice also said that the UNO possesses an international personality which enables it to bring international claims against members and non-member states for direct injuries against it, like "damage caused to the interests of the organisation itself, to its administrative machine, to its property and assets, and to interests to which it is the guardian."

The capacity of one international institution to join another or to join with the states to form a separate international organisation has been both recognised and excercised. Thus the international organisations having international personality are partial subjects of international law and are entitled to certain rights and duties.

D. Individual as Subject

According to the traditional view, states alone are the 'subjects' of international law, and individuals can only be treated as its 'objects'. While the subjects are the 'persons' to whom the law grants rights and imposes duties, the objects are the 'things' in whose favour the rights are held and duties are performed by another body. In other words, while the states are the subjects of international law with definite rights and duties, the individuals are the objects whose rights and duties under the international law are excercised and performed on their behalf by the state to which they belong.

Those who argue that states alone are subjects of the international law point out that it is the states who alone lay down rules through international conferences and treaties, bind themselves to these rules, become parties to disputes before international courts and tribunals, maintain diplomatic relations to negotiate and protect their national interests, create new rights and duties through treaties, and become members of international organisations. The individuals, they argue, cannot perform these functions and when he becomes a victim of injustice in a foreign state, he can be protected only by his own state.

Considering these facts, all classical definitions and majority of traditional writers of international law consider the state as the only subject and individual as the object of the international law. Though certain rights granted and duties imposed on individuals in such matters dealing with aliens, suppression of slavery or piracy, these rights and duties are enforceable only through their states. So Oppenheim emphatically states "Subjects of rights and duties arising from the law of nations are states solely and exclusively.... Therefore all rights which might necessarily have to be granted to an individual human being according to Law of Nations are not international rights, but rights granted by the Municipal Law in accordance with a duty imposed upon the state concerned by the international law." Though some rights and duties are permitted directly to the individuals by the international law and sometimes they are even permitted to appear before international tribunals, these writers argue, that it was only as a matter of convenience they are so permitted; but in the final analysis these individuals depend upon their states for the protection of their rights. So Sir Frederick Smith concludes "States and states alone enjoy locus standi in the law of nations; they are the only wearer of international personality."

Westlake, Kelsen and other writers consider that individuals alone are the subject of international law, because the duties imposed by the international law are ultimately the duties binding on individuals. Westlake argues, "The duties and rights of states are only the duties and rights of men who compose them." There are several instances where the international law is directly applicable to the individuals. Many recent treaties such as Geneva Convention on Prisoners of Wars, 1949, have vested rights or imposed duties on the individuals. The Permanent Court of International Justice in the Danzing Railway Officials' Case said that if a particular treaty vests rights on individuals, then such rights should be recognised and given effect to by international law and international courts.

Before the First World War, the individual was under a duty in international law to do or to refrain from doing certain acts like piracy, violation of laws of war, and individuals committing offences by violating them were tried not by any international procedure but by domestic jurisdiction of the state under whose custody they were held.

The first attempt to try an individual for certain offences under international law through an international process was made by the Treaty of Versailles, 1919, to try the German Kaiser Wilhelm II for certain crimes like aggression etc.; but he could not be tried because the Dutch Government refused to surrender him.

After the end of Second World War, the Allied Powers in the Agreement of London, 1945, decided to prosecute and punish certain individuals such as Head of States, Ministers, and high civil and military officials for crimes against peace, crimes against humanity, and other war crimes. Accordingly, two war crime tribunals at Nuremburg and Tokyo were set up for the purpose, at the end of the War.

The Nuremburg Tribunal in its judgement justified the international responsibility of individuals as follows: "That international law imposes duties and liabilities upon individuals as well as upon states has long been recognised.... Crimes against international law are committed by men, not by abstract entities, and only by punishing the individuals who commit such crimes can the provisions of international law be enforced." The judgements of both the Tribunal are of historical significance, because the Tribunals not only established the guilt and responsibility of certain individuals through an international process, but also punished them.

The trend of attaching direct responsibility to the individuals was further advanced by the Genocide Convention adopted by the General Assembly in 1948, according to which persons responsible for genocide "whether they are constitutionally responsible rulers, public officials or private individuals", are to be tried and punished by national courts or by an international criminal tribunal. Thus the Genocide Convention protects the rights of individuals to exist as groups.

In the post Second World War period, now there is a growing international awareness to vest certain rights on individuals even against his own state through international efforts. Such attempts have made the individual a direct subject of international law. The UNO Charter in Art. 1 provides for the protection of fundamental freedoms and human rights. The concept of the protection of human rights was originally confined to the domestic laws and found expression in the Magna Carta in England, Declaration of Rights of Man in

France, and the Bill of Rights in U.S.A. This concept of human rights was transformed into international arena only after the Second World War when the international community realised that international recognition and protection of human rights for people through out the world is essential to the maintenance of international peace and order. Accordingly, the General Assembly adopted the Universal Declaration of Human Rights in 1948. The Council of Europe adopted in 1950 a Convention for the Protection of Human Rights and Fundamental Freedoms which created a European Commission and a European Court of Human Rights to deal with the violation of human rights by the member states against their nationals.

Individuals are sometimes authorised to present petitions to international organisations on their own behalf or for others for the consideration of their rights and interests. Such international organisations to which individuals can petition are Trusteeship Council, Committee on Elimination of Racial Discrimination, Human Rights Committee, and International Labour Organisation etc.

Individuals belonging to minority groups in terms of race, language or religion have been protected by a Convention on Civil and Political Rights of Minorities adopted by the General Assembly in 1966, which guarantees their rights to language, culture and religion etc.

Thus today even the treatment of individuals by their own states has become the concern of international law. This transformation of individual's position is one of the most remarkable developments of contemporary international law.

6

RIGHTS AND DUTIES OF STATES

A subject under any system of law is entitled to certain rights and have to perform certain duties. Since sovereign states are subjects of international law, it is argued that they have also rights and duties. So many writers, numerous international conferences, and several international bodies such as Montvedeo Convention, 1933, and International Law Commission, 1949, have tried to formulate certain rights and duties. Such suggested rights, which are sometimes described as 'fundamental' or 'basic' are rights of independence and sovereignty, equality, territorial jurisdiction, self preservation, acquiring and holding of territory and dignity. Some of the suggested duties are duty not to resort to war, duty of non-intervention in the internal affairs of other states, and the duty to carry out treaty obligations in good faith.

But no unanimity among the writers exist regarding either the contents or the number of such fundamental rights and duties of the sovereign states. Oppenheim is of the opinion that many of the rights and duties claimed are "derived from the very membership of the community of nations. "According to Starke, "Certain of the rights and duties declared to be `basic' seem no more fundamental than other rights and duties not so formulated." Some writers point out that many of the so called rights such as right to independence and right to jurisdiction are inherent in the sovereignty of the state. Finally, many of the rights cannot be accepted as `fundamental' for the simple reason that many states frequently violate them both during war and peace time on the ground of self-preservation etc. So Oppenheim concluded," the notion of fundamental rights of states should totally disappear from the exposition of Law of Nations."

On the other hand, international tribunals often invoked certain fundamental rights or duties while deciding cases before them, such as, the Permanent Court of International Justice relied on the fundamental rights of equality and independence in Advisory Opinion relating to the status of Eastern Carelia, 1923, and the right to choose the social, economic, political, and cultural system by a state by the International Court of Justice in the Nicargua V. United States case, 1986. Thus, by virtue of the international personality and its membership of the international community, every sovereign state is entitled to certain rights and since the rights of one state become the duties of other states, these duties, too, should also be performed. In actual practice states claim certain rights and also perform certain duties.

1. Right to Independence

Sovereignty in international law has three major aspects, namely, external, internal, and territorial. The external sovereignty by which a state is free to decide its relations with other states or bodies, is also known as independence. By internal sovereignty, a state has exclusive right to decide its own institutions, enact its own laws and ensure their obedience. By territorial sovereignty, a state excercises complete and exclusive authority over all persons and things found with in its territory. Though external sovereignty is given more prominence, in fact, sovereignty in international law is the sum total of all three aspects.

A state is independent only when it is sovereign. So right to independence means a sovereign state has freedom to choose the type of constitution, the form of government, the economic system; freedom to deal with its citizens, pursue foreign policy, admit or expel aliens, enter into treaties and alliances, to make war and peace with other states, to join military or economic blocs, and claim immunities and privileges for its diplomatic agents.

To day when almost all states are members of several international organisations such as UNO, ILO, WHO etc., absolute sovereignty is no more recognised because as members of these organisations, states undertake certain restriction on their sovereignty. Similarly, through treaties states undertake certain restriction on their sovereignty. The customary international law too has imposed certain restrictions on the exclusive sovereignty of the states. Thus all modern states today surrender a portion of their sovereignty.

2. Right to Equality

From the beginning, the writers in international law have been advocating the doctrine of equality of states, which means all sovereign states, irrespective of their size, population, power, degree of civilisation, resources, prosperity, and technological advancement, are equal. Art 2 of the UN Charter states that the Organisation "is based on the principle of sovereign equality of all its members." The Declaration on Principles Concerning Friendly Relations and Cooperation Among States says "All States enjoy sovereign equality. They have equal rights and duties and equal members of the international community, notwithstanding differences on an economic, social, political, or other nature."

The legal equality of the sovereign states, according to Oppenheim, means :

(a) every state has only one vote, unless it is otherwise agreed;

(b) the vote of the weakest and smallest state has the same weight as that of largest and most powerful state;

(c) since no state can claim jurisdiction over another, states can sue in foreign courts but they cannot be sued, unless they voluntarily submit to the jurisdiction of a foreign court;

(d) the courts or other organs of one state cannot question the validity or legality of the official acts of another sovereign state.

But legal equality should not be equated with that of political equality. Politically states are not at all equal and in practice de facto inequality prevails. Theoretically though every state has one vote, the smaller states are usually guided by the influence of the Big Powers while voting. In the Security Council the Five Big Powers are permanent members having veto powers. The distinction between the developed and less developed states is expressly recognised in the GATT Agreement of 1947. In matters of diplomatic relations, while the diplomatic agents of the powerful states are given the rank of ambassadors, that of smaller states are given lower ranks. Thus, absolute equality, like absolute sovereignty, does not exist. Fenwick rightly concluded, "the whole business of equality was a legal paradox."

3. Right to Self Preservation

Since the beginning, international law allows the states the right of self-preservation and even permits a state the right of intervention in another state on the ground of self defence. But such a right to intervene in another state to defend and protect itself can only be taken in case of 'necessity'. Mr. Webster, the Secretary of States of USA defined 'necessity' on which intervention in another state can be made on the ground of self-preservation as being "instant, overwhelming, and leaving no choice of means, and no moment for deliberation." Thus the discretion is left to the concerned state to judge the 'necessity' for self defence. But this may also be used as a pretext to cover up deliberate breach of international law, unless the action of the state is judged by a political body like the Security Council or by a judicial body.

The UN Charter in Art 51 recognises the inherent right of a member state to take individual or collective steps for its self defence, until the Security Council takes action. The Charter also directs the member states to inform the Security Council immediately of the action taken in self defence.

There are several instances of states taking pre-emptive steps against another state on the ground of self-preservation and self defence. In 1807, Britain captured the Danish Fleet by bombarding Copenhegen as a measure of self defence against the anticipated French attack on her by using the Danish Fleet. During the Canadian Rebellion against Great Britain in 1937, a ship Caroline carrying arms and ammunitions for the insurgents was captured and burnt, and in the process two citizens of USA were killed. To the protest by USA, Britain justified its action as a necessary measure of self defence to prevent the imminent attack of her territory for which there was no sufficient time. After Germany invaded France in 1940, a large number of ships of French Naval Fleet escaped to the North African port of Oran, which, for the fear of being captured by Germany and used against it, Great Britain destroyed them on the ground of self defence.

4. Right to Territorial Jurisdiction

Territory being the physical basis of a sovereign state, its destruction leads to the extinction of the state itself. Hence the bulk of international laws are addressed to the territory of the state. The importance of the state territory lies in the fact that with in it a state excercises its sovereignty and authority and performs the acts of state. In other words, every state has a right to excercise jurisdiction over all persons and things found with in its territory. Lord Macmillan in the Cristina case, 1938, said that every sovereign independent state "should possess jurisdiction over all persons and things with in its territorial limits and all causes civil and criminal arising with in its limits."

Apart from the land territory, the customary international law allows a state to exercise its jurisdiction over the territorial sea, a ship bearing its flag, ports, and the aerial space. However, the right of a state to excercise jurisdiction over its territory may be restricted by the obligations undertaken by the state under a treaty or by the principles of exterritoriality.

5. Right to Dignity, Rank and Titles

According to Oppenheim every state is entitled to the right to dignity, rank, and title.

Dignity is a qualification acquired by a state through its reputation and behaviour in the international sphere. The government of a state which is upright and behaves fairly and justly in its international dealings, has a greater dignity than the one which is corrupt, unfair and unjust. The consequences of the right to dignity of a state are the exterritorial privileges to its head of state, diplomatic agents, war ships, and respect for its authority such as national flag and emblem and grant of certain titles to its representatives dealing with foreign states etc.

Though international law grants right to equality to all states, yet they are not equal in their rank. The question of the rank of a state was of great importance in the 16th and 17th centuries and was scrupulously observed. But now a days the rank of a state does not play any important role. Earlier, ranking of states was considered essential in order to determine the sitting arrangements in the international conferences, precedence, and protocols. The ranking of states created problems of precedence specially at the time of signing of a treaty. To avoid the problem of precedence while signing a treaty, several methods such as "alternate" or drawing of lots or alphabetic order of name of the states are used.

Now a days, except in few exceptional cases, states have no titles. Earlier, states like the former Republic of Venice was addressed as "Serene Republic" and even now the Republic of San Merino is addressed as "Most Serene Republic". Usually, the monarchical heads of states were addressed by such titles as 'Emperor', 'Majesty', 'Royal Highness' etc. Even now the Pope is addressed as "His Holiness".

Duties of Sovereign States

Rights and duties being corelative, rights of one state automatically becomes the duties of other states.

Every state is duty bound not to perform its acts of sovereignty on the territory of another state, to prevent its agents and subjects from taking actions which will violate the independence of another state, and not to intervene in the internal affairs of other states. So a state should not send its agents to arrest a criminal into the territory of another state to which he has escaped. Thus when the agents of French Government destroyed the ship Rainbow Warrior in the internal waters of Newzealand in 1986, France was held guilty of violation of international law and her agents were later convicted and punished by the courts of Newzealand.

Every state is under a duty to prevent within its boundaries the activities of political terrorists directed against another state. This duty was imposed by the UN Declaration on Principles Concerning Friendly Relations and Cooperation Among States in 1970 and was subsequently reinforced by the Convention to Prevent and Punish Acts of Terrorism, 1971 and the Helisinki Declaration of 1975.

Though the states are under a duty not to intervene in the affairs of another state, yet, international law however allows the states the right to intervene in another state under certain circumstances.

The states are under a duty to prevent their territory being used to harm the economic interests of neighbouring state and not to alter the natural conditions such as diversion of the flow of water of a river etc., on its territory to the disadvantage of another state. As per the Declaration on the Human Environment, states are under a duty not to cause damage to the environment of other states by their activities.

Every state is bound to observe all treaty obligations in good faith because of the principle of pactasunt servanda. All states are under a duty to respect international law and abide by its rules.

Since the Pact of Paris and the Charter of UNO have outlawed the war as an instrument of settlement of disputes, states are duty bound not to resort to war. But in case of self defence, a state is permitted to use force or even resort to war.

The doctrine of peaceful coexistence, first enunciated in the Sino—Indian Treaty, 1954 and subsequently accepted by numerous international declarations and finally adopted by the General Assembly of the UNO, has laid down the five important duties of states:

(1) Mutual respect for each others territorial integrity and sovereignty;
(2) Mutual non-aggression;
(3) Mutual non-interference in each other's affairs;
(4) Equality and mutual benefit;
(5) Peaceful co-existence.

INTERVENTION

According to Oppenheim, "Intervention is dictatorial interference by a state in the affairs of another state for the purpose of maintaining or altering the actual condition of things." According to Hall intervention means "When a state interferes in the relations of two other states without the consent of both or either of them or when it interferes in the domestic affairs of another state irrespective of the will of the latter for the purpose of either maintaining or altering the actual conditions of things with in it." Thus interference by one state in the external or internal affairs of another state with out its consent in order to maintain or change certain things by force is called intervention.

But friendly advice, cooperation, diplomatic suggestions, or general political influence of one state towards another should not be treated as intervention, because these acts are not supported by force.

International law prohibits the states to intervene in the affairs of other states, because every state has "inalienable right to choose its political, economic, and cultural systems." The International Court of Justice in Nicargua V. USA, 1986, case said that an intervention is prohibited if it:

(a) encroaches on a matter which every state is permitted to take decision freely, such as choice of political, or economic system or pursuing its own foreign policy etc.;
(b) is supported by methods of coercion or use of force such as support for subversive activities against the state subject to intervention.

Types of Intervention

1. *External Intervention:* It is an intervention by a state in the foreign affairs of another state. An external intervention is directed against hostile relations of other states, such as during war a third state can make an external intervention by entering the war in favour of either state as Italy did by entering the Second World War in favour of Germany against Britain.

2. *Internal Intervention:* The internal intervention takes

place when other states interfere in a civil war going on in a state, either on the side of insurgents or in favour of legitimate government, such as a number of states intervened in the Spanish Civil War in 1936, or as USSR intervened in Hungary in 1956 and in Czechoslovakia in 1970 to suppress the popular uprisings of the people of those states.

3. *Punitive Intervention:* This is in the nature of reprisal or retaliation, short of war, resorted to by a state when it has suffered an injury by the actions of the state intervened. This type of intervention is frequently carried out by stronger states against weaker states. This may take the form of pacific blockade to compel the other state to fulfil a treaty obligation or to redress a wrong done. The example of punitive intervention is the USA intervention in Cuba in 1964.

4. *Diplomatic Intervention:* When several states, in order to force a state, take some international actions through a treaty, it is called diplomatic intervention. In 1895, by issuing a joint demarche, Russia, France, and Germany forced Japan to return Liaotung to China from whom she extorted it through the Treaty of Shimonoseki.

5. *Subversive Intervention:* In modern times some writers are of the opinion that when a state through propaganda or other clandestine activities try to create a revolt or civil war in another state, it amounts to intervention.

Grounds of Intervention

Writers in international law make a distinction between legal and illegal interventions. While some writers consider any intervention as strictly illegal, Oppenheim and Brierly argue for intervention under certain circumstances. According to Brierly when intervention by a state is made on the grounds of self defence, reprisals, and excercise of treaty rights, it should be treated as legal.

According to Oppenheim, intervention on the following

grounds should be treated as legal:

(a) A Protector state has got a right to intervene in the external affairs of the protected state.

(b) If the internal affairs of a state is also by right the affairs of another state, that other state has a right to intervene in case the former state deals with such right unilaterally.

(c) If a state's rights such as external independence, territorial integrity or personal supremacy are restricted by international treaty, and that state violates these restrictions, the other state party or parties have a legal right to intervene.

(d) If a state violates internationally recognised international laws established by custom or treaties, during peace or war, other states have a right to intervene and force the deliquent state to follow the law.

(e) When a particular form of government or a particular monarch of a state is guaranteed by a treaty, if that type or that monarch is changed by another type or another monarch, the state parties to the treaty have a right to intervene to restore the government or monarch.

(f) Collective intervention under the provisions of the UN Charter for the purpose of restraining a state from disturbing the peace of the world as in case of Korea in 1950 and of Iraq in 1991, is legal.

(g) By virtue of the right of protection over the citizens abroad, a state may have a cause to intervene in another state to which the other state must submit.

In addition to the above grounds of legal intervention, states also intervene in the affairs of other states on the following grounds which are considered, if not strictly legal, justified:

(1) *Enforcement of Treaty Rights:* Intervention is justified

when it is found to be necessary for the enforcement of treaty rights. Such intervention does not violate the independence or the rights of the state which has violated the treaty, because that state itself had agreed in the treaty for such intervention. The examples of such intervention is the USA intervention in Cuba in 1964 as per the provisions of the Treaty of Havana, 1903.

(2) *Maintenance of Balance of Power:* The principle of balance of Power, which dominated the diplomacy of Europe since the Treaty of Westphalia, has lost its significance today because of the establishment of League of Nations and United Nations. But in the 19th century, the Anglo-French intervention in the Crimean War in 1854 to maintain balance of power in Europe is an example of such an intervention.

(3) *On Grounds of Humanity:* Usually, the treatment of a state towards its own nationals is not the concern of other states. But when such activities are related to cruel and inhuman treatment to its own people, other states can intervene in that state on the ground of humanity. In 1827, Britain, France, and Russia jointly intervened in the struggle between Greece and Turkey because attrocities committed in the war shocked the conscience of Europe. In 1971, India intervened in the civil war in Pakistan because of genocide by Pakistan over her people of the then East Pakistan.

The UN Charter also permits collective intervention on the grounds of humanity. According to Oppenheim, "The Charter of UNO in recognising the promotion and respect for fundamental human rights and freedoms as one of the principal objects of the Organisation marks a further step in the direction of elevating the principle of humanitarian intervention to a basic rule of organised international society."

(4) *To Check Illegal Intervention:* Intervention which is resorted to check or put an end to an illegal intervention is permitted by the international law such as the help given by

Britain to Portugal in 1826. Similar intervention against immoral acts or to prevent international nuissance or to defend the national honour is also permitted by the international law.

(5) *For Protection of Persons and Properties:* Intervention may also be justified when a state undertakes to protect the persons, properties or interests of its own nationals abroad when they are subjected to gross injustice or injury caused due to the unfair discrimination against them by another state.

(6) *Self Preservation:* When the preservation or defence of a state is in danger or threatened, intervention is permitted by the international law. In the Caroline case, 1837, the Secretary of States of USA, Mr. Webster enunciated the test for such intervention and justified it only in case of "instant, overwhelming and leaving no choice of means, and no moments for deliberation."

Art 51 of the UN charter recognises the inherent right of individual and collective self-defence of member states against armed attack, pending enforcement action by the Security Council, thereby leaving the ultimate authority to the Security Council. The rights of state regarding 'Self-defence' is more restricted than the earlier right of 'self preservation'. It is now generally accepted that measures of self-defence should be proportionate to the requirement of dispelling an armed attack by another state.

Monroe Doctrine

The Monroe doctrine enunciated by President James Monroe of USA in 1823 emphasises the political as distinct from legal aspects of the intervention. The Doctrine contained:

(1) a declaration that the American continent would no longer be a subject to future colonisation by a European Power;

(2) a declaration that USA would not interfere in European wars or European affairs;

(3) a declaration that any attempt by European Powers to "extend their system" to any part of the American continent would be regarded as "dangerous" to the "peace and safety" of the USA;

(4) that European Powers would not be allowed to interfere in the independence of the then South American Republics which were formed out of the Spanish colonies in which the European Powers wanted to interfere.

Thus the Monroe Doctrine was enunciated in the 19th century to prevent the European Powers from intervening in the affairs of states of South America. This theory is even now being used by the USA as it did in case of "quarantine" operation against Cuba in 1964 to prevent the construction of missile bases in that state by the USSR. In course of time the USA used the Doctrine even to intervene in the affairs of states of South American continent whenever its vital interests were endangered, as it did in Dominican Republic in 1965 to prevent the establishment of a Communist government in that state. Starke has rightly said, "a doctrine originally directed against intervention was converted into a theory justifying the intervention by the state which had first sponsored the doctrine."

The Drago Doctrine

The foreign minister of Argentina, Mr. Drago enunciated the theory in 1902 that states are duty bound not to use force or military action against the states or occupy their territories when they had defaulted in payment of their debts. The Doctrine was primarily intended for certain states of South and Central American states who had defaulted in their repayment of debts to certain European states, and as such this doctrine became a corollary to the Monroe Doctrine.

According to this theory except use of force or military action, the diplomatic intervention or recourse to the judicial tribunals by the lender states were permitted.

Subsequently, the Drago Doctrine became a part of the international law when the Hague Convention of 1907 on Recovery of Contract Debts laid down that state parties would not resort to use of armed forces in order to recover contract debts, except where the defaulter state has refused to accept arbitration or implement the arbitral award.

7

RECOGNITION

The world history produces many changes in the international community. Old states disappear, unite with other states, disintegrate, split into several states, or former colonies and dependencies become states by becoming independent. Even in the existing states, governments change due to revolution or military conquests. These changes create many problems for the international community, the most important of which is the problem of grant of recognition to the new state or government and every existing state has to face this problem at one time or other. Michel Akehurst has rightly said "The recognition is one of the most difficult topics in the international law. It is a confusing mixture of politics, international law and municipal law. The legal and political elements cannot be disentangled; when giving or withholding recognition, states are influenced more by political than by legal considerations, but their actions do have legal consequences." The question of granting or withholding recognition will arise in case of:

(a) a new state has come into being or there is territorial changes in an existing state;

(b) a new government comes to power in an existing state by other means than constitutional;

(c) Insurgents; and

(d) belligerents.

Fenwick has defined recognition as a "formal acknowledgement by an existing member or by existing members of the international community that a state or political group hither to not holding membership in the community was now entitled to it, and as an incident of membership, entitled to all of the rights and privileges of other members of the community." J.E.S. Fawcett says that recognition is "...the open acknowledgement by the political branch of government of the establishment in other country of new state or new government, an acknowledgement which entails certain political and legal consequences for the relation between the recognising state and the new state or government." The Institute of International Law has defined the recognition of a new state as "...the act by which one or more states acknowledge the existence on a definite territory of a human society politically organised, independent of any other existing state, and capable of observing the obligations of international law, and by which they manifest therefore their intention to consider it a member of international community." The Dictionary of the Terminology of International law defines recognition as "A unilateral act by which one or more states declare, or tacitly admit, that they consider that a political unit which exists in fact and considers itself to be a state, as a state having the rights and duties which follow from the statehood."

Theories of Recognition: There are two principal theories of recognition explaining the nature, functions, and effects of recognition, namely, the Constitutive Theory and the Declaratory or Evidentiary theory. The main exponents of the Constitutive Theory are Hegel, Anzilotti, Kelsen, Oppenheim, and Lauterpacht. Oppenheim has summed up the theory by saying, "Through recognition only and exclusively a state becomes an international person and a subject of international law." In other words, unrecognised states have neither rights nor duties under international law, and the rights and duties of a new state are created by recognition of existing states only.

But the Constitutive Theory may create an absurd situation when an unrecognised state may do certain things which are against the international law and the existing states may not be able to take any legal action against it because legally it does not exist. Similarly, if a new state is recognised by some and not by other states, the new state is both an international person and also not an international person and this will create an anomolous situation because the new state will have rights and duties towards the states recognising it and no rights and duties towards those states which have not recognised it. On the other hand, the practices of states show that they insist on the observance of international law by the unrecognised states and governments and by implication have accepted that such state or government do possess some status under international law.

Though the Constitutive Theory has been criticised, yet it has helped in disuading the states from annexing other states by invasion or agression or by violating international law for the fear that such acquisitions may not be recognised by the existing states. In 1932, when Japan invaded Manchuria and created a new state of Manchukuo, the Secretary of States, Mr. Stimson declared that U.S.A. could not recognise an illegal state because it was established through illegal means and in violation of international law. Later, the League of Nations endorsed this Stimson Doctrine of non-recognition by stating "It is incumbent upon the members of the League of Nations not to recognise any situation, treaty or agreement which may be brought about by means contrary to the Covenant of the League of Nations or Pact of Paris." It was of course a different matter that the members of the League ignored this resolution in order to appease Italy and Germany and recognised illegal Italian conquest of Ethiopia in 1936 and German conquest of Austria in 1938.

The Declaratory or Evidentiary Theory, on the other hand,

states that statehood or the authority of a new government exists independent of recognition and the act of recognition is merely a formal acknowledgement of an established fact. In other words, a new state or government become a member of international community ipso facto the moment it is established. Most of the contemporary writers like Hall, Wagner and Brierly advocate this theory and the Institute of International Law in 1936 said "Recognition has a declaratory effect." According to Hall "States being governed by international law, the communities are subjected to law... from the moment, and from the moment only, at which they acquire the marks of a state."

The advocates of this theory argue that recognition is only a declaration of an existing fact and a state exists as subject of international law as soon as it fulfils the conditions of statehood. Though recognition does not create a new state, yet a new state can exist without recognition. Further, the retroactive effect of recognition which means all actions of a new state become legal from the date on which it came into existence and not from the date of recognition, supports the Declaratory Theory. Art. 3 of the Montevideo Convention, 1933, states "The political existence of the state is independent of recognition by other states." Pitt Cobbett concluded "so long as a political community possesses in fact the requisites of statehood, formal recognition would not appear to be a condition precedent to the acquisition of the ordinary rights and obligations incident thereto."

The fact that a new state is generally considered to have a number of rights and duties under international law even before its recognition, is an element in a favour of declaratory theory. On the other hand, the fact that the unrecognised states and governments do not enjoy full and complete rights of foreign state or government before the municipal courts of existing states, points to the constitutive character of recognition. Now a days the unrecognised states are the objects of international claims, charges of agression and other breaches of Charter of UNO, by the very states refusing recognition such as the Arab charges against Israel and the U.S.A. charges against North Vietnam. Starke rightly said "Probably the truth lies between these two theories." Thus Svarlien concludes, "It might be said that recognition is always declaratory; that it confirms the existence of a state and recognises its legal position in the international community. But it may also, at times, constitutive in so far as it has the effect of actually creating a state where none existed" as was the case of Israel in 1949 which was recognised as a state even when its territorial boundaries were not decided.

Is Recognition a Duty?

Though the existing states are bound to respect the rights of a new state under international law as soon as it has established itself effectively, yet they are not under a duty to recognise the new state either expressly or tacitly. This is because the grant or withholding of recognition is often used as a political instrument to express approval or disapproval of a new state or government or territorial change. Pitt Cobbett has pointed out. "There is no right to formal recognition. This is something which states grant or refuse at discretion." Further, recognition is not considered as a precondition for a new state to enjoy its fundamental rights.

If granting recognition is treated as a duty, the question arises as to by whom and in what manner such a duty could be enforced. Since each duty creates a corresponding right, in this case what would be the nature of this right? Considering these problems, the Draft Declaration of Rights and Duties of States prepared by the International Law Commission in 1949 did not mention the existence of any such right or duty of states. Though Lauterpacht, an advocate of Constitutive Theory, concluded that there is a duty of the existing states to recognise a new state or government, yet, the practice of the states do not justify this conclusion. On the other hand, the existing states consider granting or withholding of recognition primarily on political grounds. Starke has concluded, "Recognition is treated, for the most part, as a matter of vital policy that each state is entitled to decide for itself." But those states who withhold recognition for sometime on political ground ensure that the state or government at least possess the required legal qualifications when they finally grant recognition and this the states consider as their legal duty. Pitt Cobbett sums up "Once a political community has achieved a certain degree of development, it has such rights as exists among states to legal treatment. In this sense, and in this sense alone, it has a right to be recognised."

The political nature of granting or refusing recognition has given rise to the question whether recognition is a necessary institution. Judge Richard Baxter of International Court of Justice felt that recognition caused more problems than it solved. In 1930, Mr. Estrada, the Foreign Secretary of Mexico said that Mexico would not grant recognition because it "considers that such a course is an insulting practice and one which, in addition to the fact that it offends the sovereignty of other nations, implies that judgement of some sort may be passed on the internal affairs of those nations by other governments, in as much as the latter assume, in effect, an attitude of criticism when they decide favourably or unfavourably, as to the legal qualifications of foreign regimes."

Mathods of Granting Recognition

(a) Express and Implied Recognition

Recognition can be granted either expressly or by taking certain actions by a state from which it will be implied that it intends to grant recognition. When an existing state either through a formal notification or declaration clearly announcing the intention to recognise such as a note addressed to the state or government which has requested recognition, it is known as express recognition.

Implied recognition takes place by taking certain action although not refering expressly to recognition, yet leave no doubt regarding the intention to grant it. But as implied recognition is a matter of intention having legal consequences, great care is taken to avoid any implication of recognition, if it is not intended, eventhough there may be limited amount of relation between the two. The following acts of a state should not be treated as implied recognition:

(1) participation in an international conference in which the unrecognised state or government also takes part;
(2) the retention and continued maintenance of diplomatic representatives for an interim period, provided there are no new appointments;
(3) the appointment of consuls and other representatives not enjoying diplomatic status;
(4) maintenance of unofficial contacts, specially with regard to routine and urgent matters;
(5) in the request for and grant of extradition;
(6) in the maintenance of contact with the insurgents in a civil war;
(7) in conclusion of a multi lateral treaty to which the unrecognised state is also a party;
(8) in becoming a member of an international organisation in which the unrecognised state is also a member.

On the other hand the following acts of a state are considered as implied recognition:

(1) a message of congratulation to a new state when it gains independence;
(2) the formal establishment of diplomatic relation, specially exchange of diplomatic agents;
(3) the issue of an exequater admitting the consul of an unrecognised state;
(4) conclusion of a bilateral treaty with the state requesting recognition;

(5) a formal declaration of neutrality between the parent government and the rebels in the recognition of belligerency.

(b) Conditional Recognition

Sometimes states and governments are recognised subject to fulfilment of certain conditions, such as honour the debt liability of the predecessor state, respect the rights of the minority, or grant of most favoured nation status to the recognising state. But such a practice is condemned by international law, because recognition is considered neither as a contractual arrangement nor a political concession but a declaration of the capacity of the new state. Further, failure to fulfil the conditions of recognition may be considered as breach of international law for which diplomatic relations may be cut off as a form of sanction, but recognition cannot be withdrawn because of non-fulfilment of conditions. In practice, very often states have extracted some concession or guarantee or undertaking or stipulations from the state or government as a price for granting recognition, and this is consistent with the political nature and unilateral act of recognition.

(c) Collective Recognition

The advantages of granting recognition by some collective international act or through an international organisation cannot be denied. In the first place it would remove many of the difficulties arising due to unilateral acts of recognition by the states; and secondly, it would remove the anomaly of new state being recognised by some and not recognised by others. The International Court of Justice in its Advisory Opinion on the Conditions of Membership of UNO argued that since the States alone can become members of the UNO, any new state admitted as member after being approved by 2/3 member states of the UNO and supported by a substantive resolution of the Security Council, tantamounts their recognition of the new member as a state. In other words, any new state admitted as a member of the UNO should be treated as to have received the collective recognition of the member states of the UNO. Of course, those states which have opposed the membership of the new state do not necessarily recognise it.

Though several attempts have been made in the UNO since 1950 for granting collective recognition, all these attempts have failed because the states do not want to renounce their prerogative of granting or refusing recognition.

Withdrawal of Recognition

As a rule, recognition de jure once granted, is irrevocable and cannot be withdrawn. The recognising state can only break off its diplomatic relation, but once recognised, the state or government would not lose its international status. Thus the British Government recognised the Soviet Government de jure in 1924, but broke off relations with it in 1927 which did not affect the international status of the Soviet Government.

But the facts on which recognition was granted may disappear in course of time, such as a state may be partitioned or annexed, a government may loose effective control and may be superceded by another, or rebels recognised as belligerents may be defeated, in which case withdrawal of recognition should be automatic. Specially, the withdrawal of recognition takes place when de jure recognition is granted to a rival government which has succeeded a previously recognised government or to a state which has annexed a previously recognised state. The mode by which recognition is withdrawn is by directly informing the state or the government from which it is withdrawn, or indirectly, by withdrawing diplomatic status from the agents of defunct state or government or granting diplomatic status to the agents of succeeding state or government. So far the belligerents are concerned, recognition terminates automatically with their defeat.

De Facto and De Jure Recognition

The states may grant de facto or de jure recognition to a new state or government. De jure recognition is granted when the new regime fulfils all the conditions laid down by the international law. According to the British practice, de jure recognition is granted when the new regime:

(a) is reasonably stable and permanent;
(b) commands general support of the population;
(c) has the ability and willingness to fulfil its international obligations.

De facto recognition is granted, if in the opinion of the recognising state, the new state or government, though independent and excercises effective power, yet has not acquired sufficient stability and permanence. So Oppenheim says, "De facto recognition of a state or government takes place when, in the view of the recognising state, the new authority, although actually independent and weilding effective power in the territory under its control, has not acquired sufficient stability or does not as yet offer prospects of complying with other requirements of recognition such as willingness or ability to fulfil international obligations." Mr. Nkambo Mugerwa says, "When in the opinion of the recognising state a new regime or authority meets some but not all requirements which are deemed essential before recognition should be granted, that state may grant de facto recognition." According to Starke, "Recognition de facto means that in the opinion of the recognising state, provisionally and temporarily and with all due reservation for the future, the state or government recognised fulfils the requirements in fact."

As regards the nature of de facto recognition, Schwarzenberger says, it is "provisional", subject to fulfilment of remaining conditions and the jurisdiction of the new authority is recognised within its own territory. Prof.

Lauterpacht is of the opinion that if the remaining conditions are not fulfilled "recognition will lapse automatically or will be finally and expressly withdrawn." Thus de facto recognition is provisional, temporary, and can be withdrawn if the remaining conditions are not fulfilled. Usually, it is granted to a new authority which has come into existence excercising undisputed authority over the territory of a state. The existing states grant de facto recognition in order to secure economic advantages like continuing trading and commercial facilities or to protect the interests of their citizens with in the control of the new state or government.

A new state or government recognised de facto is entitled to:

(a) claim jurisdictional immunity for its actions with in its own territory;
(b) claim immunity for its legislative, administrative and judicial acts in the municipal courts of the recognising state.

But a de facto authority is not entitled to:

(a) diplomatic relation with the recognising state;
(b) state property of the predecessor state situated in the territory of the recognising state by virtue of state succession; and
(c) represent its nationals before the courts of the recognising state in regard to a claim or injury done in breach of international law.

Schwarzenberger sums up the distinction between the de jure and de facto recognition: "De facto recognition is by nature provisional and may be made dependent on conditions with which the new entity has to comply. It differs from the de jure recognition of a state. There is not yet a formal exchange of diplomatic representatives. The jurisdiction of the new international person is merely recognised to exist with in its own territory and any extra-territorial effects of such jurisdiction are ignored. In contrast to de facto recognition, de jure recognition is considered to be retroactive that is to say, to date back to the time when the newly recognised entity actually came into existence."

According to the British and American practice, recognition is retroactive in the sense that their courts treat as valid the acts of the newly recongnised state or government from the date of its inception and not from the date of recognition. But in matter of retroactive operation of recognition, the British court insist on a certificate from the executive indicating its intention of granting such operation; and in the absence of such a certificate retroactive effect is excluded.

If the acts of a de facto government comes in conflict with the previous de jure government which is now displaced, the foreign courts have held that the rights and status of the de facto government to prevail over that of the de jure government. This principle has been established in the cases of Bank of Ethiopia V. Bank of Egypt and Ligouori and in S.S. Arantzazu Mendi V. the Government of Republican Spain. The certificate of the foreign office that a de facto government is in effective control of the territory is to be accepted by the court was established in the case of Luigi Monta of Genoa V. Cechofracht Co. Ltd. The declaration of the executive branch of the government on the question of recognition of a foreign state or government is always treated as conclusive and binding on the courts was held in Luther V. Sagor, the Duff Development Co. V. Government of Kelantan, and Sultan of Johore V. Abubakar Tunku cases. The principle of retroactive nature of the recognition was established in the cases of Civil Air Transport Incorporated V. Central Air Transport Corporation and in the Guaranty Trust Co. V. United States.

Recognition of Government

The continuity of state is not affected by the change of their governments because it is the state and not their government which is the subject of international law. But under certain circumstances when the governments change, such governments require recognition. There is little difference either in principle or in practice between the recognition of a new state and a new government. When a new state is recognised, its new government is also automatically recognised because not only the state cannot be formed without a government but also the state acts and speaks only through the government.

Similarly the question of a new government does not arise if it has come to power through the normal constitutional process such as a president succeeding a President or a monarch is succeeded by his heir. In such cases of change, other states usually recognise the new head of government by some formal act such as by sending a message of congratulation. Thus when the change of government is in a formal and constitutional manner, recognition by other states is purely a matter of formality. So, also when a former dependency or trust territory is granted independence and statehood by its controlling state, its recognition by other states is only a formality.

But recognition of government become necessary when the new government or its head comes to power through abnormal or violent or extra-constitutional methods such as a dictatorship over a democratic government or a coup d'etat etc. Ofcourse, the change of government does not affect the international personality of a state. In the Lehigh Valley Railroad Co. V. the state of Russia, (1927) an American court said "The granting or refusal of recognition (of a government) has nothing to do with the recognition of state itself. If a foreign state refuses recognition of change in the form of government of an old state, this latter does not thereby loose its recognition as an international person."

Thus the question of recognition of a new government arises when:

(a) there is a civil war in a state and two rival governments claim to represent the same state;
(b) after a civil war, the belligerents succeed in replacing the existing government;
(c) the constitutional government is overthrown by a coup d'etat or by unconstitutional means; and
(d) the existing pattern of government is replaced by another pattern such as a monarchy by a republican or a parliamentary by presidential form of government.

As there is no uniform principles governing the grant of recognition to a new government, the states enjoy a wide degree of discretion in the matter. Brownlie has pointed out that non-recognition of governments seem more "political" than that of states because through, it the unwillingness to enter into relation with the new government is very often expressed. States sometimes follow the test of effectiveness and othertimes the test of legitimacy before granting recognition to a new government.

According to the doctrine of effectiveness, if the new government has the ability to govern, a reasonable chance of permanence, and effectively excercises its powers with in the territorial limits of the state, such government should be recognised. On the other hand, the doctrine of legitimacy states that any government that comes to power should not only have de facto control over the state, but also should be legal according to the municipal law of that state. In 1907, Tobar, the foreign minister of Ecuader, argued that the governments which come to power through extra-constitutional means should not be recognised.

While the general practice of the states show that they follow the doctrine of effectiveness, the Tobar doctrine and the doctrine of legitimacy has been severely criticised because (1) judging the constitutionality or legality of the government of another state amounts to intervention and (2) it holds an existing system of government as sacrosanct even if it is oppressive and the people of the state want to change it.

Effects of Recognition of State and Government

The general rule is that an unrecognised state or a government do not enjoy any right before the courts of a state refusing recognition. Thus an unrecognised state or government cannot sue, nor its diplomatic or other agents can claim immunity nor there can be any diplomatic relation nor can it claim the property by way state succession in the state refusing recognition. On the other hand, recognition creates legal consequences affecting the rights, powers and privileges of the recognised state or government both under the international and municipal laws of the recognising state. The effects of recognition are as follows:

(1) After recognition, both the recognised and recognising states can establish diplomatic relationship and sign treaties between themselves.

(2) The new state or the government acquires the right of suing in the courts of the recognising state.

(3) The recognised state or government acquires the right of claiming judicial immunity for its property and diplomatic persons from the jurisdiction of the municipal courts of the recognising state.

(4) The recognised state or government can claim the property of the old state or government by way of succession, situated inside the territory of the recognising state.

(5) Since the recognition de jure has retroactive effect, with the recognition of the new state or government, the legislative, executive, and judicial decisions as well as transfer of property etc., become legal and valid from the date on which de facto recognition was granted and the municipal courts of the recognising state accept them as valid and legal from that date.

(6) In case of recognition of a new government, the treaties which were signed by the recognising state with the old state are revived automatically and they come into force.

Recognition of Belligerency and Insurgency

The question of granting recognition to insurgents and belligerents came into prominence since the Spanish Civil War of 1936-1938. In the civil war in a state, the third states consider the civil rebellion as an internal matter of the state to be handled by the state concerned in the manner it deems fit. But when the acts of rebels harm the nationals, commercial or shipping interests of the third state and the parent state is unable to control them, the third states have to redefine their attitude towards the rebels and not treat them as simple law-breakers. So depending upon the situation, the third states recognise the rebels either as belligerents or insurgents.

Generally, the rebels are recognised as belligerents by the third states when the following conditions are fulfilled:

(1) There exists a state of general armed conflict between the rebels and the parent government as distinct from that of a purely local character;
(2) The rebels occupy a substantial portion of the territory of the state;
(3) The rebels conduct their hostilities according to rules of war;
(4) The rebels are organised under a responsible authority and their armed forces under a proper command;
(5) The interests of the recognising state such as commercial or shipping interests are affected due to the act of rebels for which the parent government is unable to take any responsibility. This condition is important because if a third state recognises the rebels as belligerents even if none of its interests are harmed

or affected by the conflict, it will amount to interference in the internal affairs of another state.

Though the de facto recognition of belligerent status of the rebels is considered as an unfriendly act by the parent state, yet, by recognising belligerency, the third states simply recognise the fact that the rebels are in effective control of the territory over which they excercise their authority. Since the third states have to recognise this authority in order to protect their own nationals, commercial interests, and shipping etc. the parent state should not treat this as offensive. Usually, the third states do not grant belligerent recognition to the rebels unless they are convinced that the parent government is no more in a position to protect their interests.

The following are the effects of recognition of the belligerency:

1. the recognising state maintains neutrality between the rebels and the parent government, and the recognising state is entitled to neutral rights;
2. the rebels cannot be treated as criminals and pirates and their prisoners should be treated as prisoners of war;
3. the parent government is no more held responsible for the acts of the rebels committed over the territory occupied by them;
4. the rebels acquire certain rights against the neutrals such as the right to blockade, to seize the contraband, to visit and search and the right of their ships to enter into the ports of recognising state;
5. though diplomatic representatives are not exchanged, yet consuls may be appointed between them;
6. both the parent government and the rebels are given equal status under international law so far the conduct of the war is considered.

Thus recognition of belligerency accords the rebels an international status with limited rights and duties with regard to their conduct of war.

But when the rebels do not fulfil all the conditions required for recognition of belligerency, yet they harm the interests of the third states, they are recognised as insurgents. Thus Lauterpacht says, "Recognition of insurgency is the outcome of both of the unwillingness of foreign states to treat the rebels as simply law-breakers and of the desire of these states to put their relations with the insurgents on a regular although clearly provisional basis." The third states consider the insurgents as the de facto authority over the territory under their control and conduct their relation with them in accordance with laws of neutrality and belligerency, and thus making them subject of certain rules of international law.

The effects of recognition of insurgency are:

1. the recognising state maintains neutrality between the rebels and the parent government;
2. the rebels are not treated as the law-breakers and pirates and their prisoners are treated as prisoners of war;
3. the insurgents undertake the duty of protecting the national, the commercial interests, and shipping of the recognising state.

Insurgency is not an international status as belligerency is. The insurgents do not acquire the right of blockade, the right of visit and search etc., against other states. Thus recognition of insurgency is simply a recognition of de facto authority over a territory with out confering any privilege or imposing any duty.

8

STATE SUCCESSION

The march of history produces several changes among the existing states. Some states completely disappear from the earth either due to split, merger, absorption, formation of a federation or joining a federation, partition, cession or secession. Whenever such changes take place what actually happen is the transfer of sovereignty over the territory of one state to another state. This process of replacement of one state by another or many other states is known as State Succession.

According to Oppenheim the state succession takes place "when one or more International Persons take the place of another International Person, in consequence of certain changes in the latter's condition." O'Connell describes state succession as "the factual situation which arises when one state is substituted for another over a given territory."

When the entire territory of the predecessor state is succeeded by one or more states, leaving no trace of the predecessor state, it is called Universal State Succession. The universal state succession takes place under following circumstances:

1. When a state is completely absorbed by another by conquest or annexation such as Italian conquest of Abyssinia in 1936 and Japanese annexation of Korea in 1910.

2. When states decide to merge voluntarily, such as merger of Belgium and Congo in 1908 or when a number of states decide to form a federal union as in case of American colonies forming the U.S.A. in 1789.
3. When an existing state is disintegrated due to split or one state is divided into a number of states such as the U.S.S.R. in 1991 or Yugoslovakia in 1993.

When the predecessor state continues either in diminished or in enlarged from, either lossing a part of its territory or adding a portion of territory to it, it is called Partial Succession. Partial state succession takes place under the following circumstances:

1. When a part of the territory of state, after civil war breaks away and becomes an independent state as in case of Bangla Desh in 1971;
2. A part of the territory of one state is acquired by another state by cession as in case of Berubari or by conquest;
3. When a sovereign state decides to join a federation as Sikkim did in 1994 or when a sovereign state comes under the Suzerainity or protection of another state;
4. When a protectorate or dependency or a colony acquires independence and becomes a full sovereign state.

When state succession takes place, it creates a number of problems relating to succession to rights, obligations, assets and liabilities etc., of the predecessor state. Since international law has not laid down clear cut rules governing state succession, it creates a number of problems and controversies, particularly when one state is succeeded by a number of successor states. While some writers are of the opinion that all rights and obligations of a predecessor state comes to an end when a state is extinguished, others are of the opinion that rights and obligations of the predecessor state pass on to the successor state. Brownlie has rightly stated "State succession is an area of great uncertainty and controversy." So in many cases, these problems and contingencies are sorted out through treaties between parties.

1. Consequences of State Succession

(a) Treaty Rights and Obligations

There is no uniform rule of international law governing the succession of treaties. According to Mc Nair, " the newly established states which do not result from a political dismemberment and cannot fairly be said to involve political continuity with any predecessor, start with a clean slate in the matter of treaty obligations except as regards the purely local or real obligations of the state formerly exercising sovereignty over the territory of the new states." But some writers like Castren and Brownlie do not consider the local or real treaties as a separate category. However, all writers agree that the treaties relating to the boundary lines will be succeeded by the successor state. Similarly all international laws which have been universally accepted like the Hague Convention on Pacific Settlement of Disputes, 1907, the General Treaty of Renunciation of War, 1928 etc., are binding on the successor states. The rights and obligations arising out of the multi-lateral conventions of universal acceptance on health, and technical cooperation etc., devolve on the successor states.

Certain states, when they were colonies, enjoyed considerable freedom in the international field and exercised the rights of a subject of international law. As such they could sign treaties and become members of international organisations even when they were not fully independent and sovereign. So it has been argued that such ex-colonies, after they become independent, automatically succeed to those treaties which they signed as colonial states. But others do not agree with this view and are of the opinion that such states will succeed to such treaties only when they reaffirm them after attainment of their independence.

In case of universal succession, all political and personal treaties and treaties of alliance of the predecessor state become invalid and come to an end as the successor state is not bound by them. But in case of treaties of commerce, navigation, and extradition, it is upto the discretion of the successor state to accept or reject them.

In case of enlargement of a successor state such as when a state joins a federal union, if the rights and duties are not contradictory to the same of the federal state, they are allowed to continue. But if the enlargement of the successor state is due to the annexation, the successor state is not bound by the treaties of the annexed state excepting incase of treaties granting state servitudes.

In case of partial state succession such as when a state joins an existing federation, the existing treaties of the successor state will be applicable to the acquired territory and successor state will not be bound by the treaties of the predecessor state.

But when a state merely loses a portion of territory either due to cession or secession, its international personality remaining unaffected, the old state remains bound to the treaty, provided, the treaty is not related to the portion of territory over which it lost control.

When a treaty vested some benefit on the extinct state and the successor state is also enjoying these benefits, it become liable to fulfil its corresponding obligations.

It the successor state is only an enlargement of the predecessor state such as the German Empire after incorporation of Prussia, prior treaty rights and obligations would be binding on the successor state. However, in case of formation or dissolution of a federation, no succession to treaties take place.

2. Contractual and Concessional Rights

A large number of writers are of the opinion that a successor state is bound by the contracts and concessions granted by the predecessor state.

In case of contracts, there are no uniform rules and each case has to be decided on its own nature. Usually, such contracts terminate with the State succession if the work has not started and are not binding on the successor state if not renewed by it. But if the work has started as per contract before the succession, such contracts are binding on the successor state. The successor state is not bound to pay compensation for breach of contracts by the predecessor state; but it would be bound to pay compensation for such breach of contract if the predecessor state has agreed to pay it.

In the German Settlers' Case, the I.P.C.J. decided that when a state as the owner of the property grants certain concessions to individuals, they remain valid and survive the succession and the successor state cannot cancel those concessions. But if the extinct state had granted such concessions for the purpose of war against the successor state, the latter is not bound by the concession.

3. Public and Private Property

The public properties and funds of the extinct state are succeeded by the new state. The successor state succeeds to all the assets of the extinct state such as state funds invested abroad, movable and immovable properties both inside and outside the extinct state. It also succeeds to the right to collect taxes from the citizens which were due to the extinct state. But when a state is split into several states, the assets and funds of the extinct state are proportionately divided among the successor states.

However, no succession takes place to the proprietory rights of private individuals in which they have come to have a vested or acquired right; private proprietory rights continue as before. Similarly, the private rights of the individuals of the extinct state and their relationship with each other continue as before unless specifically changed by the successor state.

4. Public Debt

There is no common practice relating to the succession to the public debt and it usually depends on the discretion of the successor state. Normally, the successor state takes over the public debt liability of the extinct state because it also takes over the assets.

Usually, the successor state accepts the public debt of the extinct state provided the debt was not incurred by it to conduct war or other hostile activities against the succeeding state.

But when a state is split up into several successor states, the public debt of the extinct state is proportionately divided among them and distribution of public debts are made through treaties.

But the problem of distribution of public debt becomes difficult in case of partial succession when over a part of the territory of a state, a new state is created either due to partition or secession. In such cases, either the debt is distributed proportionately between the old and the new states or the successor state is made to pay that portion of the debt which was incurred for the purpose of development work over its territory.

In case of cession of a part of the territory by a state to another, the problem becomes difficult. In the Ottoman Public Debt Arbitration (1925), arbitrator Eugene Borel remarked "It is impossible, despite existing precedents, to say that a power which acquires territory by cession is legally obliged to assume a corresponding part of public debt." So in the Ottoman Debt Arbitration it was established that when a state cedes a part of its territory, it retains the whole burden of public debt with it.

In the West Rand Gold Mining Co. V. Rex it was established that when a state is annexed through conquest, the conqueror is not obliged to pay the public debt of the annexed state.

5. Torts

It is now an established practice among the states that the succeeding state is not responsible for the unliquidated claims for the damages in torts (civil cases). But the successor state is bound to pay the damages for tort, if such tort has been acknowledged by and agreed to by the extinct state to pay the compensation before its extinction.

6. Municipal Law

The municipal law of the extinct state continue to be in force even after succession. But the successor state has got the right to change the existing municipal laws.

7. Membership in International Organisation

Membership in the international organisations like UNO etc. and the rights and duties derived from such membership are not succeeded by the successor states. After partition of India in 1947, though Pakistan claimed to be a "Co-successor" state, it was finally decided by the General Assembly of UNO: "When a new state is created, whatever may be the territory and population which it comprises and whether or not they formed a part of a state member of the UN, it cannot under the system of the Charter claim the status of a Member of the United Nations unless, it has formally been admitted as such in confirmity with the provisions of the Charter." In other words, as long as the old state continues, even in diminished form, the new states created out of it shall have to apply for fresh membership and the old state will retain its membership. Thus Pakistan had applied for and admitted to UNO as a new member while India retained her old membership.

8. Nationality

The question of nationality of the inhabitants arises when a state is annexed or partitioned or a portion of territory is ceded to another state. As a general rule, the people of the annexed or partitioned or ceded territory acquire the nationality of the successor state. Often treaties between the predecessor and successor states make provision regarding the nationality of the people. Now a days, option is given to the people to choose the nationality of either the predecessor or successor state with in a certain period of time. After the expiry of the period of time, the people acquire the nationality of the successor state.

Government Succession

When an existing government is succeeded by another government or there are changes in the organisation of the government or the constitutional structure is changed inside a state, the state itself continues to be bound by its rights and duties including that of treaties under the international law. The successor governments are bound by all acts of their predecessors. So the main principle governing the governmental succession is the principle of continuity.

But under the following circumstances a successor government may not be bound by the acts of its predecessor:

(a) When a new government is established through illegal or unconstitutional means, establishing a de facto control and displacing the de jure government, that displaced de jure government may notify the states that it would not be bound by any treaty entered by the de facto government with other states when it comes back to power, that de jure government will not be bound by such treaties when it comes back to power later.

(b) Where an insurgent government is established temporarily as the de facto government over a portion of territory and is supressed by the parent government subsequently, the parent government is not responsible for the debts and deliquencies of the insurgent government.

(c) When the provision of a treaty is binding subject to the continuity of the existing form of government or constitution, with their alteration, the treaty ceases to bind the new government.

(d) When a new government comes to power which is politically, socially or economically fundamentally different than the previous one, like Bolshevik government succeeding the Tsarist government, the new government may not be bound by the acts of old government.

9

STATE TERRITORY

Territory is an essential element of state because it provides the physical basis and with in it, a state exercises its sovereignty, authority, and jurisdiction. This gives rise to the concept of 'territorial sovereignty' which means that within its territorial limits, a state exercises its authority over all persons and things which are on or enters into the territory, to the exclusion of other states and thus, they become ipso facto subject of the supreme authority of the state. According to Oppenheim, "State territory is that defined portion of the surface of the globe which is subjected to the sovereignty of the state."

No foreign state has any power or jurisdiction over the territory of another state, though certain types of persons and things of another state such as the diplomatic agents and war ships eventhough physically present on the territory, enjoy the freedom from the jurisdiction of a state due to the principle of exterritoriality.

Theoritically, only one sovereign state can exist with in one territory, and more than one sovereign state cannot co-exist with in one territory because sovereignty is considered as indivisible. But in reality numerous international practices show that more than one sovereignty can co-exist with in the same territory of a state. Thus sovereignty of a state is divisible under the following circumstances:

(a) Condominium: Two or more full sovereign states can jointly exercise sovereignty over a piece of land or water as well as the people of a territory as was the case of Anglo-Egyptian condominium over Sudan in 1899 or as it is at present in Anglo-French Condominium over New Hebrides since 1914.

(b) By Consent: when the owner state agrees to allow another state to administer a part of its territory, as in case of Cypress which was administered by Britain from 1878 to 1914 with the consent of Turkey.

(c) Leases or Pledges: States frequently lease or pledge a piece of their territory to another state as was the case of Chinese lease of Kiaochao to Germany, Port Arthur to Russia, and Hongkong to Britain in 1898 for a period of 99 years. There is also another type of lease known as perpetuity lease under which the owner state grants the use, occupation, and control over a piece of its territory to another state for an unlimited period as was in case of Panama Canal by Hay-Varilla Treaty of 1903.

(d) Mandated and Trust Territories: During the period of League of Nations and since 1945 under UNO, certain state territories were placed under them for administration and the League or UNO entrusted the administration of those territories as a Mandate or Trust to its members. Though such states were not dependent states, yet their sovereignty was exercised by the Mandatory or Trustee state.

(e) Federal state: In a federal state, the constitution divides the powers of the state between central and unit governments making them independent of each other and internally sovereign over their own sphere of powers. But both the governments exercise their internal sovereignty over the same territory and people.

Types of Land Territory and Boundary Line

(a) Types

A state territory may be real or fictional. The real territory of a state includes land surface, water, sub soil and air space, while the fictional territory includes the diplomatic premises a state has in other states and its war ships when found in high seas or in the waters of another state.

According to Svarlien "the territory of a state is composed of all land and water surface with in its boundaries and jurisdiction, all the earth and water below this surface, and all the air above it." In other words, state territory includes land surface, sub-soil upto the unlimited depth, certain waters with in the land and a part of the sea, and the aerial space upto unlimited height over its land and territorial sea.

(b) Boundary Lines

The territory of a state is demarcated by boundary line. According to Oppenheim," boundaries of a state territory are the imaginary lines on the surface of the earth, which separate the territory of one state from that of another, or from unappropriated territory, or from the open sea."

The boundaries may be natural, artificial, or strategic. When the boundary line is determined with the help of such natural features as mountains, rivers, lakes etc., it is known as natural boundary line. But where such natural features are not available, the boundary lines are determined with the help of latitudes, longitudes, highways, barbed wire fencing, signs, or pillars etc. When boundary lines are adjusted to military objectives, it is called strategic boundary line.

The boundary lines are determined on the basis of certain generally accepted principles, though special solutions are also adopted by mutual agreements of the concerned states for special problems. Generally, boundary lines on the mountain range between the two states run across the highest peaks on the basis of watershed principle. On a non-navigable river, the boundary line is drawn exactly at the centre of the river which is known as "Median Line," and in certain exceptional cases, the boundary line is drawn on one of the banks of the river, leaving the river bed and other bank to the other state. In case of a navigable river, the boundary line runs through the middle of the deepest channel, known as "Thalweg," and with the change of the course of the deepest channel, the boundary line also changes. In the case of lakes there are several possible solutions, but usually either median line or thalweg principle is followed to draw the boundary line. In case of bays, gulfs, and straits, no general rule to determine the boundary line exists as history and geography play an important role in them, but on many occasions, the median line has been accepted as the boundary line. In case of maritime boundary, the line runs along the edge of the maritime sea.

Boundary disputes arose frequently in the past giving rise to some important international arbitrations such as Alaska Boundary Arbitration, 1903, Frontier Lands Case, 1959, the Temple of Preah Vihear case, 1962, the Rann of Kutch Arbitration, 1968, and Burkina Faso (Upper Voltas) and Mali Case, 1986.

Since boundaries have always been important for international relations, the general view is that they should not be disturbed. But some of the newly independent countries of Asia and Africa raised questions about the boundaries established when they were colonial countries. But now it seems that they also have accepted the principle of uti possidetis or 'as you possess, you shall continue to possess'.

Different Parts of State Territory

(a) Rivers

All rivers, according to their position, may be divided into national, boundary, international, and internationalised rivers. When a river, from its source to mouth runs within the boundary of a single state, it is called national river. But when the river divides the territory two states and the boundary line is drawn over it, it is known as boundary river. When a river, between its source and mouth runs over the territory of more than one state, it is known as international river. The internationalised rivers are also international rivers, but they are mostly navigable and their status is determined by treaties.

So far the nature of state authority over the national rivers are concerned, the concerned state exercises full sovereignty over it, determines the use of water and regulates navigation upon it. The concerned state may deny entry of foreign ships into those rivers or may prescribe conditions for their entry. As regards the boundary rivers, if a river is navigable the boundary line is fixed by the thalweg, and if non-navigable by median line. The utilisation of water and the navigation facilities of such rivers are usually determined by bilateral treaty arrangement, failing which through arbitration or conciliation methods.

So far as international rivers are concerned, each state owns that part of the river which runs through its territory. But for very long time, a controversy is continuing regarding the navigational right of a riparian and other states in the entire river. Regarding the use of water, one general rule has emerged out of the customary international law based on the principle of good neighbourliness is that every riparian state is entitled to use the water of the river, but also under a duty to use the water in such a manner which is not injurious or detrimental to the interests of other riparian states. But the Arbitral Tribunal in the Lake Lanoux arbitration between France and Spain, 1957, decided that there was no duty on a riparian state under the customary international law to consult or to obtain the prior agreement of a co-riparian state to start new river works, although it must take into account the interests of that co-riparian state in a reasonable manner. As regards the navigational facilities, each riparian state can regulate navigation on such portion of river which they own and can certainly exclude the ships of non-riparian states.

There are certain international rivers which have been internationalised through various treaties in which freedom of navigation is guaranteed to both the riparian and non-riparian states. In Europe the rivers like Danube, Rhine etc. have been internationalised through treaties like Treaty of Paris, 1814, Congress Vienna, 1815, Treaty of Versailles, 1919, and the Paris Peace Conference, 1946, and established a regime which governs the navigation of such rivers. Now, specially for Danube, a European Commission for Danube, composed of representatives of only the riparian states, was established in 1946, superceding the previous commission, to regulate the navigation on Danube.

In other continents, the navigation on them, are governed by agreements exclusively between the riparian states. Accordingly, in Africa Nile and Niger, in North America Rio Grande, Colorado, Clumbia, and St. Lawrence, and in Asia Mekong rivers are governed as per the agreements between their riparian states. In all these rivers, as M. Sahovic and W.W. Bishop have pointed out, one general principle has emerged, namely, "In all matters of navigation the principle of free navigation is asserted but at the same time the right of riparian states to regulate the application of this regime and use of the rivers is safeguarded."

Another general principle that has been firmly established is that except in the case of national rivers, no riparian state is allowed to change the natural conditions of the river on its territory to the disadvantage of other riparian states. As such no riparian state of boundary, international or internationalised rivers is allowed to stop or divert the water or flow of the river in such a way which might cause flood, drought etc. in other riparian states.

(b) International Canals

The canals are artificially constructed water-ways meant for irrigation of navigation purposes and they are integral parts of the territory of the state. In case of canals exclusively meant for navigation purposes, international law has recognised the right of the territorial state to regulate the traffic in them as in case of Corinth Canal in Greece. But there are certain inter-oceanic canals which have been neutralised and internationalised, because they are mainly used for international navigation and traffic. Such canals are the Suez, the Panama, and the Kiel, and their territorial, states had to agree to accept certain limitations internationally imposed on their sovereignty.

(i) The Suez Canal

It is a canal of 101 miles, wholly dug up on the territory of Egypt in 1854 by the Suez Canal Company and was opened for traffic in 1869. The Canal connects the Red Sea with Mediterranean sea. The Convention of Constantinoples, 1888, which regulated the navigation in the Canal, partially neutralised and fully demilitarised it. The provisions of the Convention were:

(a) the Canal was to remain open to ships of all nations both during the war and peace;
(b) both the men-of-war and merchant ships could use the Canal;
(c) it could not be blockaded at any time;
(d) no hostilities were to be committed either with in the Canal area or beyond the limit of 3 miles;
(e) all warships were to pass through the Canal area without delay and they should not stay for more than 24 hours at the two Canal ports of Suez and Port Said;
(f) shipping or unshipping of troops, ammunitions, arms, and other war materials with in the Canal area was prohibited;

(g) permanent fortification or stationing of men-of-wars in the Canal area was prohibited; and
(h) Egypt was given the power to regulate and police the Canal.

In 1956, Egypt under Col. Nasser, nationalised the Suez Canal Company which was disputed by England and France and a combined force of England, France and Israel invaded the Canal area, which came to end because of a call given by a resolution of the General Assembly for immediate cease-fire. The Secretary General was directed to send UN Peace Keeping Forces to Suez area to disengage the fighting troops.

Finally, an agreement was reached under the auspices of the Security Council, according to which:

(a) the freedom of passage through the Canal should be maintained without any discrimination;
(b) the Canal should be "insulated" from the politics of any country;
(c) Egypt agreed to:
    (i) obey the provisions of the Constantinoples Convention and UN Charter;
    (ii) fix tolls and charges in agreement with other states;
    (iii) maintain and modernise the Canal to meet the requirements of modern navigation: and
    (iv) refer any dispute regarding the Canal administration to an arbitration committee.

In 1967, Israel troops occupied the eastern bank of Canal and Egypt closed the traffic in Suez Canal on protest. But after eight years when the peace treaty was signed between Egypt and Israel in 1975, the Canal was reopened for international traffic. Today, the Suez Canal continues to be an open channel of communication under Egyptian control and sovereignty.

(ii) Panama Canal

The Panama Canal is the second largest inter-oceanic canal, connecting the Atlantic and the Pacific oceans. As per the Hay — Pauncefote Treaty, 1901, and Hay — Varilla Treaty, 1903, the U.S.A. was granted 10 miles wide territory by the Republic of Panama in perpetuity with the right of construction of a canal. The U.S.A. agreed to pay a lumpsum of $ 10,000,000 and an agreed annual rent to Panama. The concessions granted by the two treaties to U.S.A. was little short of sovereignty. But subsequently, the Republic of Panama demanded more control over the Canal area and accordingly, the treaty was amended in 1936 granting greater jurisdiction to Panama over the Canal area.

But since the end of Second World War, the Republic of Panama was not prepared to suffer limitations on its sovereignty. So a new treaty of Mutual Understanding and Cooperation was signed granting Panama more control over the Canal area including the control over the non-American people. It was also agreed by both the parties to conclude a new treaty to end the perpetuity clause of the previous treaties. So, finally, a new Panama Canal Treaty was signed at Washington between the two Governments of U.S.A. and Panama in 1977, replacing all the four previous treaties. The provisions of this new treaty are:

1. The U.S.A. recognised the territorial sovereignty of Panama over the Canal Zone.
2. The U.S.A. agreed to relinquish its control over the Canal at the end of 1999, and hand over the Canal to Panama.
3. During the period of treaty, the U.S.A. is granted the rights of operation, maintenance, and protection of the Canal.
4. The Canal is declared as "an international transit waterway".

5. The Canal is neutralised and shall remain open both during war and peace time.
6. The ships of all nations shall be allowed the transit facilities with out any discrimination regarding the conditions and charges, of transit.

(iii) The Kiel Canal

The Canal which connects North Sea and Baltic Sea, was constructed wholly on German territory in 1896. Before the First World War, through the Canal was open for ships of all nations, yet, Germany had the power to close it at its pleasure.

But the Treaty of Versailles, 1919, declared "The Kiel Canal and her approaches shall be maintained free and open to vessels of commerce and of war of all nations at peace with Germany on terms of entire equality." However, during the hostilities between Poland and Russia in 1920, a dispute arose when a British ship Wimbledon carrying arms etc., for Poland was not allowed by Germany to use the Canal on the ground that its neutrality would be compromised. The dispute was taken to Permanent Court of International Justice which held "The Kiel Canal must be open, on a footing of equality, to all vessels of commerce, but on one express condition, namely that those vessels must belong to nations at peace with Germany."

In 1936, the Nazi Government of Germany unilaterally denouced the Treaty of Versailles, of which provisions relating to the Kiel Canal was a part. So Germany declared that though the merchant ships could use the Canal, the passage of warships of other nations was made subject to its permission to enter the Canal.

After the end of the Second World War, Kiel Canal was again opened for international navigation for both warships and merchant ships.

(c) Internal Waters

The Geneva Convention on Territorial Sea and Contiguous Zone, 1958, for the first time created "Internal Waters," to include certain parts of high sea under the territorial sovereignty of a littoral state having islands, rocks etc., nearer its coast. A littoral state can have internal water by drawing a straight base line connecting the two outer most points towards the sea. The area of sea within the straight base line shall be the internal waters. Thus internal waters includes ports, anchorages, bays, seas separated by islands and rivermouths etc.

When a bay or gulf is surrounded by the territory of one state and the distance between the two openings is not more than 24 miles, it is the internal waters of that state, such as the Sea of Azov in the Black Sea. But when such a bay or gulf is surrounded by the territory of several states, there is no generally acceptable rule to demarcate the internal waters of each state. So either the littoral states may divide the waters of the bay or gulf among themselves, such as in case of Gulf of Fonseca between Nicargua and El Salvador; or littoral states may exercise their jurisdiction over their territorial sea only, treating other parts of water as open sea, as in cases of Black Sea and Baltic Sea.

In the case of land-locked sea, it is divided on its surface by median line with equal rights for the littoral states as in case of Caspean Sea between Iran and now defunct USSR.

In case of a strait, which is a natural passage connecting two areas of high sea between the land territory of one state, and whose width is not more than 12 miles, it belongs to that state. But if the strait divides the territory of two states, it belongs to both the states, and in the absence of mutual agreement, a boundary line can be drawn in the middle, keeping every point of coast of both states at equal distance from this line. According to the judgement in the Corfu Channel Case, certain straits which are used as international maritime highway, ships of all nations shall have a right to innocent passage. This principle is also recognised by the Geneva Convention of 1958. But it is still controversial if the war ships of other nations shall have a right to passage at all times.

The Geneva Convention, 1958, provides that if by adopting the straight base line principle, a portion of water which was previously a part of territorial sea or open sea become a part of internal waters, the right of innocent passage for the ships of all nation shall exist. The Convention is silent over certain "historic" bays whose width is more than 24 miles, yet the littoral states have exercised their sovereignty by virtue of prescriptive rights which other states have accepted either tacitly or expressly, such Hudson Bay by Canada, or Bay of Peter the Great by Russia.

Unless there is a treaty provision to the contrary, littoral states can prevent foreign ships using its internal waters, lay down conditions of their entry, reserve cabotage for itself close down certain areas of internal waters to shipping, exploit the natural resources etc. The foreign war ships require special permission to enter into the internal waters of another state. When the merchant ships are allowed into the ports and internal waters, the littoral state, has literally no civil or criminal jurisdiction over the ships unless requested by the captain or consul of ship's flagstate.

(d) Sovereignty Over Air Space

Sovereignty over the air space became an important topic in international law after the first flight of Zepplin in 1900 A.D. and the crossing of the Atlantic ocean by Wright brothers in 1903.

Between 1900 and 1918 A.D., the academic lawyers suggested various theories about the legal status of the air space and the most important of them were:

(a) that the air space is entirely free for all nations;
(b) that the air space upto an unlimited height is entirely with in the sovereignty of the subjacent state;
(c) that as per the analogy of the territorial waters, there is a lower zone of the territorial air space under the sovereignty of the states and a higher unlimited zone of air space free for all states; and
(d) that the entire air space is with in the sovereignty of the subjacent state, subject to the innocent passage of civil and not the military aeroplanes of other states.

To solve the issue, France took the initiative in 1908 in convening an International Air Navigation Conference at Paris, but the Conference was adjourned without reaching any agreement and the outbreak of the First World War prevented the reassembly of the Conference. But it became clear that the states would be content only with their complete sovereignty over the air space. During the War, both the belligerents and the neutrals made it clear that their sovereignty extended into air space to an unlimited height and entry of airplanes of other states without permission would not be permitted.

At the end of First World War, a Convention for the Regulation of the Aerial Navigation, known as Paris Convention, was adopted as a part of the Treaty of Versailles in 1919. The main provisions of the Convention were:

1. Every state was to have complete and exclusive sovereignty over its air space on territory and the territorial waters. But each state was to allow innocent passage to the aircrafts of other states subject to fulfilment of conditions laid down by Convention.
2. Each state can prohibit the flying over certain areas of military importance.
3. Each aircraft must be registered in the state of which their owners are nationals. Such aircrafts, when

engaged in international flights, must also bear the registration marks, name of the owner, and his residential address.

4. The Convention distinguished between scheduled international air lines and non-scheduled air lines as well as between the aircrafts which are engaged in international flight into private and military aircrafts.
5. Every aircrafts engaged in international flight should get special permission to fly over with or without landing rights and should carry certificates of airworthiness, competency, licences for the operating crew, a list of passengers, bills of lading, log books and special wireless licences. But such aircrafts can fly in the air space of another state, with or without the landing right, only with the permission of that state.
6. All aircrafts which did not belong to the categories of aircrafts of scheduled air lines or military aircrafts, were to be treated as private aircrafts, eventhough they were government aircrafts belonging to custom or police departments. Such private aircrafts when exercising their right of innocent passage in overflying the air space of another state, must fly in the prescribed route and without landing.
7. The private aircrafts, while overflying the air space of another state, must land when ordered to do so by the subjacent state at the appointed aerodrome. The subjacent state had the right to visit the aircrafts and verify their documents both upon their landing and departure.
8. Military aircrafts were not to fly over nor land on the territory of another state without special permission. But once they were allowed, they were to enjoy the privileges of exterritoriality, normally enjoyed by the war ships of foreign states. Other state aircrafts such as police or custom aircrafts were to be treated as

private aircrafts.

9. Carriage of goods by air or air-cabotage was reserved for the aircrafts of the state concerned with in its territory.
10. The Convention established an International Commission for Air Navigation (I.C.A.N.) as a permanent Commission under the League of Nations to deal with various problems relating to aircrafts, air space etc.

Since the U.S.A. and some other states of America could not become party to the Paris Convention which was a part of Treaty of Versailles, they concluded a Convention of Commercial Aviation at Havana in 1928, in the line of Paris Convention. Another Convention was signed at Warsaw in 1929 in order to bring unification of certain rules regarding carrying goods etc., by air transport. Thus before the Second World War, the landing rights for foreign aircrafts remained with in the discretion of the subjacent states.

But due to the tremendous development in technical and navigational matters and due to the increase in the volume of commercial air traffic both before and during the Second World War, it was felt necessary to lay down uniform rules, particularly regarding air transit and landing rights of foreign aircrafts. Further, states having scheduled international air lines to distant countries wanted allocation of air traffic. So to solve these problems an International Civil Aviation Conference was convened at Chicago in November 1944, in which over 40 states represented. The object of this Conference was to conclude world wide arrangements governing commercial air traffic rights as well as dealing with the technical and navigational matters relating to international civil aviation.

The main discussion in the Conference were concerned with obtaining agreement of participating states to "Five Freedoms of Air", namely:

1. to fly across the foreign territory without landing;
2. to land for non-traffic purposes;
3. to disembark traffic in a foreign country from the state of registration of the aircraft;
4. to pick up traffic in a foreign state and carry them to the state of registration of the aircraft; and
5. to carry tragic between two foreign states.

Of the five "Freedoms," only the first two "Freedoms" obtained the support of majority states attending the Convention. Accordingly, the Conference concluded two Agreements, namely, the International Air Services Transit Agreement signed by 33 states incorporating the first two freedoms, according to which a state party to the agreement may prescribe a route to be followed with in its territory and may designate aerodromes to be used by the foreign aircrafts; and a second agreement, the International Air Transport Agreement containing all the five 'Freedoms' was signed by 19 states. Thus it was clear that the third, fourth and the fifth freedoms could not command general acceptance of states as principles of international law.

Besides these two Agreements, the Conference drew up a Convention on Civil Aviation in order to establish a permanent organisation, and accordingly, the International Civil Aviation Organisation was established as a subsidiary of the UNO and it also superseded the International Commission of Air Navigation of 1919. This Convention also provided codes for aircrafts, their personnel, on health and safety rules, and recommended custom and immigration methods and navigational facilities. The International Civil Aviation Organisation (I.C.A.O.) since its inception in 1947, has been actively functioning and has succeeded in the conclusion or adoption of several agreements and conventions governing various aspects of air navigation, safety, traffic etc.

The Chicago Convention laid down that internal air traffic or air cabotage might be reserved exclusively for the aircrafts of the state concerned. All state aircrafts, including the military aircrafts were to have no rights of over-flight or landing in the territory of another state without its special permission, except in time of war or duly notified emergencies. It also laid down the duties in general terms to be observed by the subjacent states such as equality of treatment and non-discrimination in granting permission to use the air space etc. The Convention also directed the state to take necessary steps to make air navigation safer and easier.

The Chicago Convention did not result in any material changes in the international laws of air. It rather reaffirmed many provisions of the Paris Convention and in many cases helped in removing the ambiguities or sharpening the words of Paris Convention. But Chicago Convention failed in its major task of regulating traffic, landing rights, and transit facilities. Later, the states sorted out these problems through bilateral agreements incorporating all or some of the Five Freedoms, which are neither uniform nor free from defects. But all these bilateral treaties contain a number of similar or common features which the Chicago Convention could have incorporated in a single convention. In recent years, the introduction of wide-bodied jumbo aircrafts having capacity to carry large number of passengers and cargoes and the frequency of journeys due to higher speed, have created a number of problems which are crying for solutions.

Apart from aviation, aerial space is used for many other purposes such as wireless communication, artificial rain making, and prevention of pollution etc., for which the international laws are gradually emerging through bilateral and multilateral treaties.

In respect of radio and wireless communication, the following two principles have emerged:

1. Every state has a right to prevent the injurious transmission of radio waves through its air space; and
2. Every state is under an international duty not to allow its territory and aerial space used for transmission of radio waves injurious to other states.

As regards the use of space and outer space for the purposes of testing of nuclear bombs and use of satellites, etc. certain restrictions and responsibilities have been imposed by treaties and resolutions of UNO. The Nuclear Test Ban Treaty of 1963 has banned the testing of nuclear devices in the atmosphere, outer space and under the water. The various space treaties concluded under the auspices of the UNO have banned the military use of space and outer space, emplacement of missiles etc. in moon and other celetial bodies, and have imposed definite liabilities on the states launching satellites and space objects for the damages caused to other states in case of accidents. These treaties have imposed definite duties on states in the use of their air space and outer space.

But still there are a number of problems of air space created due to the technological and scientific developments for which no international law has emerged so far, and such problems are:

(a) States who use rain-making devices in their air space, may deprive the adjacent states the benefit of rain-bearing clouds, there by causing drought in those states.

(b) The use of atomic energy for certain purposes may cause dangerous radiations due to accidents such as the Chernobyl incident of now defunct USSR, affecting the cloud, rain and air of the neighbouring states

(c) The problem of noise created by the super-sonic jets which is highly injurious to the health of people of subjacent states.

(d) The problems relating to atmospheric pollution and the environment.

But of late, the international community has become accutely conscious of this problem because of the threat of warming up of global atmosphere, melting of polar ice caps and consequent rise in the level of water of oceans causing submergence of coastal areas, and radical climatic changes causing prolonged drought or floods. Further, the serious damage caused to the ozone layer in the atmosphere which protects the earth from harmful ultra violet rays of sun, due to increasing release of chlorofluro carbons (CFC) and by the fumes released due to burning of hydro carbons, have led to laying down certain restrictions on their use. So a Convention on Protection on Ozone Layer was signed at Vienna in 1985 and a Protocol was adopted in 1987 at Montreal on the reduction of consumption of CFC and other chemicals causing similar consequences. The Toronto Conference in 1988 decided for substantial reduction of carbon dioxide from the atmosphere. After the Earth Summit at Rio de Jenerio, now there is a discernible attempt towards the adoption of a code of international law in the pattern of Law of Sea for prevention of pollution and protection of environment.

Acquisition and Loss of State Territory

In the international arena, a state's power, authority, and importance is always determined according to the territorial area which it possesses. So it is no wonder that the problem of acquisition and loss of territory always occupied an important position in the international law.

A state may acquire title to territory by two principal methods of acquisition, namely, original and derivative. When a state acquires land territory which does not belong to any other state, it is called original, and when a state acquires territory from another state, it is called derivative method of acquisition. There are five traditional modes of acquisition of territory, namely, occupation, accretion, subjugation, prescription, and cession. Starke suggests that territory can also be acquired by adjudication or award by a conference of states such as territorial redistribution in Europe at Versailles Peace Conference in 1919. Erstwhile Soviet writers suggested plebiscite as a method, but this appears more to be a preceding step to acquire than actually a method of acquisition of territory.

There are certain acquisitions of territory in the past which cannot be fitted into the traditional methods such as:

(1) territory acquired by a state as a result of an award by a boundary commission, or arbitral tribunal or International Court of Justice;
(2) territory acquired by a state by virtue of a treaty with the rulers or representatives or people of indegenous tribes who were previously its sole and exclusive occupants;
(3) long and continuous recognition by other states of a state's territorial sovereignty eventhough it was acquired through ambiguous methods;
(4) succession of a new state to the territory of its predecessor;
(5) a piece of disputed territory distributed through a treaty of compromise or settlement as was done in case of Beagle Channel between Argentina and Chile by a treaty of 1985.

The acquisition of territory by a state by any of the methods prescribed depends on the following factors:

(1) previous legal status of the territory;
(2) the way in which the possession and control of it is obtained by the state;
(3) effective control and authority has to be proved.

Different Modes of Acquisition

1. Occupation

It is one of the oldest and most important method of acquisition of unappropriated territory and territorial expansion of states. According to Oppenheim, "Occupation is the act of appropriation by a state by which it internationally acquires sovereignty over such territory as is at the time not under the sovereignty of another state." According to Lawrence, "Occupation as means of acquiring sovereignty and dominion applies only to such territories as are no part of the possessions of any civilised state."

Thus only a territory which is terra nullius, i.e. territory belonging to none or the territory inhabited by indegenous tribes who are not part of the civilised world can be acquired through occupation. Independent private individuals or corporations can acquire territory only when they are authorised to do so or their actions are subsequently ratified by a state.

Mr. Max Huber in the Island of Palmas case, 1928, said that occupation must be followed by peaceful display of authority in order to establish a state's title over it. The Permanent Court of International Justice in the Eastern Greenland case, 1933 stipulated that occupation must be 'effective' and to be effective the following conditions must be fulfilled:

(a) intention or will to act as a sovereign; and
(b) visible excercise of sovereignty.

The intention of a state to occupy the territory can be known from that state's notification to the other interested states. But a simple declaration of occupation or a casual visit to the territory or activities of the private individuals of the state etc., does not give the right of occupation to a state. But when a new territory is discovered, the hoisting of national flag or declaration of sovereignty over it gives that state "inchoate" title, which acts as a temporary ban to occupation by another state and such a title would lapse unless that state effectively occupies it within a reasonable time. If that state fail to change the inchoate title into a real title within a reasonable time, other states are free to acquire it by occupation. Further, while judging the effectiveness of occupation to grant territorial sovereignty over the occupied territory, the competing claims of other states should also be taken into account.

Since occupation to be valid should be effective, the occupying state must excercise and display its sovereignty by taking possession of and establishing administration over the territory, or by such other acts as fixing its boundaries, concluding treaties with other countries recognising its authority over the territory etc. In the Minquires and Ecrehos case, 1953, the International Court of Justice stressed the importance of "state functions", such as local administration, excercise of local jurisdiction etc., to prove the continuous display of sovereignty in order to confirm the title over the occupied territory.

Though the effective occupation is important, yet many a times the states exaggerate the extent of their occupied area. Sometimes, a state by occupying effectively the river mouth, claim sovereignty over the entire territory through which the river and its tributaries flow. Sometimes a state effectively occupy the coastal area and claim sovereignty over the entire hinterland. Sometimes after effectively occupying a territory, the occupying state claim the neighbouring territory as essential for the integrity, security and defence of effectively occupied territory. So Oppenheim says, "In truth, no rule can be laid down beyond the general principle that occupation reaches as far as it is effective."

As soon as the occupation over a territory is established by a state, it comes under the international law and no other state can acquire it through occupation. The state which assumes sovereignty over the occupied territory becomes internationally responsible for the territory and for the acts of the people over it.

In the Polar regions of the Arctic and Antarctic, the neighbouring states have put forward their claims by adopting 'sector principle'. The main justification for sector principle is that the usual rules and requirements of occupation cannot be applied to the Polar regions because of their inaccessibility, hostile climatic conditions, and lack of settlement. So the effective physical control over this territory to occupy it is not possible. But the sector claim by a limited few states is not admissible under international law because of the objections by the non-sector states, doubts of jurists about the validity of the claims, and the generally held view is that the Polar areas should be subjected to an international regime.

So far as Antarctic is concerned, a Convention on Peaceful Cooperation in the Antarctic was signed at Washington in 1959, according to which though no state has renounced its territorial claims, yet the claimant states have undertaken not to take actions individually, justifying their new demands. They have also undertaken not make new territorial claims. But this treaty has been strongly disputed by the states of the Third World, who want the UNO to deal with the affairs of the Antarctic. They want that Antarctic should be treated as a common heritage of mankind and the entire Antarctic area should be preserved as a 'World Heritage Park' because of its unique environment. They also want that any revenue derived from the exploitation of the region should be shared with the third world states.

2. *Accretion*

When the land increase through new formations created due to the geophysical changes, it is known as accretion. When such changes due to act of nature take place within the territorial boundary of a state, such as creation of an island within the national river, the question of enlargement of territory does not arise. But when such formations are created at the river mouth or with in the territorial sea, they constitute enlargement of territory. According to the customary international law, the concerned state can extend its sovereignty over such formations without taking any special steps for it.

Accretion may be due to artificial or natural causes. Artificial accretions are due to man-made reasons such as construction of embarkments, dykes, breakwaters etc., which can be constructed both in the rivers and seas. But such artificial constructions by one riparian state in a boundary river is not permitted by international law as it may cause disadvantage to the other riparian state. The states, however, may construct artificial formations far in the sea, even beyond the low water mark and any territory that may accrue can be claimed by that state.

The natural formations that are created may be alluvions, deltas, new islands, and dried up river-beds. When the soil washed up by the water is deposited on a river bank or on the sea shore, it is called alluvion. Through alluvions the territory of a state may be enlarged considerably. If such alluvion occurs on the bank of a boundary river, it becomes the part of the territory of that riparian state on whose embankment it has formed, and a new boundary line on the course of the river which has now changed, have to be drawn either through the median line or through the thalweg.

In case of deltas, which are created at the mouths of rivers due to gradual deposit of sand, stone, and earth etc., they are to be considered as the accretion to the territory of the state to which the river mouth belongs, eventhough the delta may have formed outside the maritime belt.

New islands are created in the river and both with in and out side the territorial sea. If an island is created with in a national river, it belongs to that state. But when such an island is created with in a boundary river, and if the island is with in the boundary line, it belongs to that state; but if this island is on the boundary line itself, it shall be divided between the two riparian states. If an island is created within the maritime belt of a state, it belongs to that state. But if an island is created either outside the maritime belt or in the high seas, it belongs to none and can be acquired by occupation by any state.

Sometimes, river beds dry up. If it is a boundary river, the boundary line over the dried up river shall be drawn at the middle and both the riparian states will extend their territory upto that boundary line.

3. Cession

Cession is a derivative mode of acquisition of territory. According to Oppenheim cession is "the transfer of sovereignty over state territory by the owner-state to another state." Though the cession of territory between two states is regulated by the international law, cession of territory to private persons or corporations is not.

The cession of territory by a state may be voluntary or compulsive. It may take place through peaceful means such as purchase, sale, gift, or exchange. The examples of voluntary and peaceful cession are, the sale of Alaska by Russia to USA in 1867, the exchange of Heligoland for Zanzibar between Germany and Great Britain in 1890, and the gift of Venice by Austria to France in 1866. On the other hand compulsive cession takes place as a consequence of a war either by means of a treaty or by other kinds of pressure, such as the cession of Alsace—Lorraine by France to Germany in 1871.

The acquisition through the cession shall be treated as complete only when the authority over the ceded territory is effectively transferred to the ceded state, which will assume all international responsibility, rights, and obligations for the ceded territory. As a rule, no third power has the right veto the cession of territory by one state to another.

4. *Subjugation*

It is also a derivative mode of acquisition of territory. The territory of the enemy may come under the control of the victor state through military conquest, but conquest alone ipso facto do not make the conquering state sovereign over that territory. To acquire the title over the conquered territory, the conqueror must formally declare its intention to annex the territory through note or notes to all other interested powers. Annexation turns the conquest into subjugation. As a general rule, no third power has a right of intervention when a territory is subjugated except when its interests are endangered or balance of power is disturbed. But the validity of title by subjugation of territory does not depend upon the recognition of other states.

Today, with the prohibition of threat or use of force in Art. 2 (4) of the UN Charter, subjugation cannot be considered as a legal method of acquiring territory.

5. *Prescription*

Prescription is another derivative mode of acquisition of territory. When a state acquires title over a territory on the basis of de facto excercise of sovereignty over a certain period of time, it is called prescription. According to Oppenheim, prescription is "the acquisition of sovereignty over a territory through continuous and undisturbed excercise of sovereignty over it during such a period as is necessary to create, under the influence of historical development, the general conviction that the present condition of things is in confirmity with international order." Thus a title through the prescription requires a length of time during which de facto sovereignty is peacefully excercised uninterruptedly. The adequacy of the length of time is to be decided by an international tribunal.

But prescription as a mode of acquisition of territory is controversial because of the impossibility of resolving the question of time limit.

Loss of State Territory

The state territory which is acquired by one state by any of the modes of acquisition, can also be the cause of loss of territory of another state. So dereliction, operation of nature, cession, subjugation, and prescription can be the modes of loss of state territory.

When a state, which occupied a territory, completely abandons it later, it is called dereliction. When a state abandons a territory with the intention of nothing to do with it in future, that state ceases to excercise its sovereignty over the territory for all future times, and as such loses the territory. Dereliction as a mode of losing territory corresponds with occupation as a mode of acquisition of territory.

When a state cedes a territory to another state, it loses that territory which is now acquired by another. Thus cession is both a mode of acquisition as well as loss of state territory.

Corresponding to accretion as a mode of acquisition of territory, a state may lose territory due to disappearance of land due to volcanic actions, change of the course of a river, or due to other natural causes.

In case of a territory which is conquered and subjugated, it causes loss of territory to one state and acquisition to the other.

When one state acquires a territory of another state through prescriptive rights, the former state loses and later acquires territory.

Due to civil war or revolt, when a part of the territory breaks off and form a separate state, as was done in the case of Bangala Desh in 1971, the parent state loses territory. Thus civil war or revolt followed by secession is a mode of loss of state territory.

SERVITUDE

The doctrine of servitude has been imported from Roman Law and its application in international law is of recent origin. Though some writers are of the opinion that its application in international law is not a success, yet the concept still continues to be used in the contemporary international law.

Oppenheim defines servitude as "Those exceptional restrictions made by treaty on the territorial supremacy of the state by which a part or the whole of its territory is in a certain way made to serve a certain purpose or interest of another state." Starke defines it as "an exceptional restrictions imposed by treaty on the territorial sovereignty of particular state where by the territory that state is put under conditions or restrictions serving the interest of another state or non-state entity." According to Fenwick servitude may be defined as "obligations on the part of the state in possession of the territory to permit a certain use to be made of it by or in favour of another state or states."

Thus servitude is an obligation attached to the territory of a state giving rise to corresponding right in rem to another state. These obligations are attached to territory and are generally perpetual obligations. A state under servitude undertakes certain restrictions on its sovereignty and jurisdiction by agreeing to do or refraining from doing certain acts on that territory. The acceptance of servitude, however, does not represent a negation of sovereignty, though the state under servitude is bound to observe the conditions prescribed for the territory. Since servitude is always attached to the territory of a state, no servitude can exist on territory which belongs to none such as Antarctic.

Types

Oppenheim has divided servitude into four types namely, affirmative, negative, economic, and military servitudes.

When a state grants a right to another state or its citizens to perform certain acts on its territory or on a part of it, such as granting fishing rights in its territorial waters, permitting to construct and operate railway lines, use of ports, aerodromes etc., it is called as positive servitude. But when a state undertakes to refrain from doing certain things on its territory on the demand of another state such as agreeing not to admit foreign ships into its ports, or undertake not to raise the strength of its armed forces beyond certain limits or not to fortify certain areas of its border, negative servitude exists. When a state agrees to allow the troops of another state to pass through its territory, or station troops on its territory, or create demilitarised zones, or grants concessions for establishment of naval or air bases or fortify certain areas, military servitude exists. But when a state agrees to grant certain rights in economic or commercial matters such as granting fishing rights, free navigation rights in its internal waters, or custom free zones, economic servitude exists.

Since servitude right is one in rem, it follows that the servitude remains in force in perpetuity and donot change with the change of government or territorial changes due to cession or annexation. In case of territorial changes, such obligations are binding on the successor states. Dr. H.D. Reid says, "Servitude establish a permanent legal relationship of territory to territory, unaffected by change of sovereignty in either of them and terminable only by mutual consent, by renunciation on the part of the dominant state, or by consolidation of the territories affected."

The servitude of a state can come to an end by mutual agreement between the concerned states, by express or tacit renunciation of the right by the beneficiary state, or when the beneficiary state annexes the state or portion of territory to which servitude is applicable.

10

THE LAW OF SEAS

Starke has rightly pointed out, "No branch of international law has undergone more revolutionary changes during the past four decades, and especially during the immediate past decade and half, than has the law of seas and maritime highways." To bring these revolutionary changes it took three international conferences on the law of seas under the auspices of the U.N.O and twenty seven years of hard negotiations. Finally, on 10th December, 1982, at Montego Bay in Jamaica, a comprehensive code of international law on seas was concluded, which is now known as United Nations Convention in Law of Seas, 1982, which henceforth be referred as UN Convention, 1982. The UN Convention, 1982, formally came into force in 1994.

Historical Background: The high seas or the open seas have been considered as important by the states since the dawn of civilisation. But since medieval period in general, and 15th century in particular, the statesmen and the writers had concentrated their attention on highseas. In the beginning stress was given on free navigation and free fishing rights in the high seas. But in the 15th and 16th centuries, due to great maritime discoveries by European navigators, European states claimed the right to excercise their sovereignty over large portion of high seas and sometimes over an entire ocean, such as Portugal's claim over entire Indian Ocean and Spain's claim over the Pacific Ocean and Gulf of Mexico. But simultaneously, the demand by other states for the 'freedom of high seas' also began to develop. Since "freedom" did not mean unregulated lawlessness in the high seas, certain rules come into existence though the customary international law, such as ships of all types on high seas were subject to jurisdiction and protection of the state to whom they belong, that ships sailing under an unauthorised flag were liable to be captured, and that war ships of any state were authorised to visit and search ships suspected to be sailing under false flag or engaged in slave trade or in piracy.

The littoral states started exercising their sovereign rights over a part of highsea closer to their coast on the consideration of their safety and security. This part of sea came to be known as maritime belt or territorial waters and since 1958, it is now known as Territorial Sea. The territorial waters though claimed to be under the sovereignty of the littoral states, was subject to the innocent passage of ships of all nations. By 18th century though the littoral state's sovereignty over this water was established, yet its limit was not fixed. In 1702, Bynkershoek, through his 'cannon shot principle' suggested that every littoral state was to have that width of maritime sea under its sovereigntly to which a cannon shot fired from the coast could travel, and later this distance was measured to 3 nautical miles. Though by 19th century, the 3-mile limit was accepted by major maritime states, yet it failed to become a universal rule of international law, because many states wanted a wider breadth of the territorial waters. Many maritime states, both through customary international law and treaties acquired certain right over the ships of other states such as the right of 'hot pursuit', beyond their territorial waters.

Under certain international treaties such as the Convention for the Protection of Submarine Cables, 1884, and the General Act for Repression of African Slave Trade, 1890, states mutually conceded the jurisdiction to other states over their ships in the high seas.

The first attempt to codify the laws of sea was made by the Hague Codification Conference in 1930. But this Conference failed in its task because of unwillingness of several states to accept the 3-miles rule for territorial waters and accept the concept of 'contiguous zone; i.e. an area of water adjacent to the territorial waters, over which the littoral state was to have 'control' but not sovereignty.

After the Second World War, specially during the period of 1945 to 1951, a number of states unilaterally proclaimed their exclusive jurisdiction, control, and sovereign rights over the oil, minerals and other resources of the continental shelf, i.e., the submerged sea bed, which is a natural prolongation of and contiguous to the landmass, eventhough out side the territorial waters, upto a depth of 200 metres of sea.

Again, the International Law Commission in 1949 decided to codify the various laws relating to the high seas, and in 1956, it submitted a draft on territorial sea—the term it suggested in place of maritime belt or territorial waters—to the General Assembly of the UNO. The General Assembly in a resolution in 1957 decided to convene an international conference to discuss all aspects of high seas and lay down rules of law for them.

Accordingly, the first UN Conference on Law of Seas was held at Geneva in 1958, and succeeded in adopting the Convention on Territorial Sea and Contiguous Zone, the Convention on High Seas, the Convention on Fishing and Conservation of Living Resources, and the Convention on the Continental Shelf. However, the Geneva Conference could not reach agreement on two important questions, namely, the breadth of the territorial sea and the limits of fishing. So the General Assembly decided to convene a Second Conference on Law of sea 1960 to consider these two unsettled questions. But the Second UN Conference also failed to reach agreement on them.

Since both the UN Conferences did not deal with the problems of access to sea by the land-locked states, the UN convened a conference in 1965 at Newyork, which concluded a Convention on the Transit Trade of Land Locked States.

Though the four conventions concluded at Geneva in 1985 and the New York Convention of 1965 collectively established a regime of laws governing the different parts of the high seas, yet a number of related matters, the most important of which are, the breadth of the territorial sea, right of innocent passage of war ships at all times in the territorial sea, the right of ships and over flights by aircrafts over the waters of the archipelagoes, and the problem of protection and conservation of marine species etc., remained to be solved. In addition, the International Court of Justice, in the North Sea Continental Shelf case, enunciated certain new principles regarding the division of common continental shelf between the neighbouring states. The four Geneva Conventions of the 1958 also failed to acquire general agreement of all states because of various reasons. Moreover, in the post-1960 period, due to the technological advancement, not only some of the provisions of the four Geneva Conventions became inadequate, but also certain new problems such as depletion of the fishing stock, pollution of the marine environment due to oil spills, the threat of nuclear weapons being placed on the floor of the sea bed, and the exploitation of minerals by the more advanced states in the deep sea bed required solution.

Some of these problems were dealt through multilateral treaties. Accordingly, the problem of oil pollution of the high seas was dealt with by two international conventions, namely, Convention in Relating to Intervention on the High Seas in case of Oil Pollution Casualities, and the Convention on Civil Liability for Oil Pollution Damages, were adopted in 1969 at Brussels. Similarly, the Treaty on the Prohibition of the Emplacement of Nuclear Weapons and other Weapons of mass Destruction on the Sea Bed and Ocean Floor and the Sub-soil there of, 1971, has prevented the militarisation of the sea bed. But the most important problem, that agitated majority of states was the attempt of some developed states to exploit the mineral resources on the deep-sea bed due to their technological and financial superiority to the disadvantage of the developing states. So to resolve all these problems, the General Assembly in 1970 decided to convene the third UN Conference on Law of Seas, not only to deal with the post 1960 new problems, but also to reopen the settlements which were reached by the previous UN Conferences on Law of Seas in 1958 and 1960.

The Third UN Conference on law of Seas was convened in 1973 at New York. The Conference took nine years and held twelve sessions to hammer out a final text based on the consensus of states and finally adopted a comprehensive regime on high seas, territorial sea, continental shelf, deep sea bed, and environmental issues. This United Nations Convention on the Law of Seas (UNCLOS) was finally signed by as many as 118 states on 10th December, 1982, at Montego Bay, Jamaica. By the time the treaty document was closed for signature on 9th December, 1984, the total number of signatories to the Convention was 159. Today the different parts of the high seas are regulated by the rules laid down by the UN Convention on Law of Seas, 1982, henceforth briefly to be referred as UN Convention, 1982.

The UN Convention, 1982, contains 320 articles divided into 17 parts, with 9 Annexes and 4 Resolutions. The laws relating to different parts of high seas as laid down by the UN Convention, 1982 are as follows:

1. The Territorial Sea and Contiguous Zone

The rules governing the territorial sea and the contiguous zone are dealt with in the Part II of the UN Convention, 1982 containing 33 articles.

Art. 2 grants sovereignty to the littoral states over the territorial sea including the air space above it and the bed and sub soil under it. It is located between the land territory or internal waters, or in case of archipelagoes, between the archipelagic waters, and the high seas.

Before the 18th century, the littoral states made extensive and extravagant claims of sovereignty over large streches of high seas. But such claims were gradually brought down to that portion of sea as were necessary to that states's security, safety, and capacity to dominate it. In 1702, Bynkershoek advocated the "cannon shot rule", according to which a littoral state was to have sovereignty only over that part sea adjacent to its coast to which a cannon shot fired from the coastal artillery gun could travel. Later this distance was measured to three nautical miles and all major maritime states like Britain and U.S.A. accepted it and this rule prevailed upto the beginning of the present century. But since this rule did not satisfy many states who wanted a wider breadth, three-miles limit could not become a general rule of international law. Finally, the issue was solved by the UN convention, 1982, which laid down that the breadth is not to exceed 12 nautical miles.

The breadth of the territorial sea is to be measured, in case of straight coastal lines, from the low water mark; and in case of indentured coast or if there are islands, rocks, etc., along the coast, from a straight base line drawn by connecting two outermost points towards the high seas. But the straight base line should be in the general direction of the coast. The states having mid-oceanic islands, can also claim territorial sea around such islands. The straight base line principle shall also be adopted to demarcate the territorial waters of the archipelagoes. In case of bays, if surrounded by the territory of a single state and the distance between the two mouths is not more than 24 miles, a straight line connecting the two mouths shall be drawn to enclose maximum area of water with in the line. But this principle is not applicable to "historic bays".

The UN Convention, 1982, grants rights of innocent passage to ships of all nations, but not the right of over flight to the foreign aircrafts. The passage to be considered innocent must not be prejudicial to the peace, good order, and security of the littoral state. The Convention has specified twelve categories of activities which are to be considered prejudicial to the interest of the littoral states. While exercising the right of innocent passage, the voyage of the ship must be continuous and expeditious, except in case of emergency or distress. The submarines and other underwater vehicles while passing through the territorial sea of another state must navigate on the surface and show the flag.

The littoral state may prescribe rules and regulations regarding safety of navigation, protection of the navigational aids, cables, pipelines etc., prevention of illegal fisheries, and prevention of customs, fiscal, immigration, and health offences. All ships exercising the right of innocent passage are to comply with those rules and regulations. The littoral state may designate sea-lanes for oil tankers, nuclear powered ships, and ships carrying hazardous materials. The littoral state cannot levy any charges on the ships using its territorial sea, but can collect payments for services rendered to the ships.

The littoral state may prevent the passage of a ship if it is not innocent. It can also close down certain areas of the territorial sea for passage of ships on the grounds of its security. The right to fisheries and natural resources as well as cabotage is exclusively reserved for the littoral state. The littoral state must give adequate warning against any known danger in its territorial sea.

The littoral state cannot excercise its criminal jurisdiction on board a foreign ship passing through its territorial sea either to arrest any person or to conduct any investigation in connection with any crime committed on board the ship during its passage, except when:

(a) the consequences of the crime extends to the littoral state;
(b) the crime is likely to disturb the peace of the country or good order of the territorial sea;
(c) requested by the master of the ship or by the diplomatic or consular agent of the flag state;
(d) it is necessary for the suppression of illegal traffic in narcotic drugs.

As regards the crimes committed before the ship entered into the territorial sea, the littoral state cannot take any action during its passage through the territorial sea.

Similarly, to excercise its civil jurisdiction, the littoral state cannot stop or divert the ship nor can it arrest it. But the littoral state can excercise its civil jurisdiction against a foreign ship in the territorial sea after it leaves the internal waters.

The war ships enjoy immunities from the jurisdiction of the littoral state. But if a foreign warship does not comply with rules and regulations of the territorial sea, it may be asked to leave the territorial sea immediately and its flag state is to bear 'international responsibility ' for the damages caused to the littoral state.

Each littoral state can establish a contiguous zone adjacent to its territorial sea upto a limit of 24 miles measured from the base line from which the breadth of the territorial sea is measured. The Convention allows a littoral state to excercise control necessary to prevent the violation of its customs, fiscal, sanitary or immigration laws with in its territory or the territorial sea.

2. Exclusive Economic Zone (EEZ)

The concept of Exclusive Economic Zone has

revolutionised the law of seas. Starke has rightly said, "UNCLOS will always be remembered in the history of international law as having given birth to, or at least nurture to fall strength, the concept of the exclusive economic zone."

The Part-V of the UN Convention, 1982, deals with EEZ. According to the Convention, EEZ is an area upto 200 nautical miles, beyond and adjacent to the territorial sea, over which the littoral state has sovereign rights, but not territorial sovereignty "for the purpose of exploring, exploiting, and conserving the resources of EEZ." The littoral state has also jurisdiction regarding establishment and use of artificial islands and structures, scientific research, and protection and preservation of the marine environment, subject to the rights of other states. Other states can conduct marine scientific research with the consent of the littoral state. But once such consent is granted, the littoral state can withdraw it only under the circumstances listed in the Convention. But the freedoms of high seas such as the rights to navigation, over flight, and laying cables and pipe lines of other states remain unaffected, and in case of disputes, these are to be resolved "on the basis of equity and in the light of relevant circumstances".

The littoral state has the right of construction of artificial islands and platforms, installations and structures, and utilisation of the living resources of the EEZ. The highly migratory species of fishes and marine mammals would be accorded special protection. The littoral state can excecise its sovereign rights and jurisdictions by enforcing its laws and the regulations without the right to board, inspect, and arrest the foreign ships.

The land locked and other geographically disadvantaged states can also participate "on an equitable basis" in the exploitation of the living resources, if there is any surplus, by entering into bilateral agreements with the littoral state.

The delimitation of EEZ between the opposite or the adjacent littoral states shall be made by "agreement on the basis of international law" in order to achieve an equitable solution, and in case of dispute, it shall be decided by the machinery provided by the Convention.

3. Continental Shelf

In the post war period of 1941-51, several maritime states unilaterally proclaimed exclusive jurisdiction, control or sovereign rights over the resources of the continental shelf. In 1945, President Truman of the U.S.A. claimed the sea bed beyond the territorial waters upto the depth of 100 fathoms or 200 meters. The claim of the U.S.A. and other states over the continental shelf was also supported by writers like Lauterpacht and Svarlien.

The continental shelf is the submerged bed of sea which is contiguous to the continental land mass and hence considered as its extension, located beyond the territorial sea and generally continues upto the depth of 200 meters of sea level.

The claim of states over their continental shelf was the result of the advancement of technology in the mining of oil and minerals in the sub-soil and the bed of sea, as well as in the exploitation of non-mineral resources like fishes and pearls. This claim of states over their continental shelf was finally accepted by the Geneva Convention on Law of Seas, 1958. The Geneva Convention defined it as the "sea-bed and sub-soil of the submarine areas adjacent to the coast but outside the territorial sea to a depth of 200 meters or, beyond that limit, to where the depths of the superjacent waters admits exploitation of the natural resources of the said areas; and to the sea-bed and sub-soil of similar submarine areas adjacent to the coast of the islands." But many writers criticised this definition as not being definite, unambiguous, and clear, specially the provision "admits of exploitation".

The Geneva Convention on Continental Shelf, 1958, granted sovereign rights to the littoral states for the purpose of exploring and exploiting the resources. But if a littoral state does not undertake the work of exploration and exploitation, no other state can undertake these activities without the consent of that littoral state. Further, the continental shelf need not be effectively occupied by the littoral state nor does it require an express proclamation to establish its claim. The Convention granted the exclusive sovereign rights to the littoral states to the sea bed, and sub- soil, but not over the surface water or the air space over it, as these are treated as parts of high seas. The littoral state cannot prohibit other states from laying cables and pipe lines, navigation, fishing, and scientific research without any justifiable reason. Subject to these conditions, the littoral state was allowed to construct, operate and maintain installations and structures for the purpose of exploitation of the continental shelf.

Regarding the division of common continental shelf, the Geneva Convention laid down that, in the absence of an agreement, the boundary line between two opposite states shall be the median line, and in case of two adjacent states, the boundary line shall be at equal distance from the nearest points from the base lines of the territorial seas of both the states. But in 1969, the International Court of Justice in North Continental Shelf Case laid down that division of common continental shelf should be (a) by agreement between the concerned states, and (b) the division should be on' equitable principle'.

In view of the unsatisfactory provision of 'exploitability criteria' and the judgement of the International Court in 1969, the Third UN Conference on Law of Seas, decided to revise the provisions of Geneva Convention. So the UN Convention, 1982, in Part-VI not only gave a new definition of the continental shelf, but also discarded the 'exploitability criteria'. According to Art. 76, "The continental shelf of a coastal state comprises the sea bed, sub-soil of the submarine areas that extend beyond its territorial sea through out the natural prolongation of its land territory to the outer edge of the continental margin, or to a distance of 200 nautical miles from the base lines from which the breadth of the territorial sea is measured where the outer edge of the continental margin does not extend upto that distance." This definition of the continental shelf includes the sea bed, sub-soil of the shelf, the slope, and the rise upto the continental margin, but does not include deep sea floor and its sub-soil. Though the littoral states are permitted continental shelf upto 200 nautical miles, under certain special conditions, they can also claim upto 350 nautical miles. The UN Convention, 1982, has prescribed a procedure to delineate the outer limit of the continental shelf when it is extended beyond 200 miles. Accordingly, the concerned littoral state must submit its claim along with all necessary informations to the Commission on Limits of the Continental Shelf and must also submit them to the Secretary General of the UNO who shall give due publicity to it.

As regards the rights of the littoral states, there is very little difference from that of those under the Geneva Convention. The UN Convention, 1982, grants, in addition, the right to dig tunnels in the sub-soil of the continental shelf irrespective of depth of the water above the sub-soil to the littoral states.

In the division of the continental shelf between the two opposite or adjacent littoral states, the UN Convention, 1982, accepted the principles enunciated by the International Court of Justice in the North Sea Continental Shelf Case by stating that the delimitation shall be effected by agreement in accordance with equitable principles, and if necessary, by adopting the median or equidistance lines.

Where a littoral state has made a claim beyond 200 nautical miles, it shall make payments or contributions out of the productions from this area as per as prescribed formula to an Authority to be set up for the purpose, and the amounts thus collected shall be distributed among the state parties to the Convention on an equitable basis and with due consideration for the developing, poor, and land locked states.

4. High Seas

The importance of high seas for commerce, communication, fishing and other purposes has always been recognised and has served as the basis for regulation of its legal status. In the beginning, high seas were open to all nations, but after the great maritime discoveries of 15th and 16th centuries, the powerful maritime states like Spain, Portugal, and England etc., claimed sovereign rights over certain oceans in order to maintain free communication with their far off colonies in different parts of world. Simultaneously, in opposition to such extravagant claims, the principle of freedom of high seas gained ground. Those who claimed sovereign rights over large portion of high seas based their claim on the principle of res nullius, which means the sea being outside of the occupied territory and sovereignty of states, is subject to occupation by a state who first laid its claim to it. But those who advocated the freedom of high seas advanced the theory of res communis omnium, which means those which are common to all cannot be wholly and exclusively occupied by any state, as the use of these are common to all states. Finally, the second theory prevailed and high seas were considered as free and open to all nations. Subsequently, when the laws of seas were codified, this principle was recognised in all conventions.

Today the freedom of high seas mean the freedom of peaceful use of high seas by all states and no part of it can be claimed by a state under its sovereignty, freedom of navigation, freedom to lay submarine cables and pipe lines, freedom of fisheries, freedom to conduct scientific and technical research, and freedom of over-flight of air crafts over the high seas.

But 'freedom of high seas' also means regulation of various activities of states in the high seas through laws and rules. Many of the present day rules governing high seas were first originated through the customary international law, but after the conclusion of the Geneva Convention on Law of Seas 1958, and more specifically, after the conclusion of UN Convention on Law of Seas, 1982, these rules were codified after updating and modifying them. The UN Convention of 1982 particularly revolutionised the law of seas, because of the creation of Exclusive Economic Zone. Today, the term high seas applies only to those parts of sea which are not included in the internal waters, territorial seas, EEZs, or in the archipelagic waters of achipelagoes, and the freedom of high seas is applicable only to this defined area of high seas. The UN Convention, 1982, is a comprehensive set of rules governing all aspects of seas, and the rules governing the high seas are laid down in the Part-VII of the Convention, which is divided into two sections, namely, 'General Provisions' and 'Conservation and Management of the Living Resources of the High Seas'.

Freedoms of High Seas

1. *Freedom of Navigation:* According to Art. 89, no part of the high seas can be under the sovereignty of any state and as such there is complete freedom of navigation of all types of ships of all nations. All ships sailing in the high seas must be registered in a state and states are free to lay down the conditions of the registration of the ships. After the registration the ship acquires the nationality of the state of registration and can use its flag during its navigation on the high seas. No ship can change its flag and nationality during a voyage except in case of change of owner or change of state of registration. There should be a genuine link between the ship and the state of registration. All ships shall be under the exclusive jurisdication of the flag state while on the high seas and other ships can interfere with it only under certain exceptional circumstances.

The UN Convention also grants these rights in Arts. 125 and 126 to the land-locked states. The neighbouring coastal state is to provide port facility and transit facilities to the land locked states through mutual agreements. The ships flying the flag of a land locked state should not be discriminated, but treated equally with that of ships of other states in the ports of the coastal state. However, the Convention did not grant any definitive right to the land locked states and their transit rights depend on the good will of the neighbouring coastal state.

A ship during its navigation on the high seas is subject only to the international law and the laws of the flag state. The Convention states "every state shall effectively excercise its jurisdiction and control in administrative, technical and social matters over its ships." Even when a ship is involved in collision or any other incidents of navigation on the high seas, neither the ship nor its master and crew can be arrested or detained for investigation by any state other than the flag state. The Convention imposes a duty on all ships to render all assistance to ships in case of danger, distress, or collision.

Though states cannot interfere in the freedom of navigation of ships, still under the following cases other states can interfere in the navigation of ships of other states:

(a) *During War:* When there is war, the belligerent parties attack the war ships of each other. The merchant ships carrying contraband to the enemy can also be seized.

(b) *Stateless Ship:* Any ship which has not registered itself in any state is a stateless ship. Some ships for mischievous reasons sail under the flag of two or more states and use them according to their convenience and such ships are also treated as stateless ships. All stateless ships are liable to be captured by the war ships of any nation.

(c) *Right to Visit and Search:* As a general rule, a merchant ship on the high seas is subject only to the control of the flag state. But when a war ship of a state has reasonable grounds of suspicion that a merchant ship is stateless or that the ship is of its own nationality but does not for some reasons fly the flag that state, or that the ship is engaged in certain illegal activities like piracy, slave trade, or unauthorised broadcasting etc., the war ship can stop that merchant ship, visit it, and carry out investigations.

(d) *By Virtue of International Conventions:* The state parties to certain international treaties concede to other states the right to visit and search their ships on the high seas during the peace time, to enforce the provisions of these treaties such as the Convention for the Protection of Submarine Telegraph Cables, 1884 The General Act of Brussels for Suppression of Slave Trade, 1890, and the Convention on Conservation of North Parific Fur Seal Herds. The UN Convention grants this right to states in Arts. 99 and 108.

(e) *Hot Pursuit:* For the protection of the interests of the littoral states, the UN Convention in Art. 111, has conceded to the states the right of "hot pursuit". The right of hot pursuit is meant to prevent the ships which have violated the regulations of the littoral state by escaping into the high seas. The rules of hot pursuit are that:

(a) it should commence immediately while the ship or one of its boats is still with in the territorial waters or contiguous zone;
(b) the pursuit should be continuous and uninterrupted;
(c) the pursuing ship should give audio or visual signals to the fugitive ship to stop from such a distance which can be heard or seen by it;
(d) the right is to be excercised by clearly marked war ships or government ships or air crafts specially authorised for the purpose;

(e) the hot pursuit ceases as soon as the fugitive ship enters the territorial sea of its flag state or that of a third state.

(f) *Piracy:* The pirates, since the ancient time are considered as 'hostis humani generis' or enemy of the humanity, and as such come under the universal jurisdiction of all nations. The ships engaged in piracy and their crew can be arrested by the war ships of any nation for trial and punishment. If a war ship has a reasonable ground for suspicion that a merchant ship is engaged in piracy, it may board that ship on the high seas to carry out investigation, regardless of the nationality of the ship. If the suspicion is confirmed, the pirate ship can be seized and the persons on board may be arrested for trial and punishment. For the first time, the UN Convention defined piracy in definite and precise manner in Art. 151 by stating that any illegal violence or detention or any act of depredation committed for "private ends" by the crew or passengers of a "private" ship or aircraft on the high seas or in a place outside the jurisdiction of any state, against the persons or properties of another ship or aircraft or any act of voluntary participation in the operation of a ship or aircraft with the knowledge that the act is piracy or any act of incitement or deliberate help in committing such acts. The Convention has imposed a duty on all state parties to cooperate to the fullest extent in the suppression of piracy in the high seas.

(g) *Unauthorised Broadcasting From Sea:* The UN Convention in Art. 109 deals with the unauthorised and unregulated radio and T.V. broadcastings from ship and installations stationed outside the national jurisdiction of states in the high seas. The Convention directs all states to cooperate in the suppression of such illegal broadcasting and capture the ships, installations and persons for trial and punishment. Such illegal acts can be prosecuted by the courts of flag state of the ship or the state where the broadcasting installations are registered or the state of persons' nationality or any state where such broadcasts are received or any state whose authorised radio communications are interfered by such illegal broadcastings.

B. Freedom of Fisheries

Freedom of high seas includes an unlimited freedom of fishing, which originated at a time when it was assumed that fish and other natural resources of sea were inexahaustible. But in modern times due to tremendous technological development in methods of catching the fish and exploitation of other natural resources, a fear has generated that unrestricted activities in these fields may lead to depletion and even extinction of these resources of the high seas. This realisation led the Geneva Convention to conclude the Convention on Fishing and Conservation of Living Resources of the High Sea in 1958. The UN Convention, 1982, not only confirmed the provisions of Geneva Convention, but also added a procedure for negotiation and agreement between the states for conservation measures. The UN Convention, 1982, deals with the conservation and management of living resources of high seas in the Section 2 of Part VII. The main provisions of the Convention are:

(a) All states have right to fishing in the high seas subject to the treaty obligations, but the littoral state shall have special rights and interests in the fishing and other living resources.
(b) The littoral state shall have special duty of imposing conservation measures for the fishing and other living resources on the basis of available scientific data and all other states are bound to cooperate with the littoral state in their conservation and management.
(c) The Art. 61 of the Convention requires that the littoral state shall determine the allowable catch in its EEZ. While determining the allowable catch, the littoral state is duty bound to "promote the objective of

optimum utilisation of the living resources" of the EEZ and to allow other states access to any surplus beyond its national requirement as determined by it. Thus the UN Convention allows considerable freedom to the littoral state in the utilisation and management of the living resources of the high seas.

C. Freedom to Lay Submarine Cables and Pipe Lines

All states have the freedom to lay submarine cables and pipe lines on the floor of the high seas. This freedom was first recognised by the Paris Convention on the Protection of Submarine Cables, 1884 and was later confirmed by both the Geneva Convention, 1958 and the UN Convention, 1982. Specially the UN Convention, though recognised the right of states to explore and exploit the continental shelf, yet also imposed a duty on the littoral as well as other states not to obstruct or impede in any way the laying and maintainance of the cables and pipe lines by other states. The Convention also imposes a duty on all states to make laws with the provision of payment of compensation for the damages to the cables and pipe lines by ships and persons under their jurisdiction.

D. Right of Overflight

The freedom of overflight of aircrafts of all nations over the high seas existed under the customary international law and both the Geneva Convention and the UN Convention have only recognised this right.

According to both the Conventions, the state of registration of the aircraft alone shall have jurisdiction over the aircrafts while flying over the high seas. Another state can interfere with such flight only when:

(a) an offence committed on board the aircraft has effect on that state;

(b) the offence is committed by or against its citizens ;

(c) such overflight is against its security ;

(d) the aircraft violates air safety regulations;

(e) the offence committed is under the universal jurisdiction granted by such multilateral agreements like Tokyo Convention, 1963 against hijacking of aircrafts.

11

OUTER SPACE

The first artificial satellite Sputnik was sent into the orbit on 4th December, 1957 by the USSR, and since then several states have taken to the exploration of space very seriously and have sent numerous space objects into the outer space and cosmos for various purposes of meteorology, missile detection, espionage, navigation, earth survey, remote sensing of earth and for various scientific purposes.

Today great advances have been made in the field of space technology, astronautical navigations, and in planetary exploration-both manned and unmanned space vehicles. Both USA and the erstwhile Soviet Union as well other states have conducted successful and far reaching experiments in the outer space and cosmos as a result of which man could land on moon, probing space objects could collect valuable informations on Mars and Venus, reusable space shuttles like Atlantis are now used for the journey into the space, and now plans are afoot to have a platform in the space from where the scientists can conduct research into still deeper parts of outer space. These developments require regulation of activities of states in the outer space, failing which the unregulated competition may lead to conflicts.

The UNO, through its General Assembly resolutions took initiative in conclusion of the following treaties and agreements which laid down certain basic principles relating space laws, namely:

1. The Treaty on Principles governing the Activities of States in the Exploration and Uses of Outer Space, including the Moon and Other Celetial Bodies, 1967, popularly known as Space Treaty, 1967. This is the first Code of Space laws.
2. The Agreement on the Rescue of Astronauts, the Return of Astronauts and the return of Objects Launched into Outer Space, 1968, is popularly known as Astronaut Agreement, 1968.
3. The Convention on The Liability for Damage Caused by Space Objects, 1972, popularly known as Liability Convention, 1972.
4. The Convention on Registration of Objects Launched into Outer Space, 1974, popularly known as Registration Convention.
5. The Agreement Governing the Activities of States on the Moon and Other Celetial Bodies, 1979, popularly known as Moon Treaty, 1979.
6. The Second U.N. Conference on the Exploration and Peaceful Uses of Outer Space held at Vienna in 1982, known as UNISPACE—82 discussed the demiltarisation of Outer space and certain other problems relating to outer space.
7. In addition to above treaties and agreements, the Nuclear Test Ban Treaty of 1963 has imposed a duty on the States to prohibit, prevent and not to carry out nuclear weapon tests in the atmosphere including the outer space.

From the above treaties and agreements certain fundamental rules of international law of space can be derived:

1. The doctrine of the sovereignty of the subjacent state over the air space to an unlimited height cannot work in practice so far as the satellites and other space objects are concerned. Since the beginning, these space objects have passed over the air space of other states on innumerable occasions

and since no state has ever protested that this constitutes a violation of its air space, a new permissible rule of customary international law has come into existence in this regard. Theoritically, this new rule can be reconciled with the old rule that states have sovereignty over their air space to an unlimited height but that space crafts, unlike the air crafts, have right to innocent passage. However, in various resolutions of General Assembly it is clearly stated that the sovereignty of the subjacent states do not extend to the outer space. In other words, at a particular point, the air space ends and outer space begins and opinions vary that it should be from 110 km to 300 miles from the sea level. However, this controversy is unimportant because the minimum height at which the satellites are orbited is at least twice the maximum height at which the aircrafts can fly. So states now concede the right of innocent passage to satellites and space objects launched for peaceful and scientific purposes, but not for military purposes.

2. According to the Space Treaty of 1967, no state can claim sovereignty over outer space and states are free to carry out peaceful exploration for the benefit of mankind. The Treaty also directs the states not to establish sovereignty over moon, but to use the moon and other celetial bodies exclusively for peaceful purposes. Every state sending a space object is duty bound to give notice of launching and provide other technical informations to the UNO through the Secretary General.

3. As per the Astronaut Agreement, 1968, all states are duty bound to recover and restore the astronauts and the space objects to the state of registration in case of distress, accident or emergency. The astronauts are to be considered as "Envoys of Mankind".

4. As per the Registration Convention of 1975, all space objects must be registered in a state and the space object is to bear the marks of nationality of the state of registration.

These are also to be registered with the UNO. The launching state is duty bound to inform the public and international scientific community of the nature, locations and results of the activities in space conducted by them. The launching state is also duty bound to take precautions to avoid injury to other states and against making permanent changes in the environment of earth or contamination or pollution of the upper atmosphere and outer space. A state should also not create obstacles for the scientific exploration of outer space by other states.

5. As per the Liability Convention of 1971, the launching state is internationally liable to pay compensations for damages caused to other states or their persons either on earth or in air space or in outer space. Any dispute regarding compensation are to be referred to a claim Commission.

6. The launching state retains its sovereignty over the space objects wherever they may be or wherever they may land. Other states are duty bound to facilitate the movement of space objects intended for peaceful exploration of outer space. They should also render all help to space ships making forced or emergency landings on their territory.

7. The communication satellites such as INTELSAT should be freely available to all states on a non-discriminatory basis.

8. Under the Space Treaty, 1967, the states are prohibited from placing in the orbit or in outer space or on celetial bodies any object carrying nuclear bombs or other mass destruction weapons. They are also prohibited from establishing military bases, installations, fortifications, and weapon testing and undertaking any military activity.

9. The Test Ban Treaty, 1963, prohibits states from testing nuclear bombs in the atmosphere including outer space.

But the rapid development of space technology has made

it difficult on the part of international law to keep pace with all developments and activities in the space. So the Second U.N. Conference on Exploration and Peaceful Uses of Outer Space held at Vienna in 1982 (UNISPACE-82) came to a practical conclusion that it is impossible to establish legal control over all activities related to outer space and so development of regime of laws should be left to various international and national space organisations engaged in the exploration and use of outer space.

In the recent times two types of satellites, namely, Remote Sensing Satellites and Direct Broadcasting Satellites, have generated a lot of controversies. The Remote Sensing Satellites are used for finding new sources of minerals, water sources and energy sources, locating fishes in the sea, surveying the forest areas and making survey of land areas for various purposes. But it can also be misused by the launching state for taking photographs of military installations, troop movements etc., of another state endangering the security of that state. The question arises whether the launching state should take the consent of the state on whose territory the remote sensing is to be undertaken. Similarly, under the Space Treaty of 1987, every state has a right to station a geostationary satellite which may be used for direct broadcasting and telecommunication purposes. Since broadcasting from such a satellite is likely to be received by another state, question arises whether the prior consent of that state is necessary for such broadcasts. But a number of writers who advocate freedom of information as one of the fundamental human rights argue that no such prior consent of states is necessary. However, the solution to both these problems have not yet emerged nor there is a likelihood of emerging in the near future.

12

JURISDICTION

The term' jurisdiction of a state' means the excercise of judicial and administrative processes, and the power of enforcement of law and order by a state. But there is no uniform practice of states regarding the excercise of jurisdiction While some states restrict their jurisdiction with in their own territory, others excercise it beyond their territory. Nowadays due to increasing speed of transport and communication, development of world wide commercial organisation and growing international criminal activities like drug trafficking etc., the excercise of jurisdiction of a state has become more complex and diversified. As such now almost all states excercise jurisdictions beyond their territorial limits, provided its excercise does not infringe upon the territorial sovereignty of another state. In fact, there is little or no limitation on the jurisdiction that a state can assume, except that no state would excercise jurisdiction over persons, things, or matters which is not its concern. A state can excercise jurisdiction not only over its own territory, but also in the areas which do not form a part of territory of another state. In the Lotus Case, 1927, the Permanent Court of International Justice said, "the first and foremost restriction imposed by international law upon a state is that—failing existence of a permissible rule to the contrary—it may not excercise its power in any form in the territory of another state." But the Court in the same case also said, "It does not, however, follow that international law prohibits a state from excercising jurisdiction in its own territory, in respect of any case which relates to acts which have taken place abroad...."

Broadly, the jurisdiction of a state can be classified into territorial, personal, protective, universal, and criminal.

1. Territorial Jurisdiction

The international law concedes to every state the right to excercise its jurisdiction over persons, properties, acts, and events occuring within its territory. The territory of a state, according to Brierly, is that defined portion of globe "with in which it normally excercises, subject to the limitations imposed by international law, jurisdiction over persons and things to the exclusion of other states." Many modern writers hold the view that the state territory is "an area" determined by international law for excercise of jurisdiction of that state. In the Cristina Case, 1938, Lord Macmillan said that a state "should possess jurisdiction over all persons and things with in its territorial limits and all causes of civil and criminal arising with in these limits." Thus territorial sovereignty and territorial jurisdiction are synonymous.

For the purpose of jurisdiction, besides land, territory includes internal waters, territorial sea, continental shelf, E.E.Z, ships on the high seas, and aircrafts.

(a) Internal Waters

Internal waters consists of waters of part of high seas which are under the full sovereignty of the littoral state and includes ports, anchorages, bays, internal seas, seas separated by islands and river mouths. The Geneva Convention on Law of Seas, 1958, created the internal waters by adopting straight base line principle. Accordingly, by connecting the outermost points towards the sea, the water that falls between the coast and the straight base line is known as internal waters. In case of bays and gulfs, if the distance between the two openings is not more than 24 miles, such bay or gulf is treated as internal waters.

Internal waters is under the full sovereignty of the littoral state. No foreign ship can enter into it, unless before 1958 this water was a part of the territorial sea or high seas and was used for international navigation. Foreign war ships require special permission to enter into the internal waters of another state. The littoral state can regulate the navigation, prohibit navigation in certain areas, reserve cabotage exclusively for its own nationals, and has exclusive right to exploit the resources of the internal waters. When foreign merchant ships enter into the ports or internal waters, they are subjected to the jurisdiction of the littoral state. The littoral state normally do not excercise its criminal jurisdiction for offences committed on board these ships, unless requested to do so either by the captain of the ship or the consul of the flag state. But if the offence effects the peace or good order of the port or internal waters, the littoral state can excercise its criminal jurisdiction. But war ships once granted permission to enter the internal waters, enjoy exterritorial privileges and the littoral state has no jurisdiction over them.

(b) Territorial Sea

Territorial sea is a belt of high seas which lies between the coast or internal waters and the high seas, whose breadth should not exceed twelve miles. The sovereignty of the littoral state being limited over it, its jurisdiction is also limited. According to UN Convention on Law of Seas, 1982 (UNCLOS, 1982), all types of ships of other states have a right of innocent passage through it. The passage of the ship is treated as innocent as long as it is not prejudicial to the peace, security, or good order of the littoral state, and the littoral state can prevent the passage of a ship if it is not innocent. The littoral state can also close down the navigation of ships in certain parts of its territorial sea on the grounds of security and can also lay down rules and regulations, which all ships using the territorial sea for innocent passage must comply. If a war ship does not comply with these rules, the littoral state can ask it to leave its territorial sea. But the littoral state cannot levy any charges nor can it excercise its criminal jurisdiction over the foreign ships unless requested to do so either by the captain of the ship or consul of the flag state. The littoral state is also not permitted to excercise its civil jurisdiction to arrest or detain foreign ships during their passage through the territorial sea.

The UNCLOS, 1982 also permits every state to claim a zone of waters of high seas contiguous to the territorial sea, whose breadth should not exceed 24 miles from the base line. In this Contiguous Zone the littoral state may excercise control necessary to prevent or punish for violation of its customs, immigration, health and sanitary, and financial etc., rules within its territory, territorial sea or internal waters. It is to be noted that the littoral state can only excercise control but not sovereignty over the Contiguous Zone.

(c) Continental Shelf

The UNCLOS, 1982, allows every littoral state to claim continental shelf consisting of sea bed and sub-soil of the submarine areas that extend beyond its territorial sea upto the edge of the continental margin or upto a distance of 200 nautical miles.

The littoral state has sovereign rights over the shelf only for the purpose of exploring and exploiting its natural resources. If the concerned littoral state does not exploit the shelf, no other state can undertake these activities without the express consent of that littoral state. No other state can lay its claim by way of either occupation or proclamation. The sovereign rights of the littoral state shall not extend to the superjacent water or air space and shall not effect the freedom of navigation or freedom to lay submarine cables and pipe lines of other states. The littoral state shall have the exclusive right to construct and errect artificial islands, platforms installations and structures on the shelf and can authorise drilling of the sea bed.

(d) Exclusive Economic Zone (EEZ)

The UNGLOS, 1982, allows every littoral state an area beyond its territorial sea, not exceeding 200 nautical miles of breadth as exclusive economic zone. In this area, the littoral state do not have sovereignty, but sovereign rights for the purpose of exploring, exploiting, conserving, and managing the natural resources. The littoral state, with due regard to the rights of other states, can establish and use artificial structures and islands for the purpose of marine scientific research, protection and conservation of the marine environment etc. But the freedom of high seas of other states such as freedoms of navigation, overflight, laying of submarine cables and pipe line etc., shall not be effected. The littoral state has the power to regulate the utilisation and conservation of resources of the EEZ, specially the conservation of certain marine species. But the Convention also has set the limit of the powers of the littoral states regarding enforcement of their regulations and sovereign rights.

(e) Ships on the High Seas

Every sovereign state has a right to use the high seas for navigation of all types of its ships. But every ship sailing on the high seas must be registered in a state, whose nationality it will possess and whose flag it must fly during its navigation on the high seas. Every ship can be under the flag of one state only.

The ships sailing on the high seas shall be, at every point, under the jurisdiction of the flag state, as it is treated as its "floating island". The UNCLOS, 1982 says "every state shall effectively excercise its jurisdiction and control in administrative, technical, and social matters" over the ships. The war ships and state owned and operated ships for noncommercial purposes enjoy complete immunity from the jurisdiction of other states. In case of collision and other types of crimes related to navigation, the penal or disciplinary actions against the persons involved can only be taken either by the flag state or by the state to whom such persons belong. No other state, except the flag state, can arrest or detain a ship on the high seas.

(f) Air Space and Air Crafts

International law grants exclusive sovereignty and jurisdiction over the air space on land territory, internal waters, and territorial sea to the subjacent states. Through foreign civilian aircrafts have a right of innocent overflight and land for non-traffic purposes, regular aircrafts engaged in carrying traffic etc. can land and operate with the permission of the state concerned through bilateral treaties. The subjacent state has a right to prescribe a route to be used, designate airports to land, and close down certain areas for flying for the foreign aircrafts and can reserve the cabotage for itself. But military and other government aircrafts of other states require special permission to enter into the airspace of another state.

When an aircraft, except the military and government aircraft, of another state lands on the territory of the subjacent state, that state has the right to verify the documents of the aircraft both at the times of landing and take off. According to the Tokyo Convention, 1963, if any offence is committed on the aircraft during its flight, in the air space of the subjacent state, it excercises jurisdiction over such crimes. But if the aircraft escapes into the air space of another state after commission of the crime, the state of registration of the aircraft shall have the jurisdiction. But if the criminals have landed in and captured by a third state, they can be extradited for their trial.

According to the Hague Convention, 1970, in case of hijacking of an aircraft during flight either by force or threat or intimidation, the state of registration of the aircraft or the state in which the aircraft lands shall have jurisdiction. But if they have been captured by a third state, either that state should try and punish them or they should be extradited to the state of registration for the purpose. The Montreal Convention, 1971, deals with certain other types of unlawful activities during ' in flight' or ' in service '. The Convention has directed the state parties to establish jurisdiction over such unlawful activities. But all the three Conventions of Tokyo, the Hague, and Montreal are applicable to the offences on aircrafts when committed outside the territory of the state of registration.

2. Personal Jurisdiction

According to international law, a state may assume jurisdiction over persons by following either the active nationality principle according to which the state has jurisdiction over the persons who are its nationals, or passive nationality principle according to which a state assumes jurisdiction when its nationals are suffering injury or civil damage caused by a foreign national. Thus under the active nationality principle a state may excercise civil and criminal jurisdiction over its nationals both within and without its territory by imposing taxes, ordering them to enter into military forces and by asking them to submit to its various commands. Some states like India and Germany excercise criminal jurisdiction over their nationals even if the crime was committed outside their territory. The customary international law recognises the jurisdiction of a state to apply its laws to acts done abroad by its nationals.

The states also extend their jurisdiction over the offences committed in the places which are not under the sovereignty of any state, such as high seas, Antarctic, outer space etc. Jurisdiction on the high seas is based upon the national character of the ship involved. The offences committed on board the ship in the high seas is governed according to the laws of the flag state. But when an offence is committed by a national of one state on the ship of another flag state in the high seas, both the states shall have jurisdiction over the offender. But offences committed on territory which is terra nullius, such as Antarctic, the offender shall be governed by the laws of state of his nationality. This principle is also recognised by the Antarctic Treaty, 1962.

States excercise jurisdiction over its nationals while they are executing the judgements of courts against their property inside the state, or upon them personally when they return or wait to prosecute them after their return, for the acts done abroad.

Problems arise when a person is subjected to the conflicting laws of two states—the state of nationality and the territorial state where he is found. Such a problem may arise if by the law of one state an act is considered lawful or even compulsory, while such act is considered as an offence by the other state. Usually the state of the nationality does not punish its nationals because at the time of commitment of offence he was under the physical control of the other territorial state. There seems to be a general agreement that the jurisdiction of the territorial state should take priority over the state of nationality.

3. Jurisdiction by Protective Principle

States have extended their jurisdiction to certain acts committed outside their territory eventhough the nationals of other states are involved in these acts. A resolution of Institute of International Law in 1931 says, "Any state has the right to punish acts committed outside its territory, even by aliens, when the acts constitute:

(a) an attack against its security;

(b) a falsification of its money, stamps, seal, or official marks.

This rule is applicable even when the facts considered are not punishable by the penal law of the country on the territory of which they have been committed."

Several states have asserted such jurisdiction on the

protective principle. The justification for this protective jurisdiction lies in the fact that the state excercising jurisdiction is affected by the crime, while the state on whose territory the act was committed may not consider it as an offence. Most municipal laws punish the offences relating to security, counterfeiting of money etc., eventhough committed in the territory of another state irrespective of the fact whether these acts are treated as criminal or not by that state.

4. Universal Jurisdiction

When a state can prosecute and punish persons committing certain types of crimes, irrespective of the place of the commitment of crime or irrespective of the nationality of either the victim or the offender, it is called universal jurisdiction.

Since the ancient times, the pirates were considered as 'hostis humani generis' or enemy of the humanity. Piracy jure gentium is described as an international crime, because a pirate is considered as the enemy of every state. But till recently there was no universally acceptable definition of piracy. Oppenheim defined piracy as "every unauthorised act of violence against persons or goods committed on the open sea either by a private vessel against another vessel or by mutinous crew or passengers against their own vessel." Art. 101 of the UNCLOS, 1982 defines piracy as "Any illegal act of violence, detention or any act of depredation, committed for private ends, by the crew or passengers of a private ship or a private aircraft, and directed:

(a) on the high seas, against another ship or aircraft, or against persons or property on board such ships or aircrafts;
(b) against a ship or aircraft, persons or property in place outside the jurisdiction of any state."

Earlier, the Geneva Convention of 1958 also included

"Any act of voluntary participation in the operation of a ship or an aircraft with the knowledge of facts making it a pirate ship or aircraft."

The following are the ingredients of piracy:

(a) There must be an unauthorised attack or act of violence against person or property. The Privy Council in Piracy jure Gentium case, 1934, held that actual robbery was not an essential element of crime of piracy and that a frustrated attempt to commit robbery on high seas could be considered as piracy. In the Ambrose Light Case, 1885, it was held by the U.S. Federal Court that an armed ship of unrecognised insurgents can be seized as pirate ship. The Court also said, "an armed vessel sailing on the sea in suspicious circumstances without actually committing an act of violence may be a pirate and may be seized."

(b) The act violence must be committed in the high seas or in areas which are terra nullius.

(c) The private ships or aircrafts only can commit piracy. When the crew or passengers of a public vessel have mutinied, the vessel or aircraft shall be treated as private and their acts if piratical, they shall be treated as pirates. The war ships or public ships under the command of recognised government or recognised belligerent power are not pirate ships, and if they commit any violence, redress may be sought through diplomatic channel.

All states are under a duty to cooperate to the fullest extent in the suppression of piracy in the high seas or in any place outside the jurisdiction of any state. Any state can seize a pirate ship or aircraft including its property and arrest the persons for trial by its own courts. But the seizure of a piratical ship or aircraft can only be made by war ships or military aircrafts, designated by a government for the purpose.

In addition to piracy, the UNCLOS, 1982, authorises the states to take preventive and punitive steps regarding several other crimes under universal jurisdiction. According to Art. 99, every state must take effective steps to prevent and punish the transportation of slaves. If a slave escapes and takes shelter on board any ship belonging to any state, he shall be ipso facto free. According to Art. 108, all states are to cooperate in the suppression of illicit traffic in narcotic drugs and psychotropic substances. Ships carrying these drugs can be seized and arrested by any state.

In order to prevent unauthorised broadcasting from the high seas, the UNCLOS, 1982 authorises the ship's flag state, the state of registration of the installation, the state of nationality of persons, any state where the broadcasts are received, or any state whose authorised broadcasts are interfered, to arrest the persons on the high seas and seize the broadcasting units.

The universal jurisdiction over the war crimes was recognised and reaffirmed by the Geneva Convention on P.O.Ws and Protocols I and II adopted by the Diplomatic Conference held at Geneva in 1977. In 1962, the Supreme Court of Israel tried Eichman, a war criminal, under universal jurisdiction for the crimes committed by him during the Second World War, even though the crimes were committed by Eichman when Israel was not founded nor the offences committed by him were against any citizen of Israel.

5. Criminal Jurisdiction

Though there is unanimity on a state's jurisdiction over any crime committed either by its own nationals or aliens with in its territory, or even on a state's right to assume jurisdiction over the crimes committed by its nationals outside its territory, there is no unanimity on the question whether a state can punish an alien for crimes committed outside its territory.

There are three different practices on this issue. Great Britain and U.S.A. follow the theory of territoriality of criminal jurisdiction and do not punish an alien for the crimes committed by him outside their territory. France, Germany, and many other states in addition to territorial jurisdiction over crimes, also excercise jurisdiction over crimes committed by aliens outside their territory, if such crime effect their security or financial credit. Lastly, Turkey and Italy reject the territoriality principle and follow the theory that crime, wherever committed, is a social evil and so all civilised states must punish it.

Nowadays, due to rapid development of speedy transportation and communication, a crime can be planned or started in one state, but completed in another state. The states deal with such crimes by adopting subjective and objective territorial principles, by extending their jurisdiction to prosecute and punish the crimes commenced within their territory, but completed in another state. The Convention for Suppression of Counterfeiting Currency, 1929, and the Convention for Suppression of the Illicit Drugs, 1936, authorises the states to punish the offenders if they have started their preparation or conspiracy in a state even though the final act of the crime was committed elsewhere in the world. By following the objective territorial principle, states prosecute and punish the criminals if the crime was committed in another state but completed within their territory, or such crimes produce serious harmful consequences to their social or economic systems. The objective territorial principle was approved by the Permanent Court of International Justice in the Lotus Case, 1927.

In general, the territorial criminal jurisdiction is followed by all states, because the territorial state "has the strongest interest, the greatest facilities, and most powerful instruments for suppressing crimes." Though the states have extended their territorial jurisdiction in many ways, yet from the Cutting

Case, 1887, it would appear that they are not sufficient to prosecute a foreigner who has temporarily entered into its territory for an offence committed in another state much earlier. The U.S.A., whose citizen Cutting was, objected to his prosecution by the Mexican Government on the ground that Mexican courts had no jurisdiction and the judicial treatment given to Cutting was against the customs prevalent among the civilised states. Finally, the case was withdrawn and Cutting was released. The views held by the U.S.A. in the Cutting case have been widely supported by other states.

6. Jurisdiction Over Aliens

Every sovereign state has an inherent right to admit or refuse to admit or admit on conditions the aliens. Oppenheim is of the opinion that it is upto the discretion of a state to admit or refuse admission to aliens. Aliens do not have a right to claim residence in another state. They can also be expelled by a state after their admission if they work against the interest of the state.

Once admitted, the alien comes under the territorial jurisdiction of the state just in the same manner its citizens are. If they take up permanent residence, they have to pay taxes and shoulder other burdens imposed by the state. The concerned state must give them a fair trial, protect their life and property, and must not force them to perform military duties without the consent of their own state.

The aliens are not entitled to any special protection or privileges or exemption from the jurisdiction of the state unless they prove that they are entitled to special immunity from the local jurisdiction or that the local law is not in conformity with international law.

Principle of Double Jeopardy

Once the states are allowed jurisdictions other than the territorial jurisdiction, two or more states may get the competence to prosecute and punish a person for the same offence, thereby causing double jeopardy. But fairness and justice requires that an individual should not be tried and punished twice for the same offence. Though positive international law does not probibit a second trial, many municipal laws provide that when a person is tried and he is either convicted or acquitted or pardoned, he should not be tried again by another state.

Exterritoriality

Every sovereign state, as a matter of right, excercises its jurisdiction and authority over all people and things found within its territory. But under a fictional legal principle of international law, certain categories of persons and things are exempted from the jurisdiction and control of the sovereign state, even if they are physically present within its territory. In other words, curtain types of persons and things are immune from the laws and jurisdictions of the courts or another sovereign state when they are on its territory. The principle of granting such immunities to the persons and things of another sovereign state within its territory is known as exterritoriality. The assumption behind this principle is that since all sovereign states, irrespective of their size, population, power etc., are equal under international law, it would be offensive and insulting for one sovereign state to have its legal status determined by the courts of another sovereign state. Of course, the court of another sovereign state can do so only when the immunity is waived by the recipient state.

According to Brierly, "The term exterritoriality is commonly used to describe the status of a person or thing physically present on a state's territory but wholly or partly withdrawn from the state's jurisdiction by a rule of international law."

Under this principle of exterterritoriality, both international and municipal laws have granted certain immunities on the following categories of persons and things:

1. Heads of Foreign States

In the earlier times, before the establishment of democratic states, the foreign sovereigns (monarchs) enjoyed personal immunities from the jurisdiction of the courts of other states. Today the same immunities are granted to the heads of foreign states, who are democratically elected for a fixed term.

The sovereign or head of a foreign state can sue but cannot be used in the courts of another state, even if he is living incognito in that state, unless he voluntarily submit to the jurisdiction of the court. This principle was established in a case of Mighell V. Sultan of Johore in 1893. The British Court dismissed the case brought by Mighell against the Sultan of sovereign state of Johore who was living in England in the guise of Albert Baker, for the breach of marriage. Similarly, in the Statham V. Statham and Gaekwar of Baroda, the British court dismissed the case as Gaekwar was considered as a foreign sovereign and as such no case could be filed against him. However, a case against a foreign sovereign can be brought if he waives his immunity.

2. Properties of Sovereign State

The properties which belong to a foreign state cannot be seized or its ships cannot be detained by the legal process of another state. In the Cristina case, Lord Wright observed that the principle is well settled that a foreign state or its property is not subject to the jurisdiction of courts of another state. But a foreign state can waive this immunity and appear before the court of another state, either as a plaintiff or as a defendant, by giving its consent to subject itself to the jurisdiction of a foreign court.

Though earlier the properties and ships of a foreign sovereign state enjoyed absolute immunity, today the states are reluctant to grant such absolute immunity, because the modern states, through their state-owned corporations and agencies, are in commercial activities which frequently lead to disputes and litigations with the citizens of other states. So today the states grant only restricted immunities to the property of foreign states and exclude the commercial transactions undertaken by their agencies and corporations.

3. *Diplomatic Agents*

The principle on which the immunity from jurisdiction of a state is granted to the diplomatic agents posted in that state is based on the principle that he should be free to perform official business on behalf of his state without any interference or interruption. This immunity is now recognised by the Vienna Convention on Diplomatic Relations, 1961. So he, his family, his office and residence enjoy absolute immunity from criminal jurisdiction and qualified immunity from the civil jurisdiction of the host state. The Consuls, on the other hand, are not diplomatic agents and as such are not immune from the local jurisdiction of the host state in respect of their private acts. But as per the Vienna Convention on Consular Relations, 1963, consuls enjoy immunity from judicial and administrative authorities of the host state, unless the immunity is waived by the sending state.

In case of diplomats, the immunity from jurisdiction is subject to waiver, which must be expressed to file the case and separate waiver is also required for execution of the judgement. But if the diplomat holds property in his private capacity which is involved in a dispute or he is involved in succession to private property or engaged in commercial or professional activities in his personal capacity, he is not entitled to these immunities.

4. *Public Ships*

According to Oppenheim, "It is customary rule of law of nations that men-of-war and other public vessels of any state are, whilst on the open sea as well as in foreign territorial waters, in every point considered as though they were floating parts of their home state."

Thus all armed ships and public ships of a state while in the ports, internal waters, or territorial sea of another state, are completely exempt from the jurisdiction of that state in respect of internal discipline and crimes committed on that ship except when the crime is against the citizen of that state. If an individual who is not a member of the crew take refuse in a public ship of another state after committing a crime, he cannot be arrested by the local police or removed from the ship without the consent of the commander of the ship. If the consent is refused, the remedy lies through the diplomatic channel with the flag state.

If the crew of the public ship commit any crime on the shore in their private capacity, they are usually handed over to the ship for punishment. But the crew enjoy absolute immunity if they commit any violation of law while performing their official duties. If such a ship is involved in any civil dispute, the host state cannot take any police or judicial action, but can take action for redress through diplomatic channels.

Even the private ships when engaged by a state for the purposes of state such as transportation of troops etc., are also to be treated as public ship and are entitled to these immunities.

5. *Foreign Armed Forces*

The extent of immunity enjoyed by foreign armed forces when admitted into the territory of another sovereign state depend upon the circumstances in which such forces are admitted. But the general principle laid down in the Schooner Exchange case is that the host state impliedly undertake not to excercise any jurisdiction over the members of the visiting force in such a way as to harm the integrity and efficiency of the force. Thus the foreign troops are:

(a) under the exclusive jurisdiction of their commanders for internal discipline, crimes committed within the area in which it is stationed, and for crimes committed outside the area while on official duty;

(b) free from civil and criminal jurisdiction of the host state in matters of its internal discipline.

But the members of such forces are subject to laws of the host state if they commit any crime while not on military duties.

6. International Institutions

International institutions such as UNO and its various agencies as well as to persons involved in them either as officials or as delegates have been granted immunity from the territorial jurisdiction of the states where they are located, by both municipal law of the states concerned and by international law.

13

NATIONALITY

The term nationality in law means the status of an individual by belonging to a particular state. According to Oppenheim, "Nationality of an individual is his quality of being a subject of certain state and therefore its citizen." Starke defines it as "the legal status of membership of the collectivity of individuals whose acts, decision and policy are vouchsafed through the legal concept of the state representing those individuals." According to British-Mexican Claims Commission, "A man's nationality is a continuing legal relationship between the Sovereign State on the one hand and the citizen on the other. The fundamental basis of a Man's nationality is his membership of an independent political community."

Thus nationality is very often the only link between an individual and the state through which all his rights and duties under the international law are ensured. Yet it is not the international law but the municipal law which determines who is and who is not to be considered as its national. In the U.S. V. Wong Kim Ark case, 1898, Justice Gray said that it is a prerogative of each state to "determine for itself, and according to its own constitution and laws what classes of persons shall be entitled to citizenship."

As the states lay down their own rules of nationality, there are no uniform laws, and this causes number of problems such as statelessness, multiple nationalities, and disputed nationality of the married women. So to solve these problems and to bring certain uniformity in the nationality laws, the first attempt was made by the Hague Codification Conference, 1930, by adopting a Convention on the Conflict of Nationality Laws, which laid down that each state shall make its own laws regarding nationality, but such laws are to be recognised by other states "in so far as it is consistent with international conventions and principles of law generally recognised with regard to nationality."

Importance of Nationality

According to Oppenheim, nationality is the link between the individuals and the benefits of Law of Nations. Under international law, the following are incidence of nationality:

1. The individual is entitled to diplomatic protection of his state of nationality while he is outside his state.
2. The state, in the absence of a treaty, can refuse extradition of its nationals to another state.
3. During war, the enemy character of an individual is determined according to his nationality.
4. A state can excercise criminal and other jurisdictions over the individuals on the basis of nationality.
5. Since nationality implies allegiance to the state, the state can ask its nationals to perform military duties.
6. The state becomes internationally responsible for the actions of its nationals and it must prevent its nationals from committing certain wrong acts.
7. The individual is entitled to go back to his state of nationality and the state cannot refuse to accept him back. The Convention on Civil and Political Rights, 1966, provides, "No one shall be arbitrarily deprived of the right to enter his own territory."

Though every state grants diplomatic protection to its nationals while they are in another state, under certain exceptional circumstances, one state can also extend its diplomatic protection to the nationals of another state in a third state, such as to the nationals of a protectorate or trust territory, the protector or trustee state can grant diplomatic protection in third states. Further, a state which has broken off the diplomatic relations or at war with another state, it can request a friendly state to extend its diplomatic protection to its nationals in that third state.

Acquisition of Nationality

Every state, by its own municipal law, determines the modes of acquisition of its nationality. According to Oppenheim, there are five possible modes of acquisition, namely, birth, naturalisation, redintegration, subjugation and cession.

By Birth: A very large portion of mankind acquire their nationality through birth and do not change it afterwards. But there is no uniform rules of acquisition by birth and different states follow different principles. While states like Argentina has adopted the principle of jus soli, i.e. territory on which birth takes place, the states like Germany and France have adopted the principle of jus sanguine, i.e. parentage of the child who may born anywhere in the world, and some states like Great Britain and U.S.A. have adopted a mixed principle of both according to which both place of birth as well as the parentage are considered in order to determine the nationality of a person. However, those states which have adopted the principle of jus soli, do not grant nationality to the children of persons enjoying diplomatic status, even though they are born in that state.

By Naturalisation: Acquisition of nationality by naturalisation is the second most important mode. By this process, an alien can acquire the nationality of the naturalising state. According to Oppenheim, there are six modes of acquisition of nationality by naturalisation such as marriage, legitimation, option, acquisition of domicile, appointment as a government official, and grant on application.

But there are great divergencies among the states in granting nationality to married women. The widely accepted traditional principle is that a wife automatically acquires the nationality of her husband after the marriage. But some states like U.S.A recognise independent status of women, and as such when an alien women marries a U.S citizen, she does not automatically acquire the U.S. nationality, nor when a women of U.S.A. marries an alien, she does not loose her nationality of U.S.A. This principle of independent status of women has been accepted by the Convention on Nationality of Married Women, 1957, and by the Convention on Elimination of Discrimination Against Women, 1979. So now, neither the celebration nor the dissolution of marriage by a women to an alien, automatically does not affect the nationality of the wife, unless she voluntarily acquires the nationality of her husband through the process of naturalisation.

When an illegitimate child is born outside the marriage in another state, and the parents subsequently married, the child acquires the nationality of its parents; and if no marriage takes place, it acquires the nationality of its mother.

The national of one state may leave his own state and voluntarily expatriates to state of his own choice, where he may acquire a new nationality. Though the Universal Declaration of Human Rights, 1948, grants the right to the individuals to change their nationality, many states still refuse to permit their nationals to relinquish their nationality until they fulfill certain conditions.

By Redintegration: When a natural-born national of a state has lost his original nationality due to naturalisation abroad or for some other reasons, may recover his original nationality on fulfilment of certain conditions, it is called redintegration.

By Subjugation and Cession: When a territory is conquered or ceded, the people over that territory automatically acquire the nationality of the state which has acquired the territory.

Loss of Nationality

The Universal Declaration of Human Rights, 1948, states "No one shall be arbitrarily deprived of his nationality." But the Convention on Statelessness, 1961, recognises the right of states to deprive nationals of their nationality on various grounds. In practice discretion is allowed to states to determine the grounds of losing nationality by an individual.

While Starke suggests three grounds such as release or renunciation, deprivation, and long residence abroad, Oppenheim has suggested the following five grounds of losing nationality:

1. *Release:* Some states allow their nationals the right to request for release from their nationality, and when such request is granted by the state, the individual is denationalised.

2. *Deprivation:* The municipal laws of many states have recognised several grounds for depriving their own nationals of the nationality. Some of the important grounds of deprivation are appointment or military service under a foreign government without permission, uninterrupted long residence abroad, disaffection, desertion from armed forces, and avoidance of military duties etc.

3. *Expiration:* The laws of some states provide that when a national left the state and stayed abroad beyond a prescribed length of time, his nationality expires.

4. *Renunciation:* In case of double nationality due to the simultaneous application of jus soli and jus sanguine principles by two states, the child, when comes to age, through a declaration can renounce the nationality of one of the states.

5. *Substitution:* According to the laws of some states when one of its nationals is naturalised in another state, he looses his original nationality. In case of subjugation or cession, the nationality of the inhabitants or the subjugation or ceded

territory is substituted by the nationality of the state which has annexed the territory.

Double Nationality and Statelessness

Due to lack of uniformity in rules and conflicting municipal laws, an individual may possess double or multiple or no nationality at all. When an individual possesses two or more nationalities, it gives rise to double nationality, and when he does not possess any nationality, it gives rise to statelessness.

Double Nationality: According to Oppenheim, "An individual may possess double nationality knowingly or unknowingly, and with or without intention." Double nationality may be produced by every mode of acquiring nationality, such as birth, legitimation, marriage, and naturalisation. Persons having double nationality are described as "sujets mixtes" or mixed subjects. Very often double nationality creates problems for the individual because each of the two different states claim him as its subject and demand his allegiance. If there is war between these two states, it creates conflict of duties of individual towards these states, as each state will claim him as its subject. Thoughthey cannot claim him against one another, in the third states each of them can claim as his sovereign, and can excercise the right of diplomatic protection over him. So far a third state is concerned, it can consider a person having double nationality as a subject of either of states to which he owes allegiance.

To solve the various problems and inconviniences caused due to the double nationality, the Hague Codification Conference concluded a Convention on Certain Questions Relating to Conflict of Nationality Laws in 1930 and laid down the following principles:

(1) Each of the states can claim him as its national;

(2) Each of the states cannot excercise diplomatic protection over the concerned person against the other states;

(3) A third state will recognise only the effective nationality, i.e. the nationality of the state to which he is most closely connected;

(4) If a person has acquired double nationality without any voluntary act on his own, he can renounce one of them with the permission of the state whose nationality he desires to renounce; and

(5) The Protocol attached to the Convention on military obligations of double nationality lays down that a person having double nationality can render military obligations to the state of his effective nationality and can be exempted from all military obligations to the other state. Further, if a person has lost his nationality of one state and has acquired the nationality of another, he shall be exempted from the military obligation of the state whose nationality he has lost.

Double nationality may also be caused due to the marriage of a woman to an alien. The laws of the woman's state may allow retention of her nationality even after her marriage, while the laws of her husband's state may grant her its nationality. The Hague Convention, 1930 lays down that a woman can acquire the nationality of her husband, but under certain circumstances can also retain her original nationality. But the traditional principle that wife's nationality automatically follows that of her husband, has been replaced by the theory of independent status of the wife. Accordingly, the convention on the Nationality of Married Women, 1957, laid down that neither the celebration nor the dissolution of marriage between a national and an alien, nor the change of nationality by husband during the marriage, automatically affect the nationality of the wife. But she can voluntarily acquire the nationality of her husband through the naturalisation process. This principle is now more emphatically stressed in the Convention on Elimination of All Forms of Discrimination Against Women, 1979, which provides, "State parties shall grant women equal rights with men to acquire, change or retain their nationality. They shall ensure in particular that neither marriage to an alien nor change of nationality by husband during marriage shall automatically change the nationality of the wife, render her stateless or force upon her the nationality of husband."

Statelessness

An individual is said to be stateless when he does not possess the nationality of any state. Statelessness may arise through conflicts of municipal laws relating to nationality, change of the sovereignty over a territory, birth, marriage, and deprivation. It may also occur when a person loses his original nationality without acquiring another nationality. Oppenheim rightly says, "An individual may be without nationality knowingly or unknowingly, intentionally or for no fault of his own."

Nationality being the principal link between the individual and the international law, the stateless persons are deprived of the protection of international law. Oppenheim compares the stateless persons to the ships sailing in the high seas without the flag of a state which is not entitled to any protection.

In recent years statelessness has become a major problem which prompted the Universal Declaration of Human Rights to state, "Every one has a right to nationality" and "no one should be deprived of his nationality."

The Hague Codification Conference adopted a number of provisions to reduce the possibility of statelessness, specially of children and married women. The Convention on Status of Refugees, 1933, was adopted to deal with the particular group of the stateless persons, i.e. the refugees. A Convention on the Status of Refugees was signed in 1951 to deal with all those persons who became refugees before 1st January 1951. This Convention directs the state parties to protect the refugees who are unable or unwilling to go to their state of nationality for fear of persecution for racial, social, religious, and political reasons. The states are to protect such refugees by granting them the same rights and freedom as are normally granted to the aliens. A Convention on Reduction of Statelessness was adopted in 1961 at New York, which provides that to stateless person can acquire nationality of state of his birth or one of his parents at the date of his birth. It is also that the loss of nationality is to be conditional upon acquisition of another nationality.

The subject of statelessness and necessary remedial actions are under the study of International Law Commission and the General Assembly of the U.N.O. and it is hoped that the problem of statelessness will be solved in near future.

14

ALIENS

(a) Admission of Aliens

There are various opinions regarding a state's right to admit or refuse an alien, which, broadly, are: that a state is under a duty to admit all aliens; that the state is under a duty to admit all aliens but also can exclude certain classes of aliens; that a state is bound to admit aliens if they fulfil the conditions laid down by it; and that a state is competent to refuse admission to all aliens at its will.

In practice, no state is duty bound to admit aliens into its territory and may prohibit the entry of aliens or admit them when they fulfil the conditions laid down by it. In fact, all states admit aliens under certain conditions in order to encourage tourism, trade, commerce, and international relations. Usually, aliens are allowed to enter a state through treaties of commerce and alliances, but sometimes they are also allowed, even without treaty provisions, at the discretion of the state. Generally, those aliens who are physically, morally or socially unfit, are not allowed to enter. Further, certain types of aliens like students and tourists are freely admitted, while aliens who enter as immigrants have to face strict regulations. No alien is allowed to settle in a state without having asked for and granted special permission. Sometimes, the nationals of a particular state may be refused admission for political reasons. But such an act may diplomatically be treated as an unfriendly act. People of one state for their persecution due to political, religious or ethnical reasons, very often enter the territory of another state to seek asylum and international law imposes a duty on all states not to refuse or expel or deliver them to the persecuting state.

Except the refugees, all other aliens who enter into the territory of another state must carry a valid passport issued by the authorities of their state and also obtain in advance visa or permission of the state into which he wants to enter. Sometimes the visa restrictions are waived between two states through mutual agreement on raciprocal basis, as between India and Nepal.

(b) Legal Status After Entry

After admission, all aliens except those who enjoy the exterritorial privileges, are under the territorial jurisdiction and sovereignty of that state, though they remain under the protective and personal jurisdiction of their home state. The admitting state has wider powers over the aliens who have taken residence than over those who stay for temporary period.

On entrance into a state, an alien becomes subject to its laws like its own citizens. But most states impose certain restrictions on aliens such as denial of political rights or prohibition of adopting certain professions or inheriting real property etc. But they are subject to ordinary civil taxes and custom duties, unless they enjoy the diplomatic immunities. They are exempted from compulsory military duties, except with the consent of their own states. But they have to perform civic duties for protection of people against epidemics, fires, natural calamities and other dangers. However, during the Second World War, some belligerent states compelled the resident aliens to perform some kind of services related to was even without the consent of their states. Since the First World War, many states compel the aliens to register their names after entry into the state in order to keep them under control.

The aliens, even after entry into another state, are entitled to the right of protection of their own state. But the admitting state is responsible for the protection of their life, liberty and property and must take appropriate steps to punish the offenders if any harm is done to the aliens. The admitting state must grant aliens the access to the judicial system of the state in the same way its citizens are allowed, and ensure a fair trial and impartial judgement. The aliens have a right to leave the admitting state at any time they like, provided they have cleared their local obligations like payment taxes etc., and also should be allowed to take their possessions with them.

Earlier, majority of European and American states as well as Japan demanded extraterritorial privileges from some Asian and African States for the aliens belonging to them on the ground that their laws and institutions were inferior or different than the European and American standards. So they signed treaties known as Capitulations with the Asian and African states, according to which their Consuls were to excercise jurisdiction and control over their aliens as per their own municipal laws. But now most of the Afro-Asian group have asserted their territorial sovereignty over all aliens and aliens who do not like the standard of law and institutions, are free not to enter into their states.

(c) Expulsion of Aliens

The right of state to expel or deport aliens whether temporary or residential, whose presence is considered as undesirable, is generally recognised. Like the power to refuse admission, every state is free to expel the aliens on the grounds determined by them. But expulsion must not be arbitrary but reasonable and the power should not be abused. The International Convention on Civil and Political Rights, 1966, lays down that aliens can be expelled through a legal decision except where the national security is involved; and the concerned alien must be informed of the reasons of his expulsion, as well as he must have the right to appeal to competent authorities for the review of the decision.

Expulsion must not be carried out with hardship or violence or unnecessary harrassment to the alien. Detention of an alien before his expulsion should be avoided, except when he refuses to leave or tries to escape. He should be allowed reasonable time to settle his personal affairs. He should be allowed to go to a state of his own choice and should not be deported to a state against his will where his life and freedoms are threatened because of his racial or religious or political views.

(d) Asylum

When a state grants entry to aliens to stay and settle down on its territory because he was forced to leave his own state due to his persecution for racial or religious or political reasons, or due to his support to independence movement of his country, it is called Asylum. According to Institute of International Law, "Asylum is the protection which a state grants on its territory or in some other place under the control of certain of its organs to a person who come to seek it."

The practice of asylum was followed even in ancient India, Greece, and Rome. The power to grant asylum on its territory by a state is derived from the territorial sovereignty and supremacy of that state, and by virtue of this right, every state has the power either to admit or expel aliens. According to Starke, the concept of asylum in international law involves shelter to and active protection of a refugee within its territory.

Asylum and extradition are interrelated concepts, because asylum ends where extradition begins. When asylum is granted to a political refugee, he is not extraditable. But asylum is not granted to a person who is charged by his state with common crime, and such a criminal, even if asylum was granted, can be extradited on demand either due to existing extradition treaty or due to the principle of international comity.

Freedom of state to grant or refuse asylum is recognised by international law. Though sometimes it is claimed that the individuals have a right to claim asylum in another state, the practice of states show that no such right exists. The Art. 14 of the Universal Declaration of Human rights states, "every one has the right to seek and to enjoy in other countries asylum from persecution", yet, the Convention on Territorial Asylum, 1954, and the Declaration on Territorial Asylum, 1967, have not recognised such right; rather, they have recognised the right of states to grant or refuse asylum at their discretion. Some states like France, Germany and Italy have provided a right of asylum in their constitutions to the persons who have fled their own state to escape persecutions. Thus, it can be stated that, in general, states normally grant asylum to foreign citizens who are persecuted by their own state for their political or religious or racial activities or opinions, yet no individual can claim asylum as a right nor there is any duty of a state to grant it under international law.

Asylum may be territorial, i.e. when it is granted by a state on its territory; or it may be extraterritorial, i.e. when granted in diplomatic or consular premises, or in war ships, or in the premises of international organisations. As per the current practices of states, territorial asylum can be classified into three categories, namely, (1) Political asylum granted to persons who are persecuted by their own state for holding or practicing their own political views; (2) Refugee asylum is granted to the refugees who flee their own state for the fear of persecution on racial or religious grounds, and (3) the General asylum to persons who have fled their own state only to seek better economic opportunities in other states.

The question of granting asylum to a prisoner of war who was detained by it but who is unwilling to go back to his state at the end of war is controversial. On the other hand the principle of not granting asylum to the persons who have committed war crimes such as crime against humanity, crime against peace etc., is now well established.

In recent times, the massive trans-border flow of refugees in certain parts of Asia and Africa, like large number of Bengali refugees from East Pakistan in 1970, Chakma refugees from Bangaladesh, Rohingiya refugees from Burma, Tamilian refugees from Sri Lanka, have created problems for the states into which they have entered. In such cases, some writers have suggested to adopt the principle of "non-refoulment" which means not to reject the refugees at the boundary line, but to grant them protection and to return them to their state when the situation in that state become normal. Such refugees may be granted temporary refuge and not the asylum in the strict sense of the term. If for the reasons of national security or for the protection of its own nationals against mass exodus of refugees, a state is unable to grant asylum, that state should grant temporary asylum to such refugees so that they may seek asylum in another state, instead of rejecting them at the boundary line.

But once territorial asylum is granted to the refugees, the state should grant them the human rights like freedom of religion, right to movable and immovable property, right to professional activities, right to freedom of movement in the state, and right to housing etc. The refugees also have duties towards the state which has granted them asylum. Such duties are to abide by laws and regulations of the state, to maintain public order, not to indulge in hostile activities against a foreign state, and not to take any action which might create bitter relation between their own state and the state of asylum. The state granting asylum has also a responsibility to check such activities of the refugees.

Ex-Territorial Asylum

Sometimes agents of a state grant asylum outside its territorial limit such as in embassies or consulates or in war ships to the individuals in the state where they are located. The International Court of Justice, in the Haya de la Torre case, said that there is no general right of diplomatic asylum in international law. The diplomatic missions in all states are vested with certain privileges and immunities by the host state as per the Vienna Convention on Diplomatic Relations, 1969 for their smooth functioning. The power of granting asylum in the diplomatic premises is not allowed to the diplomatic missions. Any such asylum shall be considered as intervention in the internal matters of the host state.

But the granting of diplomatic asylum is practised among the Latin American states and this right has been sanctioned by Havana Convention, 1928, Montevideo Conventions of 1933 and 1939, and the Caracas Convention of 1954. As per this practice political asylum can be granted in a diplomatic premises only on humanitarian grounds.

Starke has suggested that diplomatic asylum may be granted in the following exceptional cases:

(1) As a temporary measure, individuals can be granted asylum in embassy premises if their life is in danger due to mob violence or if the life is threatened due to extreme political corruption in the host state;
(2) If there is a long recognised local custom of granting diplomatic asylum;
(3) Under special treaty between the host state and state of diplomatic agent granting such rights, usually, to the political offenders.

The similar principles also applies to grant of asylum in the consulates or consular premises as in case of diplomatic asylum.

The war ships are treated as the floating territory of the flag state and enjoy all immunities from the jurisdiction of the foreign state in whose port or waters they are found.

Sometimes under exceptional circumstances, asylum is also granted by such war ships on the ground of humanity or if there is exceptional danger to the life of a refugee of the local state. Merchant ships, on the otherhand do not enjoy the right to grant asylum and if it has granted asylum, the refugee can be removed from the ship by the local state if the ship is within its port or territorial waters, as was done in case of Eisler, who was removed from the Polish merchant ship, Batery, by the British authorities.

(e) Extradition

Often some persons frustrate a state's attempt to excercise its jurisdiction and its right to punish them for violation of its laws, by escaping into another state. Nowadays, due to the development of international transport and communication, offenders can easily and quickly escape to far off sates after committing a crime. All states agree that serious crimes should not go unpunished; so the state to which the offender has escaped may punish the offender. But if that state is unable to prosecute and punish the offender either because its criminal law does not permit it or due to lack of jurisdiction, states agree that the criminal should be handed over to the state where the crime was committed. Moreover, the state where the crime was committed is in the best position to collect all the relevant evidence for trial as well as that state has greatest interest in the punishment of the offender. These considerations have given rise to a legal institution known as extradition. The procedure by which a criminal who has escaped into the territory of another state to avoid trial and punishment is handed over by that state to the state where the crime was committed, is known as extradition.

According to Oppenheim, "Extradition is the delivery of an accused or a convicted individual to the state on whose territory he is alleged to have committed, or to have been convicted of, a crime by the state on whose territory the alleged criminal happens for the time to be." According to the Havard Research Draft on Extradition, it is "the formal surrender of a person by a state to another state for prosecution or punishment." Starke describes it as "the process whereby under treaty or upon a basis of raciprocity one state surrenders to another state at its request a person accused or convicted of a criminal offence committed against the law of the requesting state, such requesting state being competent to try the alleged offender."

Since Grotius, every writer has held that criminals who comit a crime in one state and escapes into another, the state into which he has escaped should surrender, yet no universally accepted customary international law has come into existence making extradition a duty on the part of states. So the states conclude bilateral treaties among themselves and stipulate in them the crimes for which the extradition shall take place. Thus in the absence of a duty of the states to surrender a fugitive, extradition depends upon either on conclusion of bilateral treaty or on reciprocity or on courtsey between the states.

The states in their municipal law also stipulate the conditions under which a fugitive criminal can be extradited to another state and if these conditions are not fulfilled, extradition may be refused. Usually, if a fugitive is to be prosecuted for his race or religion or political opinion, or if there is a fear that his trial by the requesting state is likely to be prejudiced, the extradition of the fugitive may be refused. Thus international law allows discretion to the states to grant or refuse extradition.

Since extradition has effects on the rights of citizens, it is necessary to pass the required laws by the state. In practice, states enact special municipal laws, enumerating the crimes for which request to surrender the criminal to be made to other states or grant their request to return a criminal to them, according to which the extradition treaties are concluded. In the absence of required municipal law and a treaty, a fugitive would neither be surrendered nor his surrender requested.

The object of extradition is to bring back any individual who has committed a crime, be he its own subject or the subject of the requested state or the subject of a third state. While all states normally hand over a criminal who is not its subject, the practice of states are different when the concerned criminal is one its own subject.

Before a request for extradition is made through the diplomatic channel, the following two conditions must be fulfilled:

(a) the person must be extraditable; and
(b) the crime must be extraditable.

(i) Extraditable Persons

Extradition of a person is granted by a state only when it is requested to do so. Even in the absence of municipal law, a state can grant extradition of any criminal it thinks fit. But if there is no extradition treaty, the request for extradition may be refused. So far the surrender of the criminal is concerned, the civil law countries like France and Germany do not extradite their own nationals to another state for the crimes committed in that state, while the common law countries like Britain, extradite even their own nationals. However, nowadays the practice is that while states enjoy freedom to decide whether it should extradite its own national or not, each state is under an obligation to prosecute the offender if it decides not to surrender him.

No state extradites the political offenders, military deserters and persons who have committed offences against religion.

(ii) Extraditable Crime

Usually states extradite criminals involved in serious

crimes and now it is common practice of states to list the crimes for extradition in their bilateral treaties. The list of such crimes is prepared by following principles:

(1) The principle of "double criminality", i.e. the alleged crime must have been treated as an offence under the laws of both states. This principle was applied by the U.S. Supreme Court in Factor V. Laubenheimer case, 1933.

(2) Certain states like France include only those crimes in the list on the basis of a definite minimum penalty prescribed for the crimes in both states.

(3) Sometimes the principle of speciality is applied according to which the requesting state is under a duty not try or punish an offender without the consent of the requested state, for the crime other than of that for which he is extradited. This principle was followed in U.S. V. Rauscher, 1886.

A state may refuse to extradite a person who has committed a crime in whole or in part over its own territory, or committed an offence outside the territory of the requesting state, or the final judgement has already been given for the offence for which his extradition is demanded. To avoid the abuse of extradition facilities, the requested state must be convinced that there is a prima facie evidence against the person whose extradition is demanded.

As a general rule, states do not extradite the persons committing political crime, military desertion, and religious offences.

Extradition and Political Crimes

The principle of non-extradition of persons for political crimes was developed only in the 19th century, before which all extradition treaties were concluded exclusively and primarily for political offences. But the political ideals of

French Revolution developed an attitude of tolerance and liberalism, which helped in excluding the political offences from the extradition treaties and the first such extradition treaty excluding political offences was signed between Belgium and France in 1834.

Today, though the principle of non-extradition of political offender is an accepted fact, yet it is not easy to define the concepts like 'political crime' or 'having political character!' Attempts to formulate satisfactory tests to define political offence or 'political act' has not succeeded. However, the courts of Britain had tried to lay down the tests. In Castioni Case, 1891, it said, "the act is done in furthermore of, done with the intention of assistance, as a sort of overt act in the course of acting in a political matter, a political rising, or a dispute between two parties in the state." In the Meunier case, 1894, it said, "there must be two or more parties in the state, each seeking to impose the government of their choice on the other." But in the Rex V. Kolczynski case, 1955, the British court did not follow the restricted definitions given in these two judgements, but extended the definition of political crimes by saying, "The words' offences of political character' must always be considered according to the circumstances existing at the time when they have to be considered. The present time is very different from 1890 when Castioni's case was decided." This judgement has been favourably accepted by many scholars and accordingly, now, not only the offences committed to overthrow a government, but also the attempt to suppress or prosecute persons holding different political opinion, is considered as political offence.

The recent trend shows that offences involving political terrorism, war crimes and genocide are excluded from the category of political crimes. The Genocide Convention, 1948, expressly provides that genocide should not be treated as a political offence for the purpose of extradition. The General Assembly of U.N.O. in 1946 adopted a resolution directing member states to extradite the war-criminals to the states where they committed their grave misdeeds. The European Convention on the Suppression of Terrorism, 1977, and the Supplementary Extradition Treaty between U.S.A. and Britain of 1985, have excluded the terrorist violence from the list of political crimes.

Mention may be made to the so-called "attentat clause", also known as "Belgium clause", according to which the murder of a head of state or his family members should not be treated as political crime, and the offender is extraditable. But this clause was objected to by many scholars who are of the opinion that attack on a head of a state, by definition, is a political crime, and hence the offender should not be extradited. However, due to growing political terrorism, this clause is still included, as in the case of European Convention on Extradition, 1957.

The problem of defining a political crime is well summarised by Oppenheim: "Whereas many writers consider a crime political if committed from a political motive, others call 'political' any crime committed for a political purpose; again others recognise such a crime only as political as was committed both from a political motive and at the same time for political purpose; and thirdly some writers confine the term 'political crime' to certain offences against the state only such as high treason etc. Upto present day all attempts to formulate a satisfactory conception of the term have failed." So today, international law leaves to the states to decide according to their own municipal laws and practices whether an offence for which extradition is requested is a political crime or not.

Procedure of Extradition

There is no uniform procedure of extradition. But the study of various extradition treaties reveal the following procedure:

(a) request for extradition of the offender is made through diplomatic channel;

(b) on receipt of the request, the requested state takes steps to detain the offender, provided, he or his crime is extraditable;

(c) the final decision in most states lie in the hand of judiciary, which will decide whether the person is to be extradited or not and its decision is final;

(d) if the judiciary decides in favour of extradition, the executive informs the requesting state the date and place of rendition; and

(e) expences incurred by the requested state are to be reimbursed by the requesting state, unless otherwise agreed.

There is no agreed procedure when the extradition of a person is requested concurrently by more than one state, either for same offence or for different offences. In such cases, the requested state may give preference to the state where the crime was committed, or if the crime was committed by the person in more than one state, to the state whose request was received first.

15

DIPLOMATIC AGENTS

Every sovereign state, to realise its national interests and to convey its views on different international issues, formulates its foreign policy. The foreign policy is the aggregate of decisions by a government regarding a state's position in relation to other states. Diplomacy is the instrument through which the objectives of the foreign policy are achieved. Diplomacy means reaching agreement on a particular problem through peaceful negotiation without any violence. So diplomats are the persons who are appointed by a sovereign state to other sovereign states to conduct its negotiations and to maintain its international relations.

Every sovereign state enjoys the right to legation which means a state has the right to send and to receive diplomatic agents on mutual basis. Right to send diplomatic agent is known as 'active' right and the right to receive the diplomatic agents from other states is known as 'passive' right of legation.

(a) Classification

Before the 17th century, diplomats were appointed on temporary and ad hoc basis and their status, privileges, and immunities were governed by customary international law. But when diplomatic missions became permanent and the number of people involved in diplomacy increased, it was found necessary to classify them according to their rank and status. The first attempt to classify them was made by Vienna

Congress, 1815, which was slightly modified by the Congress of Aix la Chappelle, 1818. This classification continued till it was modified by the Vienna Convention on Diplomatic Relations, 1961. Today, as per the Vienna Convention, the diplomats are divided into following classes:

Class I : includes Ambassadors, High Commissioners, and Nuncios. These are the diplomats who enjoy special honours as a matter of right because they are the personal representatives of their head of the state to the head of the state of receiving state. They enjoy the right to public audience with the head of receiving state to whom they present their letter of credence on their arrival. They also have the privilege of negotiating with him personally. These diplomats are addressed as 'Excellency' as a matter of right.

Class II : includes Envoys, Ministers, and Inter Nuncios who are also accredited to the head of receiving state. But they are not the personal representatives of their own head of state. They have the right to personal audience with head of the receiving state. They are addressed as 'Excellency' only by courtsey.

Class III : includes Charges d' Affaires who are accredited by one foreign minister to another foreign minister and they present their letter of credence to the foreign minister of the receiving state on their arrival.

Every diplomatic mission is to be headed by a head of mission, who can belong to any of the three classes. Except in matters of precedence and ceremony, there is to be no discrimination between heads of mission by reason of their class. The class to which a head of a mission is to belong is mutually agreed by the concerned states. The title of ambassador or High Commissioner is normally awarded on the basis of population, power, and importance of his state. While the diplomatic representative of Pope is called Nuncio, those of Commonwealth of Nations are known as High Commissioner and all other states are known as ambassadors. In a receiving state, within a particular class of diplomats, the seniority is fixed according to their date and time of taking up of their functions. All the diplomats accredited to a particular state constitute the diplomatic corps, which is headed by a Doyen, who usually is the Papal Nuncio, and in his absence, the senior most diplomat.

In addition to the above categories of regular diplomats, the delegates to international organisations, diplomatic conferences, and the Judges of International Court of Justice also enjoy the privileges and immunities of diplomats. Sometimes, states send temporary or ad hoc missions to another state for special purposes and such diplomats carry with them a document known as 'Full Powers' indicating the purpose of visit and extent of authority given to them, which the diplomat presents to the authorities of the state or international conference with whom negotiations are to be conducted.

(b) Appointment and Reception

A good deal of ceremony and ritual is attached to the appointment and departure of diplomatic agents. A sending state announces the appointment of diplomat agent to the receiving state in document known as Letter of Credence, which he formally presents to the head of the state or the foreign minister, as the case may be, of the receiving state. But a state can refuse to accept a diplomat of another state without assigning any reason for refusal. Usually, if a designated diplomatic agent has shown his hostilities towards the people or the institutions of the receiving state, or if such a person is a subject of the receiving state to whom it does not want to grant immunities, or such a person is not personally liked by the head of the state, the receiving state can refuse to accept the designated diplomatic agent of another state. So nowadays, to avoid any upleasantness, states, before announcing a diplomat, acertain the acceptability of the person to be appointed and obtain 'agreement' or assent from the receiving state. But even after a diplomat is accepted, the receiving state has the right to declare him as persona non grata, if his activities in the receiving state are hostile to it, in which case, the sending state must recall such diplomat immediately.

(c) Termination of the Mission

A diplomatic mission may be terminated for following reasons:

1. Recall by the sending state: This is an extreme step taken by the sending state to convey its extreme displeasure on certain matters. This is a temporary measure taken when the tension between two states is not reduced otherwise.

Similarly, the receiving state can also request the sending state to withdraw its agent to indicate its extreme displeasure. But the sending state has a right to ask for the reason for such request and may recall its agent, leaving the mission incharge of a lower ranking diplomat.

2. By Notification: The sending state may notify the receiving state that the mission has ended as was done by Newzealand closing down its missions in several states, stating economic reasons.

3. Fulfilment of objectives: When a diplomat is appointed for a particular purpose such as participation in a diplomatic conference or attendance in a ceremonial function, it comes to an end after the completion of the objective.

4. Death of diplomat: When an accredited diplomat dies in his post, his letter of credence comes to an end and so also his mission. A new diplomat who will replace him must

produce a new letter of credence on assumption of office.

5. Change of head of either state: Whenever there is a change of head of either sending or receiving state due to death, new election, or abdication, the mission comes to an end and new letter of credence is necessary.

6. Extinction of state: When either the receiving or the sending state is extinct either due to annexation, merger, or split, the mission is terminated.

7. Change of rank of diplomat: When a diplomat is promoted to the higher rank, even if he is posted in the same receiving state, a new letter of credence is necessary.

8. Dismissal: A diplomat may be dismissed by his own state. He may also be dismissed by the receiving state when his passport is returned to him, which is of course, an extreme step.

9. Delivery of passport: When there is a war between the receiving and the sending states, the receiving state may deliver the passport of diplomatic agents of the opponent sending state, marking the end of the mission. Apart from war, a state may ask for the closure of the mission due to the strained relations between them.

10. Request for passport: The diplomatic agent may request for his passport from the receiving state on the ground of ill treatment.

11. Revolutionary changes: When there is a revolutionary change of government such as a republic into a dictatorship or a monarchy replaced by a republic, the diplomatic mission comes to an end, and the diplomat must receive fresh letter of credence from the new government.

12. Declaration of persona non grata: When the activities of a diplomat are considered harmful by the receiving state

such as his involvement in espionage activities etc., the receiving state can declare such a person as persona non grata and he must be recalled by the sending state.

(d) Functions of Diplomatic Agents

According to Oppenheim, a diplomatic mission performs only three functions, namely, negotiation, observation, and protection. But in modern times, a diplomat has to perform many more functions, namely:

1. He being a representative of his head of state, acts as the spokesman of his state and government in the receiving state.
2. He interprets the policy of his government to the government of receiving state.
3. He maintains the prestige, reputation and image of his state and create the goodwill of the receiving state for his own state.
4. He maintains good relation between his state and receiving state.
5. He acts as the channel of communication between his state and the receiving state.
6. He closely observes and reports the happenings in the receiving state which are relevant to his own state.
7. He protects and safeguards the persons and properties of his state in the receiving state and takes steps to redress any wrong done to nationals of his state.
8. He registers the births, deaths, and marriages of the nationals of his state in the receiving state.
9. He issues passports to the citizens of his state under certain circumstances and visas to the citizens of the receiving state who want to visit his state.
10. He looks after the promotion of export of goods from his state and maintains good relations through propaganda.

Diplomatic Immunities and Privileges

The principles governing diplomatic immunities and privileges are among the most ancient and universally recognised rules of international law and now international law has granted the diplomats certain privileges and immunities from the excercise of jurisdiction of the receiving state in the Vienna Convention on Diplomatic Relations, 1961.

The theoritical basis of diplomatic immunities has changed from age to age. Under the "representational" theory of the Middle Ages, the ambassador was recognised as the personal representative of the foreign sovereign and hence arresting him or filing cases against him was considered tantamount to such actions against the foreign sovereign himself. Under a fictional theory of "exterritoriality", the embassy was considered as a part of the territory of the sending state and as such the buildings and persons over it were considered beyond the jurisdiction of the local authorities. The more recent "functional" theory is simpler and more rational as it is based on the proposition that a diplomat should be free from the interference by the local authorities so that he can perform his duties without any hindrances.

From the ancient times, the privileges and immunities granted to diplomats on mutual basis had been recognised by states and as such a number of customary laws had come into existence. Now the immunities and privileges have been codified in the Vienna Convention on Diplomatic Relations, 1961. Further, diplomatic privileges, as distinguished from the immunities, had a less solid foundation in the international law. Earlier, these privileges were granted by the states on the principles of comity and reciprocity than on international law, and now they are granted by the Vienna Convention of 1961.

Long before the Vienna Convention, international law recognised the immunities of diplomats from the civil and criminal jurisdiction of the host state; guaranteed their freedom of movement, communication and of religious worship; and inviolability of the mission's premises and archives. Now, the Vienna Convention grants full immunity to the diplomats from the excercise of criminal jurisdiction of the host state. As regards the civil and the administrative jurisdictions, they enjoy only qualified immunity. The diplomats do not enjoy immunity in the suits relating to (1) real property held on the territory of the host state in their private capacity; (2) succession to the property on the territory of the host state in which the diplomat is personally involved; (3) professional and commercial activity in which the diplomat is engaged outside his official capacity. Art. 32 of the Convention gives the option of waiver to the sending state and such waiver in civil and administrative cases should be express. Further, separate waiver which should also be express, is required for the execution of the judgement.

The Vienna Convention provides that the person of a diplomat shall be inviolable and as such he is not liable for arrest or detention. In the case of Republica vs. De Longchamps, it was observed "the person of a public Minister is sacred and inviolable. Whoever offers any violence to him, not only affronts the sovereign he represents, but also hurts the common safety and wellbeing of the nations; he is guilty of the crime against the whole humanity." The mission's premises, its archives as well as the residences of diplomats are also immune from search, seizure, requisition or attachment. In the case of the U.S. Diplomatic and Consular Staff in Teheran (1980), the I.C.J. upheld the principle of the inviolability of the premises of a diplomatic mission and the corresponding duty of the host state to protect the premises, documents and archives of the mission. The host state is under an obligation to protect the personnel of the mission; and as such the I.C.J. held the Iranian Government responsible for failure of its duty to protect them from the attack of a group of Iranians. The Court directed the Iranian Government to free the hostage U.S. diplomats and to pay reparation to the U.S.A. for the injury caused to the diplomatic persons. The question of inviolability of diplomatic premises arose in England in 1984 when gun shots were fired from the Libyan People's in London on demonstrators, killing a women police officer. But the British Government, instead of entering into the premises of the Libyan legation, insisted on the recall of Bureau's staff.

The Convention has conferred a new right to the diplomats to move and to travel freely in the territory of the host state, except in the prohibited zones. It also guaranteed the freedom of communication, including the use of couriers and coded messages as well as the inviolability of the diplomatic pouch when used for diplomatic documents and articles intended for official use. The diplomatic pouch also enjoys freedom from custom's inspection. But if this facility is abused, the immunity will be withdrawn and the diplomatic pouch can be inspected by the officers of the host state.

The Convention exempts the diplomats from paying the social security taxes and military obligations. He is also exempted from being summoned by a court as a witness. The diplomats are also exempted from paying direct taxes imposed by the national or local governments of the host state. But they have to pay all indirect taxes; estate, succession and inheritance taxes; taxes on private income and investments; charges for specific services; registration, court and record fees; and stamp duties.

The Convention grants freedom of worship and celebration of religious functions to the diplomats within their premises even though that religion is proscribed in the host state except that the subjects of the host state cannot be invited to such worship or celebration, if the law of the state does not permit.

These privileges and immunities are enjoyed not only by the ambassadors and public ministers but also by all diplomatic personnel. This was established in Ghose vs. D'Rozario case (1962) when the Judge said "It is necessary that the embassy staff, as well as the ambassador, should be immune. The immunity belongs to the state, and not to its representatives individually. There is no difference in principle between the ambassador and humbler members of his staff."

These privileges and immunities are also extended to the members of the immediate family of the diplomat, provided they are not nationals of the host state. Similarly, the domestic servants of the diplomat who are not nationals of the host state are entitled to such immunities as are extended by the host state at its discretion.

The Convention further specifies that the nationals of permanent residents in the host state who have diplomatic status are entitled to inviolability, immunities and privileges only for official acts performed in course of their duties.

These immunities and privileges are enjoyed by the diplomats from the moment they enter into the host state and continue to enjoy them during the period of their mission. Even when the mission is terminated, the diplomat is allowed to enjoy them for a reasonable period time to enable him to wind up his affairs.

The Vienna Convention allows the enjoyment of these immunities and privileges to the diplomatic agents, their families, their official communications, couriers, technical and administrative staff in the third states during their transit enroute to and from their diplomatic post and their home state. However, the diplomats are not entitled to these immunities in the third states if they are on private visit. But if the third state is at war with the host state of the diplomat, he can be arrested if he is found in that third state.

16

CONSULAR RELATIONS

The Consular relationship between the States is more ancient than the permanent diplomatic relations. The Greek City states appointed an official called Proxenoi to perform the consular functions. Originally the Consuls were elected by the merchants who were residents in a foreign state and his function was to act as a judge of their commercial disputes. The modern system came into existence from sixteenth century when states appointed their own officials as consuls to different countries. Following Industrial Revolution and the opening of China and Japan to the Western countries, international trade, shipping and travel increased considerably, and with that the importance of Consuls was also increased. The Consular institution was developed primarily for protection of trade and commerce; but in course of time they were entrusted with several other responsibilities by their home states. Due to their increasing importance, by the end of last century almost all states established consular services and as such uniform customary international laws grew up. These customary laws are now codified and updated in the Vienna Convention on Consular Relations, 1963.

Consular and Diplomatic Services

Consular service, in most countries, is different than the diplomatic services, though both of them are controlled by the Foreign Ministry. While the diplomatic mission is located at one particular place, Consuls are appointed in more than one city or district in the state to which they are sent. While diplomatic representatives are issued with Letter decredence, the consular officials are appointed by commissions or patents by their own state and receive exequatur or authorisation from the receiving state. While diplomatic agents enjoy complete immunity from the local jurisdiction of the receiving state, the Consuls do not. Like the diplomats, the consuls do not represent their state and are not accredited to the host state. Though the functions of diplomatic and consular agents are different, yet many states found it convinient to combine both the offices in one person. So Starke has noted "The modern tendency of states is to amalgamate their diplomatic and consular services, and it is matter of frequent occurance to find representatives of states occupying, interchangeably or concurrently diplomatic and consular posts."

According to the Vienna Convention, 1963, Consular posts are divided into four classes: Consuls General, Consuls, Vice-Consuls, and Pro-Consuls. Some times, honorary consuls are also appointed by a foreign state from among the citizens or residents of the receiving state.

The Consular relation between two states is established through bilateral treaty. A person is appointed as a Consul by his state by a commission or patent and the receiving state recognises him by granting exequatur. Normally a consul does not enter into his duties until the receiving state has granted him the exequatur. When the receiving state has granted exequatur to the head of the consular post, it also means that all other consular staff are also acceptable to it. The size of consular staff each state will maintain is determined by the treaty which established the consular relation.

The consular services are terminated due to the death of consul or withdrawal of the exequatur or recall or dismissal of the consul or if war break outs between the states. According to Vienna Convention, a sending state can close down its consulate at any time by notifying the receiving state and similarly the receiving state can notify the sending state that a member of consular staff is persona non grata and hence to be recalled.

Today consuls perform a large number of important non-political and technical services on behalf of their own state. The Vienna Convention has listed these functions which may broadly be catogerised into following groups: (1) protection and promotion of trade, (2) assistance to ships, aircrafts and crews and help in the inspection of ships in accordance with the health, sanitation and other laws of the receiving state, (3) providing services to the nationals of the sending state such as by helping them in protection of their rights and interests before the courts and authorities of the receiving state, and (4) performance of various administrative and material functions for the nationals of both the sending and receiving states such as issue of passports and visas; registering marriages, births and deaths etc. Additional functions can also be entrusted to the consuls if both the states so desire in the consular treaty.

The duties and functions of consuls being limited in nature, they do not enjoy complete immunity from the jurisdiction of the receiving state like the diplomatic representatives. In fact so far as the immunities are concerned, they enjoy a position in between the diplomats and the ordinary aliens. The Vienna Convention has included certain privileges and immunities for effective functioning of consular posts which the states are at liberty to confirm, supplement and expand by concluding treaties between them. If there are matters which are not regulated by the Vienna Convention, they are to be governed by the customary international laws.

The privileges and immunities are granted to the sending state and not to the consular posts. The consular archives and documents are inviolable and most consular treaties also recognise the inviolability of the consular premises, but not the private residence of the consul. The officials of the receiving state are prohibited from entering into official consular premises without the consent of the head of consular post or his head of the diplomatic mission. But in case of disaster or emergencies, such consent shall be pressumed and officials of the receiving state can enter into the premises. The receiving state is under an obligation to protect the consular premises from damage, intrusion, riot or any attack on their dignity. The consular premises and its property are immune from requisition by the receiving state, but can be taken over by it by paying adequate compensation promptly.

According to the Vienna Convention, the consular officials shall not be arrested or detained except for "grave crimes" and that too on the decision of competent judicial authority. Very often they are exempted from prosecution of minor offences.

The freedom of movement of the consular staff is guaranteed subject to the law of the receiving state. The consular staff has the freedom to visit the nationals of their own state who are detained or in prison of the receiving state. It is also the duty of the authorities of the receiving state to inform his consular post if an alien who is detained or arrested requests to do so.

The consular staff enjoys freedom of communication which includes sending of couriers or coded messages and right to use diplomatic and consular pouches. But if there is a suspicion that the pouch facility is abused, the officials of the receiving state can open and examine the pouches in the presence of the consular officials.

As regards the financial privileges and immunities, the consular staff enjoy the same facilities as are granted to the diplomatic representatives under Vienna Convention on Diplomatic Relations, 1961. Thus they enjoy exemption from direct taxation, custom duties and inspection, payment of social security tax etc.

The immunities granted to the family members of consular officials, their employees and service staff and their domestic servants are much less than enjoyed by the diplomats. If the nationals of the receiving state have been appointed as consular officers with its express consent, their privileges and immunities are limited only to their official acts and duties.

17

TREATIES

The importance of international agreements or treaties lie in the fact that through them inter-state relation is maintained and in the absence of any international legislature, the rules of international law are created. It is only through the treaties international cooperation and understanding is achieved.

Treaties are the international agreements between the states which are binding upon them by virtue of the principle of Pacta sunt Servanda. But all international agreements are not called treaties; rather they are known by several names such as Conventions, Capitulations, Protocols, Agreements, Arrangements, Proces Verbal, Statutes, Modus Vivendi, Exhange of Notes, Concordats, and Final Act etc. Generally, the term "treaty" is used to describe the formal agreements relating to peace, alliance, transfer of territory or some other fundamental matters. So far the international law is concerned, there is no difference in nature except only with regard to the procedure of these various terms, and all of them are equally binding on the parties. But the different nomenclatures have different effects under the municipal laws, such as, in U.S.A. while a treaty requires ratification by 2/3 majority of Senate, an agreement does not require ratification.

(a) Definitions

According to Oppenheim "International treaties are agreements, of contractual character, between states or organisations of states, creating legal rights and obligations between parties." According to Clive Perry, "The essence of a treaty, whether be regarded as an instrument or transaction, is that it is a specific source of obligation of international law, voluntarily undertaken by one international person towards another or other, giving rise to raciprocal rights in that other or another." J.E.S. Fawcett defines it as "a written agreement by which parties establish international legal relation between them in a particular field or for a particular purpose." Starke defines it "as an agreement where by two or more states establish or seek to establish a relationship under international law between themselves."

(b) Types

There is no uniform basis of classification of treaties. However, various writers have adopted different bases to classify them. On the basis of the binding nature of the provisions of a treaty on one, two or many states, treaties are divided into unilateral, bilateral or multilateral treaties. Similarly, on the basis of number of parties to the treaty, they are divided into bilateral or multilateral treaties. Vattel has divided them into Equal and Unequal, and Real and Personal treaties. Oppenheim has divided them into Law-making treaties and treaties for other purposes. Calvo has divided the treaties on the basis of their Form, Nature, Object and Effect into Permanent and Temporary, Personal and Real, Equal and Unequal, Simple and Conditional and treaties of Political, Social, Commercial, Neutrality, Extradition etc. But the classification of Prof. Mc Nair appears to be more scientific such as, treaties having characteristics of Conveyance, treaties having characteristics of Contract, treaties establishing charters of incorporations such as establishment of International Postal Union, and Law-making treaties which are further subdivided into Pure Law-making treaties and Treaties creating Constitutional Law such as Statute of I.C.J.

(c) Capacity to Conclude Treaties

To conclude a treaty, the political organisation as well as

the person must have capacity. All sovereign states and many International Organisations possess the capacity to conclude the treaty and on their behalf a person can sign the treaty if he has the authority from the Constitution or the Charter and as well as from the municipal law. While all Sovereign States have the capacity to conclude the treaty through their accredited representatives, the capacity to do so by an international organisation depends on the powers given to it in its Charter or Statute or Constitution. But the Part or Non Sovereign States can enter into treaties only with the consent of their controlling state. As a general rule, the units of a federation do not have the capacity to conclude treaties. But some federations like Switzerland and the erstwhile U.S.S.R. had given the capacity to a limited extent to their units in their constitutions. The neutralised states, on the other hand, possess limited capacity to conclude treaties as per the neutralisation treaties. The Holy See possesses full capacity to conclude treaties known as Concordats, with other states. The capacity of the vassal and protected states to conclude treaties depend upon the freedom granted to them by their suzerain or protecting states.

On behalf of a state, normally, treaties are negotiated and signed by either the head of the state or head of the government or foreign minister or accredited permanent diplomatic representatives to that state. But when a separate diplomatic agent is sent to negotiate and conclude a treaty either with another state or at a diplomatic conference, he is to carry a document known as Full Powers from the competent authority of his state. When the treaty is to be negotiated and concluded by the head of the state or head of the government or the foreign minister personally, they do not require the document of Full Powers.

(d) Conclusion of a Treaty

Earlier, different aspects of treaty making were regulated by the customary laws, but after the conclusion of the Vienna

Convention on Law of Treaties, 1969, all aspects of treaty making are now governed by it.

There is no specific method of conclusion of a treaty. Sometimes, even an oral agreement between the authorised representatives of states is enough to bind the concerned states to it. But treaties being legally important, it is desirable to conclude them in the form of a document. When a treaty is formally concluded, it has to follow the following steps:

1. *Accredition:* The states who want to become parties to a treaty appoint accredited representatives to negotiate it. Each accredited representative carry with him a document known as Full Powers to prove his bonafides and to indicate the limit of his powers relating to conclusion of the treaty. In case of a bilateral treaty, the Full Powers documents are exchanged between representatives and in case of a multilateral treaty, the representatives submit the document to a Committee on Full Powers. But when the head of the state or head of the government or the foreign minister is personally negotiating the treaty, the document of Full Powers is not necessary.

2. *Negotiation and Adoption:* The terms and conditions of a treaty are negotiated by mutual discussion between the representatives, in case of bilateral treaty, and among the diplomatic representatives in a conference in case of a multilateral treaty. During negotiations, the representatives usually are in close touch with their government and if necessary seek fresh instructions.

As per Art. 9 of the Vienna Convention, the provisions of a multilateral treaty are adopted by 2/3 majority of votes of the conference. Sometimes, a treaty is adopted by an international organisation and then kept it open for acceptance and ratification of member states.

3. *Authentication:* The draft of a treaty which has been negotiated and agreed upon is authenticated by the signatures

of the representatives. In case of multilateral treaty, a formal session of the conference is held where the representatives append their signatures on the draft treaty. But if a treaty is to be authenticated by signatures, it is important that the representatives sign the treaty on the same day, place and time and before each other. The date of the treaty is usually taken to be the date of on which the treaty was signed. Sometimes a treaty is authenticated by a resolution of an international organisation. Nowadays, a negotiated treaty is kept open upto a certain date not exceeding a period of nine months in order to obtain more number of parties to the treaty.

If a treaty is not subject to ratification and approval of the concerned states, usually the treaty becomes binding on the parties from the date of signature. But bilateral treaties usually come into effect after the signed treaty documents are exchanged between parties. While many bilateral treaty documents are exchanged immediately, others are exchanged after ratification.

4. *Ratification and Reservation:* Ratification of a treaty means the approval of the signature of the representative as well as the draft of the treaty by the concerned state. Earlier, ratification was an essential part of treaty making process. But today, ratification is considered as a simple act of confirmation by which the state concerned declares its consent to be bound by the treaty.

The objects of ratification are that a state may want to reexamine and review the treaty and if on second thought, it does not want to be a party, it may withdraw. Further, ratification also provides time during which the concerned state may have to amend its laws to implement the treaty or seek the approval of the legislature or consult the public opinion. According to Art. 14 of the Vienna Convention, ratification of a treaty is essential if:

(a) the treaty expressly provides for it; or
(b) the negotiating states agree that it is necessary; or
(c) the treaty was signed subject to ratification; or
(d) the document of Full Powers indicate the desire of the state for ratification.

According to Brierly, a state is neither legally nor morally bound to ratify a treaty signed by its representative; but refusal to ratify a treaty should not be on frivolous grounds.

Ratification may be express or tacit. When a state implements a treaty without expressly declaring its ratification, it is called tacit or implied ratification. But when a state, specially its foreign minister, signs a document indicating its approval of the treaty, it is called express ratification.

Sometimes ratification is granted with reservation. It means a state is willing to be bound by the treaty except for some of its provisions. Such ratification with reservation being conditional in nature, it modifies the treaty. According to Oppenheim "conditional ratification is not ratification at all, but is equivalent to refusal of ratification coupled with a fresh offer." Such reservation by a state party must be acceptable to the other state parties as their consent is necessary for such conditions and modifications. If other parties agree to the reservation, it becomes a new treaty as the old treaty becomes null and void due to the conditional ratification.

In case of multilateral treaties, the position of a state with reserved ratification is not clear. However, the Advisory Opinion of I.C.J. on the Reservations to the Convention on the Prevention and Punishment of Crime of Genocide, observed "Reservations compatible to the objects of the treaty, if not objected by members, the reserving state is considered as a party to the treaty. But if the reservation is not compatible with the objects of the treaty, the reserving state may be considered as not a party."

When ratification of a treaty is required, such ratifications must be exchanged between states in case of a bilateral treaty; and in case of multilateral treaties, they are deposited at a central headquarters, usually the foreign office of the state where the treaty was signed or with the Secretary General of the U.N.O.

5. *Accession and Adhesion:* When a state did not sign a treaty at the time of its conclusion, it can join the treaty at a later date either through accession or adhesion.

When a new state becomes a party to all provisions of an existing treaty with all rights and obligations, it is called accession. Such accession by new states can take place only with the consent of original state parties.

But when a new state want to join an existing treaty with regard to only certain provisions or principles, it is called adhesion. Thus while a new state can become a full member to a treaty through accession, it can become a partial member to that treaty through adhesion.

6. *Entry into Force:* Many treaties come into force on the date of signature, if no ratification is required. But where ratification is required, such a treaty comes into force only after exchange or deposit of ratification by all parties. In case of a multilateral treaty, it comes into force as soon as ratification by a prescribed number of states deposit their ratifications. Sometimes, a particular date is fixed for bringing the treaty into force irrespective of number of ratifications received.

7. *Registration and Publication:* Art. 102 of the Charter of U.N.O. provides that all treaties and international agreements entered by member states are to be registered with the Secretariat of the U.N.O. as soon as possible and be published by it. It also provides that no state who is a party to an unregistered treaty or agreement can invoke it before any organ of the U.N.O. such as the I.C.J., or General Assembly.

Starke has observed "Apparently the provision does not invalidate an unregistered treaty, or prevent such a treaty from being invoked before bodies or courts other than United Nations organs." The purpose of registration is to prevent secret treaties and agreements between states.

The U.N. Secretariat publishes the treaties and agreements registered with it from time to time in the U.N. Treaty Series. A failure to publish a treaty does not make it unenforceable.

8. *Application and Enforcement:* The final stage of conclusion of a treaty is the actual incorporation of the treaty provisions into the municipal laws of the state parties for their application. Sometimes, the supervision of or administration by international organs is required which is usually done by setting up special committees or commissions.

(e) Invalidity of a Treaty

According to the Vienna Convention, treaties may be declared invalid under the following circumstances:

1. If the treaty was signed by a state which do not have the capacity such as a Vassal state or if its representative has signed the treaty exceeding the powers given to him by his state in the Full Powers document.
2. If there is mistake or error of facts and circumstances on the basis of which the treaty was concluded. But the entire treaty cannot be invalidated if the error is of minor nature or related to the wordings of the text of the treaty or the error was committed by a state party itself.
3. If a state party was persuaded to conclude the treaty by another state by fraudulent methods.
4. If a state's consent to the treaty was procured through direct or indirect corruption of its representative by another negotiating state.

5. If the consent of the representative was obtained by coersion or threat, or a state's consent to the treaty was obtained by the threat or use of force. But peace treaties signed between the victor and vanquished at the end of a war cannot be invalidated.
6. If the treaty comes in conflict with jus cogens, which is defined as certain fundamental rules of international law which have been accepted by the entire international community.
7. If the treaty comes in conflict with the provisions of UN Charter, according to Art. 103, such treaties will be invalid.

According to the Vienna Convention, a state party which wants to invalidate a treaty on the above grounds must notify the other state parties, so that a process of judicial settlement, arbitration or conciliation can be started to solve the dispute.

(f) Doctrine of Pacta Sunt Servanda

The states are bound by the provisions of a treaty to which they have given their consent and must implement the treaty in good faith. The principle under which the treaties are considered binding on the parties to a treaty is known as pacta sunt servanda which means the states must respect the agreements concluded between them in good faith. According to Judge Anzilotti this principle is a "supreme norm" and is the exclusive source of the obligatory character of treaties. Thus when a state agrees to fulfil certain obligations under a treaty, it is both legally and morally bound to fulfil its obligations.

The importance of the principle of pacta sunt servanda cannot be underestimated because not only the treaties but also the entire regime of international law being created on consent, agreement and understanding of states, the treaties and international laws are considered binding because of this principle. If this principle is not strictly followed, the entire structure of international law would collapse. Thus Fenwick rightly says, "Philosophers, theologians and jurists have recognised with unanimity that unless pledged word of a state could be relied upon, the relation of entire international community would be imperilled and law itself would disappear."

These considerations have compelled the writers and jurists to grant the pre-eminent position to the principle of Pacta Sunt Servanda in international law. This principle has been affirmed by both the Charter of U.N.O. and the Vienna Convention on Law of Treaties.

(g) Interpretation of Treaties

The frequent disputes relating treaties arise about their interpretation and much of the time of the international courts are engaged in the work of interpreting treaties than anything else.

The question of interpretation arises because words have several meanings and these meanings may also change in course of time. Further, words may have both a common and a technical meaning. Similarly, a phrase may mean one thing when considered in isolation, but when qualified by the next phrase it may mean something else. Two clauses when considered literally, may be found to be opposed. Very often treaties are drafted in two or more languages such as the U.N. Charter was drafted in five languages. In some cases the treaty text in a particular language is declared as authentic while in other cases, such as the U.N. Charter, all languages have been declared as equally authenticate. In such cases the terms of each treaty text are pressumed to have same meaning and while interpreting, the object and purpose of the treaty should be kept in view and the treaty text should be reconciled accordingly.

The following general principles are followed in interpreting the treaties:

1. The plain and natural meaning of words and phrases should be accepted. The grammatical interpretation, if leads to absurdity or inconsistency or is beyond the intention of the parties, should not be accepted.
2. As far as possible, the treaty should be interpreted within the four corners of the treaty text itself. But if the treaty text is not clear about the intention of parties, the preparatory works, such as the records of discussion of the conference, draft amendments, the preliminary draft of the treaty etc., as well as the interpretative protocols, resolutions and reports of committees should be referred.
3. Treaties should be interpreted in accordance with the objects and purposes of the treaty which can be ascertained from the Preamble and annextures to the treaty.
4. Treaties should be interpreted in such a way as to give the words and phrases a reasonable and consistent meaning.
5. Interpretation of terms of a treaty should not be made in such a way as to restrict the sovereignty of a state party.
6. A treaty should be interpreted in such a way that it will not make a provision of the treaty meaningless or ineffective. On the other hand, a treaty should be interpreted in such a way which will help in achieving the purpose of the treaty.
7. If a word or phrase or provision of a treaty can have more than one interpretation, the interpretation which will have less obligation on the parties should be accepted.
8. While interpreting, the treaty text as a whole should be read so that the doubt or ambiguity of a clause can be clarified with the help of another clause.
9. Interpretation of a treaty should be made in the light of legal understanding of parties as well as the

meaning of the terms at the time when the treaty was concluded and not according to those of at the time of interpretation.

10. If there is a conflict between a general provision and a special provision in the treaty, the special provision should regulate the general provision, unless the parties intended to give greater importance to the general provision.

(h) Revision of Treaty

Revision, as distinct from replacement, of a treaty means modification or amendment to an original treaty. The term 'revision' was used before the Vienna Convention on Law of Treaties and the terms 'amendment' and 'modification' are used since then.

The process of amendment or modification of a treaty is not a unilateral process; so all parties to the treaty should be involved in the process. Most treaties nowadays provide for amendment or revision of the treaty according to the changing circumstances. They also prescribe a procedure of amendment in the treaty text itself. Such a procedure usually provide that the amendment may be initiated by one or number of parties which may be approved by the remaining state parties. Though unanimity of all state parties is required for adoption of any amendment to treaties, since 1945 a trend has emerged according to which multilateral treaties can be amended by majority of state parties. Usually, the treaty itself prescribes a period of time after which amendments can be made to the treaty.

The Vienna Convention has prescribed the following principles regarding the procedure and effect of amendment of multilateral treaties:

(a) that the proposal of amendment must be notified to all state parties;

(b) that all state parties are entitled to take part in process of amendment;

(c) that every state party to the original treaty has the right to become party to the amended treaty.

All amended treaties require ratification of the parties and if an original state party refuse to ratify the amended treaty, it shall be excluded.

(i) Termination of a Treaty

A treaty is terminated when the parties to it are released from further obligations. In case of a bilateral treaty, when one state party is released of its obligation, the treaty is terminated. But in case of a multilateral treaty, a situation may arise in which one or two parties are discharged from the obligations of the treaty while the treaty continues in full force between the remaining parties. But if such a multilateral treaty provides for certain number of parties to continue and if the number becomes less, the treaty is terminated. It is to be noted that no state party can unilaterally terminate a treaty at its discretion without informing other state parties.

A treaty can be terminated under following grounds:

1. Treaties which are concluded for a fixed period, terminates automatically at the end of the period. Even in such treaties, sometimes a state party is allowed to withdraw after a fixed period after treaty is in force, in which case the treaty is terminated even before the end of the period.
2. Some treaties may become obsolete or meaningless and become incapable of application in course of time, such treaties, for all practical purposes, are treated as terminated.
3. Some treaties are concluded to achieve certain specific objects and after the achievement of those objects in full, such treaties are terminated.

4. In case of bilateral treaties, if one of the state party is extinct due to merger, split, dissolution, annexation or conquest etc., the treaties with that state are terminated. But treaties relating to boundary or territory of the extinct state are not terminated.
5. A treaty may be terminated or a state party may be allowed to withdraw from the treaty with the consent of other state parties.
6. If an existing treaty comes in conflict with a newly developed fundamental rule laying down norms of international law (jus cogens), that treaty becomes illegal and is automatically terminated.
7. A treaty is considered terminated if all parties to it conclude a new treaty covering the same subject matter.
8. When war breaks out between parties to a treaty, there is no uniform pattern affecting the treaties. The general opinion as observed by Justice Cordozo in Tocht V. Hughes case, is "Provisions compatible with state of hostilities, unless expressly terminated, will be enforced, and those incompatible rejected." Usually all political, commercial and extradition treaties are terminated after the outbreak of war.
9. According to Art. 103 of the U.N. Charter, if obligations under any treaty to which a member state is a party, comes in conflict with that of U.N. Charter, the Charter will prevail and the treaty will be terminated.
10. When certain material or essential conditions of the treaty are violated or not performed by a state party, in case of a bilateral treaty, the other state party may terminate or suspend the treaty. But in case of such violation by one of the state parties to a multi-lateral treaty, other state parties may either terminate the whole treaty or terminate it only for the defaulting state party.
11. When it is impossible for a state party to perform the

obligations of treaty due to permanent disappearance or destruction of an object which was indispensable for the execution of the treaty, the treaty can be terminated. But if this impossibility is created by that state party either due to violation of an obligation under that treaty or due to any other international obligation undertaken by that state party, the treaty cannot be terminated.

12. A treaty can be terminated by a state party by invoking the doctrine of rebus sic stantibus, according to which if there is a fundamental change of facts and circumstances which existed at the time of conclusion of treaty, a state party can invoke the doctrine to terminate the treaty or withdraw from it. This doctrine is also recognised in Art. 62 of the Vienna Convention of 1969. According to this Convention, the doctrine can be invoked by a state party if the following conditions are fulfilled:

    (a) the circumstance which is claimed to have changed, must have constituted an essential basis of the consent of that State to be bound by the treaty;
    (b) the changed circumstances radically changes the obligations under the treaty.

But as per the Convention, the doctrine cannot be invoked to terminate a treaty if:

(a) it establishes a boundary;
(b) the fundamental change is due to violation of an obligation under the treaty or any other international obligation by the state party invoking the doctrine.

The state party invoking this doctrine for the termination of the treaty must give notice to the other state parties stating the reasons for termination. In other words, there is no automatic termination of a treaty by a state party by invoking the doctrine.

(j) Suspension of a Treaty

The application of the treaty to one or all parties to it may be suspended under the following grounds:

(a) if a provision of the treaty provides it; or
(b) if all parties to the treaty agree to it; or
(c) if by concluding another treaty, the parties want to suspend the earlier treaty.

In case of a multilateral treaty, two or more parties may suspend its application between them alone, if it is provided by the treaty itself.

18

SETTLEMENT OF INTERNATIONAL DISPUTES

For maintenance of international peace and security it is essential that all international disputes should be settled in a fair and just manner between the involved state parties. Earlier, many disputes were settled by use of force; but since 1945 under the Charter of UNO, the use of force by individual states as a means of settlling their disputes is no more permitted.

The rules and procedure of settlement of disputes without using force have been laid down partly by custom and practice and partly by the Hague Conventions of 1899 and 1907 and the UN Charter of 1945. But there is no obligation under international law on states to settle their international disputes without the consent of the involved parties. Broadly speaking the methods of settling international disputes may be divided into:

(a) Peaceful or amicable method of settlement, and
(b) Compulsive or coersive means short of war.

(A) Peaceful Settlement of Disputes

The following are the various peaceful methods of settlement of international disputes:

(i) Negotiation, Good Offices and Mediation

These are less formal methods than the method of judicial

or arbitral settlement. The methods of good offices and mediation frequently accompanies with the method of negotiation. Nowadays, the legal frame work has been established for the twin processes of consultation and communication to facilitate the method of negotiation.

Both Good Offices and Mediation are methods of settlement in which, usually, a friendly third state assists in bringing an amicable settlement of a dispute between the parties, as was done by the U.S.A. to settle the dispute between Egypt and Israel and between P.L.O. and Israel. Mediation can be made either by an individual or an international organ such as Security Council which acted as a mediator in a dispute between the Netherlands and Indonesia in 1947.

In case of good offices, a third state tender its services in order to bring the disputing parties together with a suggestion to reach a settlement without itself participating in the negotiations. But in case of mediation, the mediating state has an active role and it actually participates in the negotiations and it may also make suggestions which may or may not be accepted by the disputing parties.

However, the scope of both good offices and mediation is limited.

(ii) Conciliation and Commissions for Enquiry

Conciliation may be defined as the submission of disputes to a previously constituted commission, enjoying the confidence of the disputant states, whose duty it was to examine all aspects of the dispute and to submit to the parties a solution based on equity and mutual concession, which they are free to accept or reject. According to Judge Manly O. Hudson "Conciliation... is a process of formulating proposals of settlement after an investigation of the facts and an effort to reconcile opposing contentions the parties to the dispute being left free to accept or reject the proposals formulated."

The Hague Conventions of 1899 and 1907 had provided for Commissions of enquiry or Conciliation Commissions. Such commissions can be set up to enquire and report on facts. Though the commission can be set up by a special agreement between parties, the findings of the commission are not binding on the parties.The object of an enquiry commission is to establish the facts and there by prepare the way for a negotiated settlement. This method is more suitable in cases of boundary disputes where the commission can enquire into historical and geographical facts which are subject of controversy between the disputing states and help in clarifying the issues for a peaceful agreement on the boundary line.

(iii) Arbitration

An international dispute can be referred to certain persons called arbitrators who are freely chosen by the parties and these arbitrators make an award without strictly following the legal considerations. The procedure of arbitration is as old as Indian, Greek and Roman civilisations. During Christian era, the disputes between the princes and rulers of different states of Europe were submitted to the arbitration of Pope. During 19th century the procedure of arbitration grew in prestige and authority after the successful arbitration of the Albama Claim Case in 1872 between the U.S.A and Britain. In modern times, it was at the first Hague Conference in 1899 that arbitration received recognition as a formal international procedure of settlement of disputes. This Convention for the Pacific Settlement of International Disputes, 1899, stated that the object of arbitration is "the settlement of differences between states by judges of their own choice and on the basis of respect for the law." The second Hague Convention of 1907 established the Permanent Court of Arbitration, which is an institution of peculiar character. In fact, it is neither "permanent" nor is it a "Court". The members of the "Court" are appointed by the states who are parties to the Hague Convention. Each such state may appoint four persons having qualifications in international law. All such persons so appointed, constitute a general list of competent lawyers out of which the disputant parties appoint two arbitrators each. These four arbitrators then choose an Umpire and all the five arbitrators then constitute the tribunal, where the award is given by majority vote. Each tribunal thus created shall have to function according to the arbitration agreement in which the subject of dispute, the tribunal's jurisdiction, the procedure to be followed, and the rules of law and the principles according to which its decision is to be given, are specified.

Since the foundation of Permanent Court of Arbitration several important awards have been given by it such as the Pious Fund Case of 1902, North Atlantic Coast Fisheries Case, 1910, the Savarkar Case, 1911 etc.

Arbitration is essentially a consensual procedure and so the states cannot be compelled to arbitrate unless they agree to do so in regard to a specific dispute. However, even without any compulsion states submit various types of disputes for arbitration; but they normally exclude disputes in which their vital interests or matters relating their domestic jurisdiction are involved.

The arbitral process has several merits such as, it is more appropriate than the judicial process for settlement of technical disputes, it is less expensive, it can be conducted without any publicity, and, finally, its procedure is flexible than the judicial process.

(iv) Judicial Settlement

When a properly constituted international judicial body settles disputes by applying rules of law, it is called judicial settlement. At present there is one only general judicial organ—the International Court of Justice at the Hague—to settle international legal disputes judicially.

This Court is completely different from the Permanent Court of Arbitration in many respects. While the I.C.J. is a permanently constituted tribunal, governed by a Statute and have its won body of rules of procedure which are binding on parties to a dispute before it. It has a permanent registry which receives documents and acts as a channel of communication with governments and other bodies. Its proceedings are public. The Court is open to all states for judicial settlement of all cases which the states may want to refer to it. The 15 judges of the Court represent the principal legal systems of the world and are elected separately both by the General Assembly and the Security Council for a term of 9 years. Since only 1/3 of judges are elected once in every 3 years, 2/3 judges maintain continuity and consistent practice in its proceedings.

The Court, which is an integral part of the U.N. Charter excercises jurisdiction over the states which are parties to its Statute. So the Court ipso facto exercises jurisdiction over all members states of the U.N.O. The non-member states can also approach the Court, if they submit a declaration to the Registrar of the court indicating acceptance of its jurisdiction and its decisions.

The Court excercises Voluntary, Obligatory, and Advisory jurisdictions. Under Voluntary jurisdiction, the state parties to a dispute, through an agreement, refer the case to the Court. Similarly, only one party may refer the case to the Court, while other party may indicate its assent to such reference. Under the Obligatory jurisdiction, certain types of disputes between the state parties are automatically and compulsorily referred to the Court. Such disputes which must be referred to the Court are concerning (1) interpretation of treaties (2) any question of international law (3) any fact whose existence, if established, would constitute a breach of an international obligation, and (4) the nature or extent of the reparation to be made for the breach of an international obligation. Under Advisory jurisdiction, the Court may give legal opinion on any legal question referred to it by the

Security Council or General Assembly. The other organs of the U.N.O. and the specialised agencies can also seek the Advisory opinion of the Court with the approval of the General Assembly.

The record of the Court over the years since its inception has been impressive, particularly, in the field of tendering Advisory opinion to U.N.O. by enlightening it as to the course of action it should take on a dispute.

(v) Settlement Under Auspices of U.N.O.

One of the fundamental aims of the establishment of U.N.O. is the peaceful settlement of disputes and differences between states. So under Art. 2 of the Charter, the member states have undertaken to settle their disputes by peaceful means and refrain from threats of war or use of the force. For this purpose wide powers have been given to the General Assembly and more specifically to the Security Council. The General Assembly has the authority to recommend steps for peaceful adjustment of any situation which is likely to harm the general welfare or friendly relations among the nations.

The Security Council is given more extensive powers so that it should act quickly and decisively. The Security Council acts in (1) disputes which may endanger international peace and security; and (2) cases of threats to peace or breaches of peace or acts of aggression. While in the first category of disputes the Council may recommend parties to settle their disputes by peaceful methods such as arbitration, judicial settlement etc., there is no restriction on the type of action the Council can recommend or take which it may decide are necessary. It may, in the second type of disputes, either recommend any peaceful methods of settlement of disputes or also may decide to give effect to the coersive methods such as economic sanctions or may even decide to use armed forces against the states which decline to be bound by its decision.

(B) Compulsive or Coersive Procedure of Settlement of Disputes Short of War

When the two states fail to resolve their dispute through peaceful means, resort may be taken to certain coersive methods, short of war, to bring physical pressure without actually using the force. Though war itself is a recognised method of settlement of disputes, yet coersive method is less drastic through which the same purpose can also be achieved. It is obvious that this remedy of coersive procedure, as a rule, is always resorted to by a stronger power against weaker states.

The following are different Coersive methods usually adopted to settle disputes:

(i) Retortion

It is a method of retaliation by a state against another state for certain discourteous or unfriendly acts towards it. Usually, retortion is resorted to as a measure of retaliation by an agrieved state when certain harmful, though legal, actions by another state is taken against it. The retaliatory action of the agrieved state though is harmful yet it should also be legal.

Retortion is distinct from reprisal in the sense that both the offending and the agrieved states remain within the boundaries of law, eventhough their actions are harmful to each other.

The methods that are adopted in retortion are expulsion of nationals, levy of special customs duties, denial of port facilities to the ships, withdrawal of diplomatic privileges from the diplomatic representatives and recall of its diplomatic representatives etc., from the offending state.

The use of retortion by a member state of the U.N.O. has become limited by the provisions of the Charter, because retortion under certain circumstances may endanger the international peace and security, in which case it becomes illegal under the U.N. Charter.

(ii) Reprisal

Reprisals are the retaliatory actions by an agrieved state against another state to compel it to agree to a settlement of dispute created by that state due to its illegal or unjustified conduct.

The distinction between reprisal and retortion is that while retortion consists of certain retaliatory actions which are legal, reprisal consists of certain retaliatory actions by the agrieved state which though are illegal, yet are taken to compel the offending state to abide by the law.

Earlier, the agrieved state used to seize the persons and property of the offending state. Today, reprisals may assume various forms such as boycott of goods of the offending state, an embargo, a military or naval demonstration, or bombardment etc.

Starke has pointed out that reprisal as an international practice is controversial because the law relating to it are unsettled. Today, reprisal is considered as justified only when the state against which it is taken is:

(a) guilty of international delinquency;
(b) agrieved state's request to rectify the wrong done was ignored by the offending state;
(c) as established in the Naulilaa case 1928, it should be proportionate to the injury suffered; and
(d) reasonable to secure the settlement of dispute.

Some writers are of the opinion that reprisal is justified only when negotiations for the settlement of dispute fails and the actions taken by the agrieved state are meant to bring about a settlement of the dispute.

The U.N. Charter in Art. 2 (4) directs the members to refrain from the threat or use of force against another state. The Security Council in a resolution in 1964 condemned reprisals as being "incompatible with the purposes and principles of U.N.O." The General Assembly in a resolution on 24th October 1970 declared "States have a duty to refrain from acts of reprisal involving use of force." In other words, the U.N. considers armed reprisal against other states as illegal and, by implication, permits the reprisals not involving force and such reprisals are permitted only when negotiations and other peaceful means of settlement of dispute have failed. But the Charter in Art. 51 permits the states to take armed reprisals that are taken in self-defence against armed attack.

The reprisal taken by a belligerent state against another belligerent during the course of the war is different than the reprisals taken by a state during peacetime. The aim of the reprisal during war is to restrain the enemy belligerent state from violating the laws of war. During the Second World War, Britain captured the neutral merchant ships carrying German goods to other countries as a reprisal for sinking of British merchant ships by Germany by using illegal magnetic mines in the sea.

(iii) Embargo

Sometimes an agrieved state impose embargo on the ships of the offending state which are found in its own ports. But the embargoed ships cannot be confiscated until finally the offending state refuses to settle the dispute. Some times, as an act of embargo, the ships of the offending state are also captured on the high seas. But when the agrieved state, gets redress or satisfaction from the offending State, the ships under embargo must be released.

(iv) Boycott

It is also a sort of reprisal. In the practice of boycott, the citizens of the agrieved state collectively suspend trade and commerce with the citizens of the offending state. So long boycott is adopted voluntarily by the citizens of the agrieved state, it does not violate international law. But if the citizens of the agrieved state resort to boycott due to the pressure or persuation of their state it becomes 'economic aggression' and as such becomes illegal under the international law.

(v) Pacific Blockade

During war blockade of a belligerent's ports by the naval forces of another belligerent is a normal affair. But pacific blockade is imposed during peace time by an agrieved state in order to compel an offending state to give satisfaction to it. The concept of pacific blockade originated in 1827 when England, France and Russia, without declaring war, imposed a blockade against Turkey to bring pressure on it. Usually blockade during the peacetime is used by a very powerful state having strong naval forces against a weaker state.

According to the practices of some states, which is also supported by many writers, during pacific blockade, the agrieved blockading state has no right to seize the ships of the third states when they try to break a pacific blockade, which a blockading state can do during the war time.

But due to the restrictions imposed by Art. 2 (4) of the U.N. Charter on its members, pacific blockade imposed by a member state against another state has become illegal under international law. However, Art. 42 authorises the Security Council to adopt pacific blockade in order to "maintain or restore international peace and security." Thus, today, pacific blockade can be employed collectively under Security Council but not individually by the states.

(vi) Armed Intervention

Intervention which is defined as a dictatorial interference in the domestic or foreign affairs of another state is traditionally divided into three types, namely, internal, external, and punitive. Nowadays a fourth type, namely, subversive intervention has come into existence which means by propaganda, sabotage, sending armed infiltrators etc., by one state into the territory of another state for creating either revolt or civil strife in that state for its own purposes.

The international law allows states the right of intervention under certain circumstances such as self-defence, reprisals, enforcement of treaty rights, maintenance of balance of powers, and protection of persons and properties etc. But the U.N.O. has imposed rigid restrictions on the right of intervention by a state through the General Assembly Resolution of 1965 which states "No state has a right to intervene, directly or indirectly, for any reason whatever, in the internal or external affairs of any state." On the other hand, the chapter VII of the Charter allows collective intervention, i.e., intervention under the authority of the Security Council. Such collective interventions may be made on humanitarian grounds, to enforce the treaties, to check illegal intervention, to remove international nuisance and such other issues which threaten peace and security in the world.

Starke has enumerated the following exceptional cases when a state can have legal right of intervention under international law:

(1) Collective intervention according to the Charter;
(2) To protect the rights and interests as well as personal safety of its citizens abroad;
(3) For self-defence, if intervention is required to meet the actual armed attack;
(4) In the affairs of a protectorate under its control; and
(5) If the state in which intervention is to be made is guilty of gross violation of international law in regard to the intervening state.

19

WAR

A. Attempts for Renunciation of War

For centuries, war was considered as the permissible method of settlement of disputes between states when all other methods failed to get redress for the alleged wrong done to them. Till the 1920, there was no effective international organisation through which their conflicts could be settled, threats prevented, or commission of wrongs punished. In the absence of such an organisation, the individual states took law into their own hands and prosecuted the offenders by waging wars.

Earlier writers considered war as a sovereign right of a state. But the ruthless use of force, cruelty, wanton destruction of life and property led the statesmen and writers to believe that steps should be taken to prevent or abolish war; or if it could not be abolished, at least it could be regulated through laws. The Christian theologists, particularly, St. Thomas Acquinas, took initiative in the middle ages to develop laws of war on the basis of principles of humanity, morality, and chivalry. They also distinguished between a Just and Unjust war, and by implication, the unjust war being immoral should not be undertaken by a state. Later, the writers in international law like Grotius, Vattel, Von Clausewitz etc., succeeded to a large extent in bringing about a high degree of order in war by suggesting the detail rules in regulating the conduct of war. These laws originally started as customary laws, later codified in a number of instruments like, Geneva Convention of 1864, Declaration of St. Petersburg of 1864, the two Hague Declarations on 1899, and in eleven documents signed as the Hague Convention of 18th October, 1907, the Geneva Protocol of 1925, the London Protocol of 1936. The most recent addition to the law in restricting the freedom of parties to a war was the Hague Convention of 1954 for the protection of cultural properties during the armed conflicts.

One of the major defects of international law upto the end of twentieth century was that it failed to provide a machinery to which state parties to a dispute could approach for a peaceful solution, as a result of this failure the states frequently resorted to war even to decide minor disputes. However, the first such machinery was provided by the Hague Convention on the Pacific Settlement of Disputes, 1899. But this convention also failed to prevent the outbreak of First World War.

At the end of the First World War, the concept of sovereign right to make war by the states was greatly restricted and the Pact of Paris gave a call for the renunciation of wars as an instrument of national policy. The formation of the League of Nations provided new hopes for the eradication of war. The League, for the first time, provided an institutional frame work for resolution of international conflicts, by making its member states duty bound to submit to it any dispute which was likely to lead to 'war' or 'resort to use of force'. A Permanent Court of International Justice was established at the Hague for judicial settlement of disputes between the states. The League, to certain extent, guaranteed the political independence and territorial integrity of member states and proclaimed that any war or threat of war was its concern and the Covenant of the League authorised it to take appropriate actions to prevent them. Thus the principle of collective responsibility of the member states of the League to prevent war or threat of war was established. But due to certain organisational defects, the League was not very successful in preventing wars, and finally the outbreak of Second World War sounded the death knell of the League.

However, during the life time of the League certain important measures were taken to rectify some of the defects. The Geneva Protocol of 1924 provided for compulsory arbitration of those disputes which the League Council failed to resolve. The most significant achievement during this period was the Kellogg - Briand Pact which finally abolished war as a legal institution which led to the conclusion of the General Treaty for Renunciation of War, 1928, and the parties to this treaty undertook to renounce war or threat of war as an instrument of national policy and accepted the duty of submitting all their disputes for pacific settlement.

But the provisions of the League as well as other laws laid down through treaties, including the Renunciation Treaty, were overtaken by the advancement of science and technology, and these rules became ineffective and inapplicable, as a result of which the Second World War broke out.

The devastating and disastrous consequences of the Second World War, finally led the states to take effective steps to eradicate war. The victorious Allies created a new international organisation to replace the ineffectual League of Nations by United Nations Organisation. With the adoption of the Charter of the U.N.O. the war lost its dignity as a legal institution and war was formally outlawed. Clive Perry has rightly said that with the adoption of the Charter, "the long career of war as a legal institution ended with almost miraculous case." In this respect, two factors helped; firstly, the International Military Tribunals, which for the first time, brought individual leaders and officials who were responsible for starting the unlawful war to trial in order to fix their personal responsibility and punish them for committing certain war crimes. In future, all the leaders and persons will be individually responsible for the war and its consequences and they cannot take the shelter under the doctrine of Acts of

State. Secondly, the Charter of the UN imposed an obligation on member states to renounce war and always to seek pacific settlement of their disputes. Thirdly, the Security Council of the UN was entrusted with the responsibility of maintaining peace and security in the world and was authorised to take effective steps to deal with threats to peace, breaches of peace, and acts of aggression.

Thus today, the Charter of the U.N.O. has ruled out "the right to make war" as illegal and the Security Council and the General Assembly have alone the prerogative of using force for maintaining peace and for guaranteeing security to all states through the system of collective security.

B. Legal Nature of War

The contest between two or more states in which their armed forces are engaged in mutual act of violence is known as war.

According to Von Clausewitz, war as a struggle on an extensive scale is designed to compel one party or to compel its opponent to fulfill its will. Oppenheim considers war as a contention between two or more states through their armed forces for the purpose of overpowering each other and imposing the conditions of peace according to the wishes of the victors. To Starke, war is "a contest between two or more states primarily through their armed forces, the ultimate purpose of each contestant or each contestant group being to vanquish the other or others and impose its own conditions of peace."

In order to be considered as a 'state of war', an armed conflict must have the following conditions:

(i) a hostile relationship between the contesting parties;
(ii) declaration of war to create a state of war;
(iii) a contest between two or more states through their armed forces; and

(iv) the ultimate purpose of each contestant is to vanquish the other and to impose its own conditions of peace.

But the General Treaty for Renunciation of War, 1928, and more specially, after adoption of UN Charter, certain prohibitions have been imposed on the states' power of resorting to war. Nowadays, armed conflicts between states sometimes do take place, but states for the fear of violating the Renunciation Treaty, and more particularly, the Charter of UNO, do not call these conflicts as war, but by other names such as 'non-war conflicts'; breach of peace', 'act of aggression', hostilities', 'conflicts' etc.

Non-War Hostilities

In the post—Second World War period since 1945, no 'war' in the legal sense of the term has occured till today. But several major armed conflicts had taken place since then such the Korean hostilities of 1950-53, Indo-China conflict of 1956, border conflict between India and China in 1962, hostilities between Indonesia and the Dutch in 1962, India Pakistan armed conflicts of 1965 and 1971, the Suez Canal Conflict of 1956, and the Vietnam hostilities of 1965, etc. These armed conflicts though were fought on the scale of war, yet they are described as 'non-war armed conflicts.'

The reasons for development of non-war conflicts, instead of wars are:

(a) the desire of the states not to violate the Renunciation treaty and the Charter of UN;
(b) to localise the conflict and to prevent the disastrous consequences of a general war;
(c) to prevent the uninvolved third states from declaring neutrality which might create hindrances in their conduct of the hostilities because of the laws of neutrality.

The development of 'non-war conflicts' in the postwar

period was foreseen by the San Fransico Conference which drafted the Charter of the UNO and also made provision in the Charter in Art. 39 to deal with such non-war conflicts arising out of "threat to peace, breach of peace, or acts of aggression." However, whether a particular armed conflict be considered as a "state of war" or a "state of non-war conflict" depends on the following factors:

(i) The dimension of the conflict: If the use of force is general and unlimited, it is a state or war; but if it is limited and the area of conflict is also limited, it is a non-war conflict.

(ii) The intention of the contestants: The intention of the contestants towards the conflict will determine the status of conflict as war or non-war hostilities. But the problem arises when one of the contestants considers the conflict as war, while the other considers it as non-war conflict as was the case of India-Pakistan conflict of 1965.

(iii) The attitude and reactions of third states: if the conflict affects the interests and the rights of the uninvolved third states, they may have to redefine their relation with the contestants either by recognising them as belligerents or declaring their own neutrality, irrespective of the intentions of the actual contestants.

The evolution of non-war conflicts have revolutionised the laws of war, as while only some of these laws are applicable, yet many others are not applicable. The laws which are applicable are the laws of military warfare and use of weapons, the laws relating the protection of victims of war, and laws relating to humanitarian principles. But the laws relating to private property and confiscation of property of the enemy and the laws of neutrality are not applicable.

C. Types of War

Since the time of Grotius, writers in international law

have tried to classify the wars into just and unjust, public and private, perfect and imperfect, formal and informal wars. Nowadays two more types of war, namely, the total war and the guerilla war have been added. In the total war everything is made subordinate to the requirements of war regardless of any laws, rules, regulations, and treaties etc., with the sole purpose of defeating the enemy by any and every means. The guerilla war is fought by the unorganised armed bodies of people not belonging to any organised armed forces on the territory which is occupied by the enemy.

D. Commencement of War

The state of war, according to the Hague Convention No. III of 1907, "must not commence without previous and explicit warning, in the form either of a reasoned declaration of war or of an ultimatum with conditional declaration of war." In other words, a formal declaration is essential to establish a 'state of war'. The neutral countries must be notified immediately after the declaration of the war.

But the practice of states between 1935-45 shows that little regard was paid to this rule of giving warning to others through a declaration of war or by issuing an ultimatum. Instead, surprise attacks without any warning, like the Japanese attack on Pearl Harbour in 1941 or German attack on Russia in 1941, became the practice. But non-observance of this rule of declaration of war does not in any way reduce its importance.

Some times, states declare war, although actual hostilities may not actually take place between them. This was observed during the Second World War when more than 50 states though formally declared war, yet less than half of these states actually participated actively through their military forces against the enemy.

E. Nature of Modern War

From the experiences of the last two World Wars, the

following nature of the modern wars can be deduced:

1. A formal declaration of war establishes a 'state of war';
2. States declaring war need not actually engage their military against the enemy in active hostilities;
3. In the modern total wars, not only the armed forces of the belligerents, but also their entire population were involved;
4. Propaganda, disinformation, and psychological warfare have become as much part of the war as the weapons, armed forces, and civilian population;
5. More than the combatants, the civilian population had become the victims of war because of air bombardments, shortage of food and other essential articles, and other harrassments;
6. Civilian population were exposed to mass destruction due to the explosion of atomic bombs; and
7. The end of armed hostilities did not necessarily terminate the state of war, as, though Germany and Japan surrendered unconditionally to the Allies in 1945, yet legally they were at war with Allies until the peace treaty was signed with them in 1951 and after.

F. Conduct of War

The failure of the international community to abolish the war and to prevent the states from settling their claims and disputes by force, the statesmen and writers in international law tried to regulate it by creating a body of rules called "laws of war" which are in the nature of restrictions and limitations on States resorting to war. Today, those rules of international law deal with the relations between the states which are at war or engaged in actual armed hostilities, in an undeclared war. The relations between the belligerents or states at war and the neutrals or states which are not party to the war are governed by "laws of neutrality".

Before twentieth century the rules of war and neutrality were laid down by customs. But the two conferences at the Hague in 1899 and 1907 took major steps to codify the laws of war and neutrality. Particularly the Second Hague Conference in 1907 was attended by largest ever number of statesmen and concluded altogether thirteen Conventions regulating hostilities, neutralities, and avoiding unnecessary suffering and loss of life and property. Those aspects of war which were not codified in these Conventions, were to be governed by the customary laws.

The following are some of the basic principles to regulate the conduct of war and hostilities that emerged out of the Hague Conventions:

1. All belligerents are subject to the laws of war. These laws also recognise the military necessities of the belligerents when they may not be followed strictly; but actions under "military necessity" must also be taken in accordance with these laws. Since war is only a means to an end, the use of force against the enemy should not exceed the required necessities and when the enemy surrenders, the war must come to an end.
2. Though the development of laws and their codification cannot keep pace with the rapid scientific and technological progress and invention of new weapons, yet "the right of belligerents to adopt means of injuring the enemy is not unlimited." So some absolute and other conditional prohibitions have been imposed by the customs and usages of war. The absolute prohibitions such as poisoning of wells, killing of prisoners, misuse of flag of truce etc., are applicable under all circumstances, irrespective of any situation. But the conditional prohibitions are left to the

discretion of the belligerents as they are subject to "the conduct of military operations permits."

3. Considering the principle of humanity, the belligerents are forbidden to use arms, ammunitions, weapons, projectiles and materials which might cause unnecessary suffering. The victims of war such as the sick, wounded, and captured soldiers as well as civilian population must be granted maximum protection. Further, the laws of humanity prescribes that the belligerents must refrain from extreme cruelty which might destroy the foundation of human relationship and might make the return to peace impossible.
4. The belligerents must distinguish between armed combatants and non-combatants or civilian population, defended and undefended positions, between belligerents and neutral states and their people, and in case of aerial warfare, between military and non-military objectives, and deal with them as per the law. A belligerent should not attack the civilian population of the enemy unless they are engaged in hostile activities against the belligerent. Similarly, the ships and persons belonging to the neutral states are immune from interference except under laws of neutrality; but when they participate in actual hostilities or violates the laws of neutrality or engaged in un-neutral services, they can be attacked and seized.

But since the First World War, it has been observed that these fundamental principles are either violated or disregarded by the belligerents in the actual conduct of the war. The First World War saw the unrestricted submarine warfare, use of gases, and economic warfare against the entire population in direct violation of several provisions of the Hague Conventions. During the Second World War the abuses, lawlessness, and atrocities of the belligerents reached the climax. The technological developments made the Second World War a total war which affected all aspects of life and in which every enemy national was involved in one way or the other. It was characterised as war of 'unlimited war aims' and was fought till 'unconditional surrender' of the enemy. To defeat, as much devastation as possible was inflicted on the enemy in order to destroy its military and economic potentialities. In the process, this total war completely ignored the principle of humanity by use of such new mass destruction and devastating weapons as nuclear bombs and biological weapons. The distinction between the belligerents and neutrals also collapsed because the radio-active fall-outs of nuclear bomb not only effect the enemy but also the neutrals. The distinction between the combatants and civilians, defended and undefended positions, and military and nonmilitary objectives became irrelevant due to economic warfare, blockade, starvation, bombing of civilian population and targets far away from the front line, destruction of merchant ships by submarines, and use of long distance rockets and neuclear bombs.

Though in the present era of technological advancement and the total war it is very difficult to apply the laws of war and neutrality, yet, in the words of one writer, "in times of armed conflict that law, however imperfect and ill-adapted to present day conditions, exercise beneficial restraints on the emotions of men-in-arms and on the aims of the governments."

G. Effects of War

Once the state of war is created, as a direct effect, the relations between the belligerents undergo serious changes. Immediately after the declaration of war, the armed forces of the belligerents acquire the right to start the hostilities according to the laws of war. In case of the undeclared wars, the state parties must also follow the rules of war in the conduct of their hostilities. The effect of war on the relations of belligerents are as follows:

(i) Effect on Diplomatic Relations

When war breaks out, the diplomatic and consular relations between the belligerents cease and diplomatic representatives, consuls, and their staff are handed over their passports by belligerents to enable them to proceed to their home state. According to the Vienna Convention on Diplomatic Relations, 1961, such diplomats and consuls must be allowed immunities till they depart. They must also be provided all facilities by the receiving state to enable them to leave the country at the earliest.

(ii) Effect on Treaties

The effect of war on the existing treaties to which the belligerents are parties is, in the words of Justice Cordozo, "one of the unsettled problems of law." Even the Vienna Convention on Law of Treaties, 1969, is silent on this issue. Starke has suggested two tests to determine the effect of war on treaties, namely, subjective and objective tests. According to the subjective test, it is to be found out whether the parties to the treaty intended to be bound by it even after the outbreak of war. According to the objective test, it is to be found out if the application of the treaty is incompatible to the conduct of war.

In 1985, the Institute de Droit Internationale or Institute of International Law adopted a resolution with eleven articles, according to which some treaties to which the belligerents are parties, are terminated, while some treaties are suspended during the period of war, and still some treaties are considered to be in force. According to this resolution, the effect of war on treaties are as follows:

(a) All political treaties such as treaties of alliance and friendship are abrogated at the beginning of the war.

(b) Treaties which lay down rules regarding the conduct of war and hostilities such as the Hague Conventions of 1899 and 1907 are to continue, if the belligerents are parties to them.

(c) Treaties of permanent nature such as boundary treaties, treaties of cession, neutralisation treaties etc., are to continue to be in force inspite of the war.

(d) Multilateral law making treaties which establishes international organisations are to continue in force. But other law making treaties dealing with drugs, health, protection of industrial properties etc., are either suspended during the war to be revived after the termination of the war or implemented partially.

(e) If the treaty itself has a provision regarding the position of the state parties in the event of outbreak of war, such a treaty is either suspended or abrogated or allowed to continue as per the provision.

(f) With regard to other classes of treaties, such as treaties of extradition and commerce, in the absence of clear intention of parties to continue them, are suspended.

(g) If a treaty is incompatible with the action to be taken as per the resolution of Security Council regarding threat to peace or breach of peace or acts of aggression, a member state who is a party to that treaty must either terminate or suspend that treaty.

When a treaty is suspended during the war, it is not automatically revived when peace is established. The practice of states show that clauses are included in the peace treaty at the end of war to remove doubt as to which treaty is to continue and which is to be abrogated.

(iii) Effect on Contracts

Regarding the contracts between the nationals of the belligerent states, the belligerents are entirely free to cancel or suspend or allow them on the outbreak of war. There are however, certain uniformity in the practices of states such as no fresh contract can be entered between the nationals of belligerent states during the period of war, the contracts entered into before the war are either suspended or dissolved, the contract between a belligerent national and a neutral national regarding a work to be performed on enemy territory is suspended during the war, the contracts regarding sale of goods and agencies to the enemy are dissolved, the contracts of executory nature are dissolved, and the contracts of insurance are suspended during the war.

(iv) Effect on Commercial Relations

The belligerent states usually pass a legislation such as Trading with Enemy Acts of Britain and U.S.A. during the two World Wars for regulation of trade and commerce with the enemy. Generally, trade and commerce cease between the belligerents on the outbreak of war.

(v) Effect on Debts

If the debt is incurred by a belligerent state from the nationals of another belligerent state before the outbreak of war, the repayment is only suspended and the creditors get the right to recover the debt after the war. But the debts incurred during the war between the enemies are not justiciable and can not be recovered even through the judicial process. The private debts to be paid to enemy nationals are suspended.

(vi) Effect on Enemy Property

The effect of war on the enemy property differs according to their nature.

If the enemy state is the owner of such property which is found with in the territory of a belligerent state, it can confiscate the movable property. But if such movable enemy state property is located on the portion of enemy territory under the occupation of the belligerent state, such property can be appropriated if it is useful for its military purposes.

If the immovable enemy state property such as houses, forests etc., is found over the portion of territory under the occupation of the belligerent, such property can be used and if they are of military character such as barracks, forts etc., they can be destroyed but not acquired or disposed of. On the other hand, both warships and state owned merchant ships found in the sea may be seized and confiscated if they are not used for religious or scientific or philanthropic purposes or used as hospital ships.

In case of private property owned by the private citizens of the enemy state found within the territory of a belligerent, its status is controversial. But the general practice of the states appears to be that such property cannot be confiscated but can be seized during the period of war, leaving their disposal to be settled by peace treaties. But enemy private property found on the occupied territory cannot normally be taken over unless it is essential for local military purposes. The plunder of such enemy property is prohibited. On the other hand, enemy private ships and cargoes belonging to enemy private citizens found on sea can be confiscated by a belligerent. But if the cargo of an enemy private owner is found on a neutral merchant ship, such cargo cannot be confiscated unless such goods are likely to be used for war by the enemy.

20

ENEMY CHARACTER

After the commencement of war, certain persons, properties, and corporations of the belligerents acquire enemy character and are subjected to a number of restrictions. The nationals of the neutrals are considered neutral and are not subjected to these restrictions as long as they do not help the enemy directly or indirectly or engage themselves in unneutral services.

Every belligerent state usually define the enemy through legislation such as Trading with Enemy Act, 1913 of Great Britain and Trading with Enemy Act, 1917 of the U.S.A. According to Lord Hailsham, in Great Britain "An alien enemy is one whose Sovereign or State is at war with Sovereign of England or one who is voluntarily resident or who carries on business in an enemy's country eventhough a natural-born subject or naturalised subject."

The following persons or properties acquire enemy character:

1. Individuals

In general, all individuals of the belligerent state acquire enemy character after the commencement of the war. Earlier, while Anglo-American courts determined the enemy character of an individual on the basis of his domicile or residence, the Continental states like France and Italy determined it on the basis of nationality. But nowadays there is little difference between the two tests because the Anglo-American courts have also accepted the test of nationality.

According to Lawrence the following categories of individuals of one belligerent can be treated as having enemy character by the other belligerent:

(a) the persons engaged as crew in the merchant ships of the enemy;

(b) the armed combatants and residents of the enemy state;

(c) the followers of the enemy army such as journalists and contractors etc.;

(d) the neutral nationals domiciled in the enemy state for the purpose of trade;

(e) persons living on the territory occupied by the enemy;

(f) persons of a neutral state having trading houses on the enemy territory which is known as commercial domicile. On the other hand, nationals of the enemy state do not acquire enemy character if they reside and carry on trade in a neutral state.

Usually, after the commencement of the war, the belligerent parties allow the nationals of the enemy to leave their country within a stipulated period; but Germany did not allow the nationals of enemy belligerents to leave the country at the out break of both the First and Second World Wars.

2. Ships

The enemy character of a ship, in general, is determined by its flag. Not only the ships of a belligerent but also those of the neutral states acquire enemy character if:

(i) a ship owned by a neutral national but chartered by the enemy or navigated by the crew of the enemy;

(ii) a neutral ship flying the enemy flag or controlled by enemy agent;

(iii) a ship owned by an enemy owner but sailing under the neutral flag when engaged in carrying troops etc., along with the innocent cargoes;

(iv) a neutral ship which takes direct part in the hostilities or under the control of an enemy agent or in the exclusive employment of the enemy;

(v) a ship resists the legitimate exercise of the right of visit and search.

3. Cargoes

Generally ownership is the basic criterion for establishing the enemy character of the cargoes of a ship. If the owners are of enemy character, the cargoes will be treated as enemy property. All cargoes found on an enemy ship is pressumed to be enemy cargoes unless otherwise proved by the neutral owner. The London Naval Conference of 1908 was of the view "the neutral or enemy character of goods found on board an enemy vessel is determined by the neutral or enemy character of the owner." But the Conference failed to lay down whether the nationality or the commercial domicile principle was to be adopted to determine the neutral or enemy character of the owner.

4. Corporations

The enemy character of a corporation is determined by its domicile. According to Pitt Cobbett "the domicile of a corporation is the place where the brain which controls the operations of the company is situated." Thus in case of corporations the guiding factor is the domicile of the persons who directs the operations of the company. In the case of Daimler Co. Ltd. V. the Continental Tyre and Rubber Co. Ltd. (1916), Lord Parker ruled that the enemy character of a corporation may be assumed if "its agents or the persons in de facto control of its affairs" are "residents in enemy country, or, wherever resident, are adhering to the enemy or taking instructions from or acting under the control of the enemies."

Thus the place of registration or incorporation and the place where the business is carried, are the two tests applied to determine the enemy character of corporations. During last two World Wars, England, U.S.A., and many other countries by passing legislations prohibited the corporations incorporated in those countries from entering into business with the enemy.

21

LAWS OF LAND WARFARE

The customary laws relating to war on land have been codified in a number of declarations and conventions such as the Declaration of St. Petersburg, 1868, the Hague Declaration of 1899, the Hague Convention Nos. IV, VII, VIII, and IX of 1907, Geneva Protocol of 1925, the Geneva Conventions of 1929 and 1949, the Hague Convention of 1954, and the Convention adopted by the General Assembly of the UNO in 1972. From this long list of instruments the following rules and features of the land warfare can be deduced:

1. Combatants and Noncombatants

The laws and customs of war are applicable to the combatants who are actually involved in the war. The combatants are divided into lawful and unlawful combatants. The lawful combatants may be killed, wounded or captured in the battle. The spies, who according to the Hague Convention No. IV of 1907, are a category of lawful combatants can be punished by death if captured. The unlawful combatants are those persons who are members of the regular armed forces of a belligerent, but are in civilian clothes such as the saboteurs, and are liable to capture, detention, trial and punishment by the military tribunals for their offence. On the other hand, the mercenaries, according to the Geneva Convention of 1949, are neither treated as combatants nor are entitled to be treated as prisoners of war when captured.

The noncombatants are the unarmed citizens and they are not subject to attack by the belligerents, if they do not take part in the hostilities.

The irregular forces such as the militia, volunteer corps and the organised resistance movements are protected by the laws of war if they fulfill the following conditions:

(a) they are organised under a commander;
(b) they can be recognised from a distance by a distinctive sign;
(c) they carry arms openly; and
(d) they conduct their operations according to the laws and customs of war.

The levee en masse which include the inhabitants who rise spontaneously and take up arms to resist the invading troops of the enemy on their territory, are to be regarded as belligerents, if they carry arms openly and follow laws and customs of war.

2. Use of Ruses

Ruses of war are the strategies practised on the enemy in order to deceive or mislead him and the Hague Regulations permit them. Laying ambushes and traps, concealing military operations, diversion attacks, and withdrawals etc., are the examples of such ruses of war. The use of military uniforms and ensigns of the enemy can be used to deceive him, but cannot be used during the actual war.

On the other hand, the use of flags of truce or Redcross flag to deceive the enemy, assassination of the head of the state, military generals or soldiers are not considered as ruses of war but as perfidy and are illegal.

3. Use of Weapons

Due to the technological progress and rapid inventions,

new military weapons come into existence and so it is difficult to lay down rigid rules regarding the legality of use of such weapons. By new weapons it is meant that new means and methods of injuring the enemy which were not in use when the laws of war were codified. The absence of any express prohibition on the use of such new weapons does not mean that they are legal. Such new weapons, in order to be lawful, must conform the fundamental principles of war and neutrality, the principle of humanity, and the distinction between the armed forces and civilians. Thus all weapons which don't conform these fundamental principles and which produce uncontrollable effects must be treated as illegal.

Use of poison in war in any manner "be it to poison wells or food or arms" is prohibited by Hague Convention. The Declaration of St. Petersburg prohibited the use of projectiles under 400 gms., which are explosive or charged with inflamable of substance. The Hague Declaration of 1899 prohibited the launching of projectiles and explosives from the balloons as well as the projectiles diffusing asphyxiating or deleterious gases. The use of 'dumdum' bullets were also prohibited. The Washington Treaty, 1922 and the Geneva Protocol, 1925 prohibited the use of poisonous or other gases which are aphyxiating. The bacteriological warfare is also prohibited.

The invention of nuclear weapons and its use by U.S.A. during the Second World War against Japan at Hirosima and Nagasaki with most devastating effects, raised the legality of the use of such weapons. It is now clear that the nuclear weapons in kiloton range and above cannot conform to the principle of humanity and the immunity to the civilian population. Further, the radio active fall out of the nuclear explosion also harm the future generation permanently. So the General Assembly in a resolution in 1961 prohibited the use of nuclear and thermo nuclear weapons. The dangerous and uncontrollable effects of such weapons of mass destruction led to the conclusion of Nuclear Test Ban Treaty in 1968 and the treaty Prohibiting the Emplacement of Nuclear and other weapons of Mass Destruction on Sea Bed and Ocean Floor in 1971.

A Convention on Inhuman Weapons was concluded in 1980 according to which certain conventional weapons like incendiary bombs, bobby traps and land mines are prohibited from being used against the civilian population and objects.

An International Conference on Chemical Weapons met at Paris in 1989 and unanimously agreed to draw up a convention to prohibit the development, production, stock piling and transferring of chemical weapons.

4. Protection of Civilian Population

According to the Hague Conventions, attack or bombardment of undefended towns and villages, residential houses and buildings are prohibited except in case of military necessity. But this rule broke down during the First World War and was completely ignored during the Second World War because of indiscriminate bombing by aeroplanes, use of rocket bombs and finally by explosion of atom bombs. In both the World Wars, the civilian population was worst effected.

The killing or wounding of the enemies who have surrendered or laid down arms is prohibited. The Geneva Convention of 1949 has provisions for establishment of hospital, safety, and neutralised zones with proper markings where such civilian persons as the sick, aged, expectant mothers, mothers with young children and wounded civilians can take shelter.

At the initiative of International Red Cross, a resolution was passed at its Vienna Conference in 1965 declaring that:

(1) the right of belligerent to injure the enemy is not unlimited;

(2) the attacks against the civilian population is prohibited.

These principles were endorsed by a resolution of General Assembly of the UNO in 1968.

5. Prohibition on Wanton Destruction

Unnecessary destruction of property such as buildings, villages and town etc., are prohibited. Destruction is considered as wanton if such destruction is not connected with offensive or defensive operations. The Hague Convention has specified that certain buildings and monuments connected with religion, arts, science and charity, if they are marked with certain visible signs, are not to be attacked. The Hague Convention of 1954 has made provision for protection of cultural property from attack.

However, all the detailed rules laid down by various Conventions broke down during the First World War and were completely decimated during the Second World War. Many of the distinctions such as between combatants and non combatants, defended and undefended areas, armed forces and civilians etc., have lost their relevance in the total wars where winning the war at any cost was the aim. Finally, the use of atom bomb during the Second World War has wiped out the last vestige of these rules.

6. Treatment of Prisoners of War

In the ancient time, the prisoners of war were used as slaves by the victorious belligerents. After the spread of Christianity, these prisoners were held as hostages for collection of ransoms by the units of the army or their commanders who captured them. The Hague Conventions laid down that the prisoners of war (POW) were "in the power of the hostile government" instead of individual army units and they must be "humanly treated". The government whose army captured the prisoners was under the obligation to maintain them by providing food, clothes, and shelter. The P.O.Ws, except their officers, could be engaged in various works connected with war, but they must be paid for their services. The captor state must set up agencies to provide informations to the relatives of P.O.Ws and must also allow the charitable organisations of the state of the P.O.Ws to provide relief to them. The P.O.Ws were to be allowed to rejoin their families at the end of war.

But during the First World War, it was clear that these provisions became inapplicable due to changed nature of the war. So to rectify the inadequacies of the Hague Conventions regarding the P.O.Ws, new rules were added through the Geneva Convention of 1929. The Geneva Convention not only reaffirmed the fundamental principles of the Hague Conventions, but also laid down new rules to protect the prisoners from abuses which occured during the First World War. But these provisions of the Geneva Convention also could not prevent Germany and Japan from violating them during the Second World War.

So under the influence of the International Red Cross, the Swiss Government convened an International Conference at Geneva on 12th August, 1949, which adopted a number of Conventions dealing with the protection of victims of war. The Convention No. III which deals with the P.O.Ws is a revision of Convention of 1929. The Convention of 1949 widened the scope to include not only the combatants, but also the journalists who reported on the war, and the civilian members of the crew of the military aircrafts. It also added a provision to provide food to the prisoners sufficient in quality, quantity and variety so as to maintain their good health. However, during the Korean War, there were complaints by the Soviet Union that inhuman practices were followed by the U.N. Forces towards the P.O.Ws. At the end of the Korean War a new problem arose at the time of exchange of P.O.Ws between the parties, because a number of P.O.Ws refused to return to their own state. So the Armistice Agreement that followed the Korean War in 1953, provided that no force or threat was to be used against the prisoners who did not want to go back to their own country.

7. Care of Sick and Wounded

Before 1864, there was no uniform state practice regarding the care of sick and wounded enemy. The Geneva Convention of 1864 laid down that the sick and wounded soldiers should be cared by the belligerent in whose power they were, irrespective their nationality. The hospitals and their personnel engaged in caring the sick and wounded were to be identified by the emblem of Red Cross.

But during the First World War, it was found that many of the provisions of this Convention were not practicable, even if the belligerents wanted to implement them. So the Geneva Conference of 1929 adopted a new Convention in which protection was given to mobile as well as fixed medical units. It also laid down that persons engaged in the care of sick and wounded were to be respected under all circumstances and were not to be taken as P.O.Ws; aircrafts engaged in medical work were to be painted in white with Red Cross emblem on it; and the names of not only the wounded but also the dead were to be communicated to the belligerents.

But during the Second World War, the hospitals and vehicles bearing the Red Cross emblem were attacked and bombarded. At the end of the war, the Japanese war criminals were charged and punished for "mistreatment of the sick and wounded, medical persons, and female nurses."

So the Geneva Convention of Sick and Wounded of Armed Forces, 1949, revised the earlier Conventions in the light of experiences during the Second World War and enlarged the scope of the Convention by including other persons than the actual combatants. It also made rigid provisions against the commercial use of Red Cross emblem.

8. Relationship Between Belligerents

During the last two World Wars it was observed that a considerable amount of non-hostile communications between the belligerents passed through the diplomatic representatives of the neutral states. Each belligerent used to send its communication in an indirect way through the neutral diplomatic representative who was looking into its interests in the state of the other belligerent.

But since the ancient times, direct relations between the commanders of the belligerents on the battle field through a flag of truce is a common feature and the inviolability of the person of the bearer of the flag of truce is one of the oldest and universally recognised rule of international law. The Hague Conventions of 1907 not only recognised this customary rule, but also included other people who would accompany the bearer of the flag in the same category. But both customs and laws of war also recognises the right of a commander to refuse to receive them.

The misuse of the flag of truce to deceive the enemy is considered as one of the most serious crimes and may lead to reprisals.

22

BELLIGERENT OCCUPATION

When a territory which was previously governed by an enemy government is occupied by a belligerent by either defeating or driving out the original government is known as belligerent occupation. The belligerent can occupy either a part of the territory or the whole state. International law has laid down separate rules which governs the belligerent occupation and its activities over the occupied territory.

Though Grotius did not make any distinction between the temporary rights of an occupied army and the permanent rights of a belligerent conqueror, by the middle of 17th century, a distinction came into existence between the temporary authority of an occupation army and the final status of the territory to be determined at the end of war through a peace treaty. The army of occupation, by virtue of its de facto control over the territory, excercise temporary legal authority, and the scope of this authority is determined by two factors namely, the needs and necessities of military operation of the belligerent occupant, and the needs and welfare of the civilian population.

According to the Hague Regulations of 1907, only when the territory "is actually placed under the authority of the hostile army" and it is in the firm possession of the territory, the belligerent occupation is established. In distinction from invasion, which is a preparatory stage of military occupation to gain control over a territory, belligerent occupation includes invasion plus possession of the enemy territory and holding it under its control for a temporary period. Thus due to temporary and provisional nature of authority, the belligerent occupant does not either displace or transfer the sovereignty of territory to it. Further, belligerent occupation neither involves the change of nationality of the local people nor the occupant can annex the occupied territory. Since the belligerent occupant simply establishes a temporary military administration and can demand obedience and temporary loyalty of the inhabitants of the occupied territory with regard to maintenance of public order, safety of the occupying forces, and to the laws and regulations which are essential for the administration of the territory.

The Hague Regulations of 1907 laid down the duties of a belligerent occupant, which were grossly violated by the belligerents during both First and Second World Wars. Moreover several new developments that took place during the Wars, necessitated the revision of these duties. So the Convention on the Protection of Civilian Population in time of War was concluded at Geneva in 1949, which not only revised the earlier Hague Convention but also added few more duties of the belligerent occupants. Today, the following are the duties of a belligerent occupant:

1. Not to destroy or seize the religious, scientific, educational, cultural institutions and the historical monuments.
2. Not to prevent the local inhabitants from pursuing their normal lawful occupations.
3. Not to compel the nationals of the occupied territory to take up arms against their own state and not to compel them to enlist themselves in the army of the occupant.
4. Not to compel the inhabitants to take an oath of allegiance to it.
5. Not to take hostages nor impose collective penalties

on the inhabitants for acts of individuals, such as sabotage, for which all of them cannot be held responsible.

6. Not to transfer the inhabitants by force, either individually or en mass, to another territory.
7. Not to requisition food and medical supplies of the civilian population for its own use.
8. Not to arrest or prosecute or convict the protected persons for any act they might have committed before occupation.
9. Not to collect contributions from the inhabitants unless ordinary taxes collected are insufficient for the purposes of administration.

The inhabitants on the occupied territory also have a duty to obey the occupant and they can be punished for their conduct against the security and public order and also for espionage or for their interference in the occupant's military operations. The Geneva Convention has permitted the belligerent occupant to prohibit certain activities of the civilian inhabitants and the occupant is under a duty to give wide publicity to these prohibitions before punishing the inhabitants who undertake such activities.

The belligerent occupant has certain rights granted by the Conventions. The occupant can requisition the supplies of articles of daily use as well as other supplies from the inhabitants; but such supplies should be actually required for the occupation army and the supplies requisitioned should be proportionate to the resources of the occupied territory. The occupant is entitled to collect all taxes and revenues for the benefit of the occupied territory. The occupant may compel the inhabitants to render such services which are not directly connected with war. The occupant is under an obligation to maintain the courts and status of judges and continue to maintain the old penal laws.

As regards the public and private property as well movable and immovable property, the Geneva Convention has laid down specific rules. The private property must be respected and cannot be confiscated by the occupant, though the neutral private property found within the occupied territory can be taken over by payment of compensation to the neutral owner. Plundering of the private property is strictly prohibited. But private houses can be requisitioned by the occupant for providing quarters to its soldiers. If the necessity of actual military operation so requires, the occupant can destroy the private houses. So also, if the inhabitants harrass the belligerent occupants by firing on them or indulging in other hostile activities from the private houses, the occupant can destroy them. In case of private movable properties, they are immune from seizure except in case of such properties as arms and other war materials; but even in case of such seized materials, they must be restored and compensation paid to the owner after the termination of the hostilities.

All public movable properties such as cash, funds, securities, arms, stores, supplies and means of transportation, being the state properties, can be taken over by the occupant and can be used for its operation of war.

All the lawful acts of the belligerent occupant will be recognised and accepted after the occupation is terminated either by reconquest or restoration to the original government; but its unlawful acts can be punished as war treason.

23

LAWS OF NAVAL WARFARE

The laws of naval warfare owes its origin primarily to the traditional international law. So these laws are contained partly in rules of customary international law, and partly in the Declaration of Paris, 1856, partly in the Hague Conventions of 1907, Nos. VI, VII, VIII, IX dealing with Naval Bombardment and X, XI and XIII dealing with Neutral Rights and Duties in Maritime War, and partly in the London Protocol on Submarine rules of 1936.

In the naval warfare, the belligerents are entitled to capture not only the enemy property but also their surface ships, submarines and aircrafts engaged in the naval warfare. The belligerents may even destroy the merchant ships if they refuse or resist their right of visit and search in the national or international waters, but not in the neutral or neutralised ports and waters.

The following are the rules of naval warfare derived from both customary and treaty laws:

1. Privateering Outlawed

Upto early 19th century, it was the common practice among the belligerents to supplement their public armed ships with privately owned and privately manned ships voluntarily offered by their owners. These ships known as 'privateers' joined the war after receipt of letter of marque from that belligerent state. The privateers were granted the right to property by the state over the prizes taken by them during the war. In actual practice, these privateers were no better than the pirates whose main aim was to acquire as many prizes as possible to take themselves. So the Declaration of Paris, 1856, abolished privateering by declaring "Privateering is and remains abolished."

2. Conversion of Merchant Ships into Warships

During the war, the belligerents are allowed to convert their merchant ships into warships, provided the conversion is made in a port within the belligerent state and not in a neutral port or on high sea.

3. Rules Regarding Merchant Ships

Before the First World War, there was a clear difference in the treatment of enemy warships and enemy merchant ships. While the enemy warships could be destroyed the merchant ships on the high seas were subjected to visit and search to determine the nationality and ownership of the ship and the cargo. But if a merchant ship tried to resit this right by use of force or refused to allow the right of visit and search, the belligerent was at liberty to destroy such a merchant ship. Carrying of arms and refusal of the right of visit and search was common during days of privateering. But after the abolition of privateering, the merchant ships normally do not carry arms on them and do not resist the belligerent's right of visit and search by force. However, if a merchant ship was to be destroyed in an emergency, it was the duty of the belligerent to ensure that the passengers and the crew of the merchant ship were removed to a safer place before such destruction.

During the First World War, the German submarines not only attacked and destroyed the enemy warships but also the merchant ships and were described as "Commerce destroyers". The advantage of a submarine was that it could approach a ship unseen and could destroy an unsuspecting ship without warning. So when the submarines attacked the merchant ships, they did not give any warning to remove the passengers and the crew to a safer place. Though this action violated the existing laws of naval warfare, Germany tried to justify the action by arguing that these unarmed merchant ships also carry food and ammunition for the enemy belligerent and as such deserved to be destroyed. Since no previous warning to the passengers and crew to move to safer place could be given by the submarine, the only alternative was not to attack such unarmed merchant ships, to which Germany did not agree.

So far the armed merchant ships were concerned, Germany argued that they could be attacked without any warning, because with arms they were as good as war ships and any prior warning to them could invite counter attack on the submarine itself. Further, the instructions of the British Government to its merchant ships to carry arms and destroy the German submarines on sight, strengthened the stand taken by Germany.

The London Protocol on Submarine Rules, 1936, though accepted the right of a submarine to sink a merchant ship or make it incapable of further navigation, yet it reemphasised the older rule that the passengers and the crew of such merchant ships should be removed to safer place before the destruction of the merchant ship.

But from the very beginning of the Second World War, German submarines indiscriminately destroyed the merchant ships and completely ignored the rules of London Protocol, and similar actions were also followed by the submarines of Britain and U.S.A.

4. Enemy Character

In general, the ship and cargo of an enemy subject, is enemy property. As regards the nationality of a ship as distinct from its cargo, it was determined by the flag of the ship. So

Declaration of London laid down that enemy ownership of the ship do not subject it to capture if the ship is registered, flies the flag and carries the papers of a neutral state. But a ship owned by a neutral citizen but registered in and flies the flag of an enemy state is liable to capture.

As regards the cargo, while the enemy character is determined by the domicile of the owner according to Anglo-American practices, the continental countries like France, Germany etc., determine it on the basis of his nationality.

5. Exemption of Certain Types of Ships

According to the Hague Convention No. VI of 1907, the following types of enemy ships may be exempted from confiscation:

(i) If an enemy ship was found in the port of a belligerent at the commencement of war, it is allowed to depart freely, either immediately or with in a specified period.

(ii) Those enemy merchant ships which left their home ports before the war began and were ignorant of declaration of war, but now entered into the ports of the belligerent, may also be allowed to go freely.

(iii) Those ships of the enemy which left their home ports before outbreak of war and were encountered on the high seas while still ignorant of the war, were not to be confiscated by the belligerent.

The Convention allows a belligerent to detain the enemy ships in its ports without paying compensation. It also allows the belligerent to destroy these enemy merchant ships which were ignorant of the outbreak of war, if it was found necessary, by paying compensation.

But these provisions were not followed by all belligerents during both World Wars and innocent enemy ships found in their ports were either detained or confiscated or operated without paying any compensation.

According to the Hague Convention No. XI of 1907, ships engaged in religious, scientific works, the cartel ships engaged in the exchange of prisoners, and the small ships engaged in fishing or coastal trade are immune from capture as long as they do not take any direct or indirect part in the hostilities.

6. Hospital Ships

Special provisions have been made by several conventions for the hospital ships. Both the Hague Conventions of 1899 and 1907 exempted the hospital ships from attack or capture because of their humanitarian work. The Conventions also prescribed that such hospital ships should be painted in white and must fly the flag of Red Cross.

But during the First World War, the German submarines attacked and sunk a number of hospital ships on the ground that many such ships were indistinguishable and that they were also engaged in military works. During the Second World War, Japan made several attacks of the hospital ships causing death of many sick and wounded soldiers and sailors.

So the Geneva Convention on Sick and Wounded Prisoners of War, 1949, in Art. 14 granted a belligerent party the right to demand the surrender of sick, wounded or ship wrecked sailors of a military or civil hospital ship, provided they are in a fit condition to be moved. But the belligerent taking them over should provide necessary medical treatment. In Art. 15, the Convention has laid down that if the sick, wounded or ship wrecked sailors are taken on board of warship of a neutral state, that neutral state should ensure that these people do not take any further part in the war.

The persons on the hospital ship and their crew must be protected and respected, and ordinarily, they should not be captured.

7. Naval Bombardment

The Hague Convention No. IX of 1907 has prohibited the bombardment of undefended ports, towns, villages, and buildings, unless the local authorities refuse to fulfil the demands of requisition of provisions and supplies. But military or naval establishments, depots of arms, stores of war materials etc., can be bombarded.

But while bombing, the belligerents must, as far as possible, avoid the destruction of the buildings connected with public worship, science, arts etc., if they are indicated by visible signs.

8. Giving Quarters

Belligerents are under an obligation to give quarters to the surrendering ships and their crew.

9. Submarine Warfare

The submarines introduced by Germany in the First World War, created a new situation. These submarines were lawful combatants and it took advantage of its working under the surface of the water to attack the enemy ships and even enter into the enemy ports and territorial waters unseen. But as per the existing laws, the submarines could not give warning to the ships and its crew before sinking them by its torpedoes. Sometimes, there were difficulties in identifying the character of the ship as a result even the hospital ships were also sunk. Germany argued that any previous warning to a ship or its persons would expose the submarine itself to grave danger, because if the ship, was armed, it would shoot the submarine. This danger was real because the British Government ordered its merchant ships to shoot down a submarine on sight. So Germany argued that neither any previous warning to the ship and its persons nor any protection to the people could be given.

The Washington Conference in 1921-22 decided that the

existing rules of naval warfare also apply to the submarines and if the submarines could not follow these rules, then it should not attack the merchant ships. This principle was reaffirmed by London Submarine Rules Protocol of 1936.

Though several conferences made efforts to control the submarines, all these efforts proved to be ineffective during the Second World War and submarines of both the belligerent parties went on sinking the merchant ships of each other in the utter disregard of all the rules of naval warfare including the law humanity.

10. Postal Correspondence

The Hague Convention No. XI of 1907 granted inviolable immunity to the postal letters of the enemy. If an enemy ship carrying postal letters was captured, it was the duty of the captor to send the letters to their destination as soon as possible. But this immunity was not extended either to the ship carrying them nor to the postal parcels.

11. Use of Mines

The Hague Convention No. VIII distinguished between anchored and unanchored mines and laid down that the unanchored contact mines should be constructed in such a way that they become harmless after on hour after the person who laid them ceases to control them. The anchored mines should also become harmless as soon as they are broken from their moorings. The torpedoes should also become harmless if they miss their targets.

But in both the World Wars these principles were ignored by the belligerents completely.

12. Use of Deceptions

In maritime warfare, as in case of land warfare, use of deceptions but not perfidy, was an accepted part of the strategy. The use of false flag of either the enemy or of a neutral in order to attract the enemy into action or to escape from him is permissible. But at the time of actual attack the ship must disclose its identity by flying its own flag. Even, the disguise of a war ship as merchant ship or to attack under the cover of darkness in order to take the enemy by surprise is permissible. But false signs of distress or urgent appeal for help as a means of attract the enemy ship and then to attack it amounts to perfidy.

Post-War Developments in Naval Warfare

In the post-Second World War period, new naval weapons, introduction of nuclear powered ships and submarines carrying nuclear missiles, use of aircrafts and hellicoptors from aircraft carrier ships, and use of 'homing' missiles on the enemy ships from the aircrafts, have shown that most of the previous rules of maritime warfare have become out dated and unworkable. Further, the Iraq—Iran Conflict of 1980-88 has shown that the merchant ships and oil tankers can be destroyed on the sea from the land-based missiles and aircrafts from hundreds of miles away from the sea.

In the era of total war, the entire area of high sea became the theatre of naval war. So to reduce the area of naval warfare, some belligerents have started the practice of establishing naval "War Zones" or as in case of Falk Land Conflicts "Exclusion Zones" within which any ship found would be liable to be sunk at sight.

As regards the submarines, two new developments have taken place. Firstly, now that surveillance and intelligence gathering have become an integral part of any naval warfare, the submarines are used for the purposes with the help of highly advanced electronic devices. Secondly, the satellites in the space and outer space have been equipped with devices to detect and to locate the submarines under the surface of the water and thereby help in targeting them for destruction with sophisticated weapons and missiles.

24

AERIAL WARFARE

The twentieth century witnessed tremendous progress in the technological development in the aircraft industry. The main reason for this revolution is the increasing use of aeroplanes in the warfare. Though aircrafts play an important and devastating role in the war, till now no comprehensive rules of aerial warfare has evolved. Before the First World War, the only rule that existed regarding aerial warfare was in the Hague Convention, 1907. The extensive use of aircrafts in the First World War in indiscriminate bombing had necessitated the regulation of aircrafts and bombing in the air warfare. So the Washington Conference, 1922 appointed a Commission of Jurists to draft a set of rules for air warfare. The Commission prepared a Code of Air Warefare Rules, which are though not ratified by the states, yet are often referred by them either to justify or to defend their action even today.

The Draft Code of Air Warfare stated that aerial bombing is legitimate only when it is directed at the specified military objectives such as military forces, arms factories, and military establishments etc., but not against the civilian targets. The use of incendiary and explosive projectiles, though prohibited in the land warfare, is permitted in the aerial warfare. While the Code permitted attack on the disabled aircraft and their crew, it prohibited any attack on the crew when they are trying to escape from the disabled aircraft with the help of parachutes. The Code permitted firing on enemy civilian aircraft only when it tries to fly over the territory or found in the immediate vicinity of war front on the land or the sea. Such civilian aircrafts and the goods carried in them are liable to be captured. The Code also prohibited the arming of private aircrafts even for self defence. The code prohibits aerial bombardments for terrorising the civilian population and for damaging for destroying private civilian property. The bombardment of undefended places as well as noncombatants is also prohibited. The Code provided that care should be taken to see that towns, villages, hospitals, places of public worship, historical monuments and civilian populations are not harmed or injured while bombing the military targets. The Code also directed that if it is found impossible not to harm them, in that case the bombardment of military targets are not to be taken up.

When the League of Nations came into existence, it adopted a resolution in 1938 prohibiting deliberate bombardment of civilian population and directed not to harm the civilian population in the neighbourhood while bombing the military targets.

In the beginning of the Second World War, Britain and her allies declared to which Germany also agreed that aerial bombardment was to be directed against "strict military objectives in the narrowest sense of the word" and the civilian population was to be saved at any cost. But after indiscriminating bombardment of Warsaw, Roterdam and other cities of Europe by Germany, Britain and her allies took retaliatory steps and did not confine their bombing strictly to military objectives. The use of rocket bombs by Germany on different cities of England created widespread devastations. These bombs were fired from the coast of Holland and were dropped without any warning on civilian areas. So, Lauterpacht rightly said, "the practice of Second World War reduced to the vanishing point the protection of civilian population from bombardment."

The dropping of atom bombs by allies in 1945 by aircrafts on Hirosima and Nagasaki caused enormous civilian casualties and devastations. The purpose of these aerial attacks was not to destroy the military objectives but to demoralise the enemy through large scale destruction of civilian lives and properties. Since in the era of total war the civilian morale has also become a military objective, now it has become difficult to give any protection to civilians.

An attempt was made by the Geneva Convention of 1949 for the Protection of Certain Persons in Time of War to protect certain types of civilian noncombatants from bombardment from air, land and water during a war. The Convention suggested the establishment of hospital, safety and neutralised zones for the protection of sick, aged, children, expectant mothers and mothers with young children. The Convention directed the belligerents to clearly mark these zones and prohibited bombarding them.

The Lucerne Conference on the Use of Conventional Weapons, 1974, unanimously condemned the massive use of incendiary bombs, mainly from aircrafts, against the civilian centres, which was later approved by the General Assembly of UNO.

It is to be noted that though since 1923 till to date the international community through various conferences, conventions and resolutions has laid down several guidelines against aerial attacks on civilian population, yet at time of war, these rules are violated with impunity. The absence of firm rules of International Law governing aerial warfare has led to such gross violations.

25

TERMINATION OF WAR AND HOSTILITIES

Very often the actual fighting and armed hostilities may stop, but the 'state of war' continues until it is formally terminated. There are several methods of terminating the state of war and armed hostilities in order to restore peace.

Termination of State of War

The usual method of terminating the state of war is by concluding a peace treaty in which all matters such as prisoners of war, evacuation of territory, indemnities, and reparation etc., are dealt with between the belligerents.

The war can be terminated by stopping the hostilities by the belligerents between them as was the case of Sweden and Poland in 1716 and between France and Mexico in 1867. But this is not a satisfactory method as it leaves the future relations of the belligerents in doubt and the exact date of termination of war cannot be fixed.

Similarly, war can be terminated by unilateral declaration of one or more victorious Powers terminating the state of war as was done by the all Allied Powers except the Soviet Union in 1947 and 1951 towards Austria and West German Republic respectively.

But when the conquest is followed by annexation or

subjugation by a belligerent, the conquered belligerent loses its sovereignty and its international personality and as such there can be no state of war between it and its conqueror.

When a non-state is involved in a war, an agreement or agreements are signed between the parties to end the war and restore the peace, as was done by the Four Powers Agreement of 1973 to end the Vietnam War to which a non-state entity, the Vietcong, was a party.

Termination of Hostilities

The methods of terminating hostilities as distinct from the 'state of war' are applicable to both state of war and non-war armed conflicts and these are:

1. By armistice to bring about a temporary suspension of hostilities which can be resumed at the end of the period of armistice. According to Lauterpacht, "Armistice, in the wider sense of the term, are agreements between belligerent forces for a temporary cessation of hostilities." Armistice may be general when all armed hostilities are suspended; or it may be partial or local whose effects are restricted to only a part of armed forces or to a certain areas. While general armistice is concluded either by diplomatic representatives or by commander-in-chiefs of the concerned parties and is subject to ratification by their respective states, partial or local armistices are negotiated by the local commanders of the parties and these are not subject to ratification by their states. Nowadays a general armistice is used not only for temporary suspension of hostilities, but also for termination war, to be later confirmed by the final peace treaty, such as the General Armistice of 1918 was later confirmed by the Treaty of Versailles of 1919.
2. By unconditional surrender or other forms of

capitulations containing terms of peace, but not as result of any treaty or agreement, the hostilities are ended.

3. By a Truce—a term which has been used by the UNO practice such as the Truce established by it in Palestine to end the hostilities.
4. By a Ceasefire, which is also a frequently used term by the UN Security Council to order or request the parties to end the hostilities such as the Indo-Pak Ceasefire of 1965.
5. By Agreement of Cessation or Suspension of hostilities between parties, which is a step towards a durable peace such as the Geneva Agreements of 1954 which ended the fighting in Laos, Cambodia, and Vietnam.
6. By Joint Declaration by parties for restoration of normal, peaceful and friendly relations such as the Tashkent Declaration of 1966.

26

WAR CRIMES

The Hague Conference 1899, for the first time declared certain offences during war as war crimes and upto the First World War such crimes were usually granted immunity and amnesty through the peace treaties concluded at the end of wars. But the Treaty of Versailles, 1919, decided to set up military Tribunals to try Germans and certain officials who had violated the laws and customs of war. However trials could not commence because of certain legal objections as well as the refusal of the Dutch Government to surrender the German Kaiser who sought asylum in that state.

There was no precise definition of war crimes and writers defined them differently. It is to be noted that every violation of the rules of warfare is not a war crime. According to some jurists the term "war crime" should be applied only to those acts which are condemned by the common conscience of mankind due to their brutality, inhumanity or wanton destruction of property.

These crimes during wartime can be committed by civilians, armed forces, or persons who are sympathetic to the enemy. Similarly, persons in authority who fail to control their subordinates committing attrocities are also to be treated as war criminals.

As per the Hague Convention IV of 1907, a belligerent state is liable to pay compensation for any violation of

International Law by its armed forces and such compensation in the form of reparation from that belligerent state is determined at the end of war when peace treaty is concluded.

According to Hans Kelsen, "violation of the rules of warfare are called war crimes. General International Law obligates the states to punish their own war criminals and authorises any belligerent state the prisoners of war in its power for having violated the rules of warfare prior to capture. Hence, General International Law imposes upon individuals as private persons the obligation to refrain from committing war crimes and establishes individual criminal responsibility for the commission of such crimes by private persons." But Oppenheim has widened the definition when he said that war crimes are such hostile or other acts of soldiers or other individuals as may be punished by enemy on capture of the offender.

According to Oppenheim there are four kinds of war crimes, namely:

(1) Violation of laws of war by members of armed forces such as use of poison, forbidden arms and ammunitions, killing the sick and wounded, illtreatment of prisoners of war, unlawful bombardment of prohibited places etc.

(2) All armed hostilities committed by individuals who are not members of enemy armed forces.

(3) Espionage and war treason which are committed in favour of enemy.

(4) All acts meant to plunder and wanton destructions committed by soldiers or civilians.

In addition to above, the following war crimes have been added at the end of Second World War through the Charters of Military Tribunals of Nuremburg and Tokyo.

(1) Crimes against peace such as adoption of war as a

national policy violating Pact of Paris, 1928, and aggression etc.

(2) Crimes against humanity such as murder, extermination of races, enslavement and deportation etc., against the civilian population.

Though the provisions of war crimes were made in the Hague Convention 1907, Versailles Treaty, 1919, Locarno Pact 1925 and Pact of Paris, 1928, they could not be enforced. But towards the end of Second World War the Allies signed an Agreement in 1945 and annexed a charter for establishment of International War Crime Tribunals to try and punish persons of Axis Power, acting as individuals or members of organisations for committing (1) conventional war (2) crimes against peace (3) crimes against humanity and (4) conspiracy to commit these crimes. In accordance with this charter, two War Crime Tribunals were established at Nuremburg and Tokyo.

1. **Nuremburg Trial:** An International Military Tribunal was established as per the Charter attached to the Agreement of 1945 to try individuals and organisations of Axis Powers who were responsible for committing crimes against peace, crimes against humanity and other conventional war crimes.

The crimes against peace included planning, preparation and starting of a war of aggression or a war in violation of treaties, agreements or assurances and participation in a common plan or in a conspiracy to achieve the ends. The crimes against humanity included murder, genocide, extermination, enslavement, deportation and other inhuman acts committed against any civilian population either before or during war, and persecutions on political, religious, social or racial grounds. The traditional war crimes included violation of laws and customs of war including murder, ill treatment to or deportation for slave labour or other purposes of civilian population of occupied territory, ill treatment of prisoners of war, killing of hostages, plunder of public or private property, wanton destruction of towns, cities and villages not justified by military necessities.

Twenty two Germans and six organisations were charged with war crimes before the International Military Tribunal, which started on November 20, 1945 and pronounced its judgement on September 30, 1946. Of the 22 accused Nazi leaders, three were acquitted, twelve sentenced to death, three to life imprisonment and four were sentenced to long term imprisonment.

The Nuremburg Trial rejected the argument advanced on behalf of the defendants that they were prosecuted for international crimes under ex post facto laws because before 1939-40 such crimes as crimes against peace had not been defined or made punishable under international law; but the Tribunal pointed out that the defendants must have known that their actions were illegal and wrong and violative of international law. The governments of Germany, Italy and Japan, specially some of their officers must have known that war was outlawed by Pact of Paris, 1928 to which their states were parties. They must have known that invasion of and aggression on other states was against international law. The defendants submitted that International Law is concerned with sovereign states and individuals cannot be punished for the Acts of state. The Tribunal rejected this submission and observed "Crimes against international law are committed by men, not by abstract entities, and only by punishing individuals who commit such crimes can the provisions of international law be enforced." The defendants also submitted that they were acting on orders of superiors or in obedience to laws and regulations of the state was also rejected on the ground that the acts were considered as criminal by International Law and "universally known to be against the law", but such facts may be considered in mitigating the punishment.

The Nuremburg Trial is an important landmark in International Law. It created new principles and new precedents. It did not follow the traditional view that individuals are protected by the plea of Act of State, but on the other hand, observed "crimes against international law are committed by men, not by abstract entities." Again for the first time in the history of Law of Nations, the war crimes which were envisaged in many previous treaties, were enforced. Finally, the Trial helped in dispelling the general belief that international law is "weak and ineffective". The trial affirmed that resorting to aggressive war is criminal, would prevent any future aggressor for committing acts which Hitler or Mussolini committed. The trial also helped in enunciating several important principles of international law relating to conduct of war, belligerent occupation, treatment of prisoners etc.

But the Tribunal was also criticised. The first objection was that the judges of the Tribunal were drawn from the states who were parties to Agreement of 1945 or from those Nineteen states who adhered to this Agreement. So it can not be characterised as and "International" Tribunal. Secondly, some jurists criticised the ex-post facto application of laws. A writer said "the Charter applies with retrospective effect a rule which is contrary to municipals law of all civilised nations and therefore in violation of international law." Thirdly, Prof. H.A. Smith is of the opinion that the trial has violated the fundamental principle of impartiality because all the judges were from victorious countries. Finally, those responsible for dropping atom bombs on Hirosima and Nagasaki causing wanton destruction of civilian life and property which was described as the most inhuman act of war were not punished but were honoured as heroes of war.

2. **Tokyo Trial:** Under the Charter for Military Tribunal for Far East, a Tribunal was established at Tokyo, consisting of eleven judges representing states at war with Japan including India.

There were twenty eight persons accused of various war crimes, the trial started on June 4, 1948. Some of the accused were sentenced to death while others were punished with various terms of imprisonment. India was represented by Dr. Radha Benode Pal who gave a dissenting judgement.

The Tokyo Tribunal conducted its proceeding according to the principles which guided the Nuremburg Trial.

27

NEUTRALITY

The concept of neutrality was not known to Grotius. Though the term 'neutrality' was in use in the 17th century, it was left to Bynkershoek and Vattel to formulate a systematic doctrine of it in the 18th century, according to which the independent states had a right to stay aloof from the war and that they should be under a duty to maintain impartiality between the belligerents. Thus upto the First World War, neutrality of a state was meant as a legal position of aloofness in a war between two or more states while maintaining certain rights against and performing certain duties towards the belligerents as per the prescribed international law. Accordingly, Oppenheim defines the status of neutrality as "the attitude of impartiality adopted by third states towards belligerents and recognised by belligerents, such attitude creating rights and duties between impartial states and the belligerents." In other words, neutrality was a legal status connected with the state of war, which described the position of states who do not participate in a war.

After the war was declared, immediate notification of neutrality by the concerned states was necessary and the belligerents were to be informed of the same.

Neutrality Under League of Nations

The codification of the traditional laws of neutrality was left to the Hague Conference of 1907, which it did in drawing up the Convention No. V dealing with the rights and duties of neutral states in war on land and the Convention No. XIII dealing with such rights and duties in a naval war. But some of the problems relating to blockade and contraband control could not be solved at the Hague Conference, which were later solved by the London Naval Conference in 1908, which however, could not be ratified due to the outbreak of the First World War.

But during both the World Wars, all the recognised rules of neutrality were found to be outdated and in many cases inapplicable that it had led some writers like Starke to question "whether it is in the general interest to preserve an institution of uncertain value."

The emergence of League of Nations at the end of the First World War put an end to the traditional principles of neutrality. Articles 10 and 11 of the Covenant of the League of Nations made its members collectively responsible to find ways and means to preserve peace in the event of "any war or threat of war", leaving no scope to any member to remain neutral.

The Kellogg-Briand Pact, which is known as Pact of Paris for Renunciation of War, 1928, according to which the state parties agreed to renounce war as an instrument of national policy, literally outlawed war. This Pact, according to many jurists definitely restricted the status of neutrality, because question of neutrality will arise only if there is a war. Prof. Quincy Wright went to the extent of saying that the Pact of Paris made neutrality illegal and hence ended the duties of a neutral state.

The outbreak of Second World War in 1939 temporarily revived the traditional law of neutrality. But before the war began, there was a fundamental change in the attitude of most of the states towards the status of neutrality. The neutral states, instead of insisting on their rights or duties of the belligerents were prepared to appease the belligerents to avoid any chance of clash. This attitude was noticeable in the non-intervention policy of England and France in 1936 towards the Spanish Civil War and Neutrality Act of 1937 passed by the Congress of U.S.A. But this attitude again underwent a change after the German conquest of neutral states of Norway, Denmark, Holland and Belgium, and when the neutral U.S.A. took a series of steps which were against the classical concept of impartiality of the neutral states such as transferring destroyers, supplying arms and ammunitions, and through the Lend-Lease Act, 1941, providing and equipping the armed forces of Great Britain and her allies against Germany and Italy. This action of neutral U.S.A. gave rise to a new concept of neutrality called "qualified neutrality", because of the discrimination of one belligerent against the other who had violated the international law.

Neutrality Under the United Nations

After the Second World War, the UN Charter of 1945 "finally marked the end of neutrality as a legal system." Under the Collective Security system of the U.N.O., the member states do not have the right of neutrality.

According to Art. 39 of the Charter, the Security Council has the responsibility of maintaining peace in the world by taking action against a state whose action becomes "threat to peace or breach of peace or act of aggression". According to Art. 41 all member states are duty bound to take measures as per the decision of the Security Council against a state guilty of violating peace. Further, Art. 2 (5) of the Charter imposes an obligation on all members to extend every assistance to the U.N.O. and to refrain from assisting the states against which the preventive or enforcement actions are being taken by the U.N.O. Even while such actions are being taken by the Security Council, certain member states may not be called upon to take these measures or may even be exempted from taking these actions. The status of such states who are not called upon or exempted from taking measures may be described as "a status of non-belligerency" or "qualified neutrality". In fact, due to the principles of collective security and various provisions of the Charter, there is little scope for any member state remaining neutral. Thus Oppenheim rightly said, "In principle no member of U.N. is entitled, at its discretion, to remain neutral in a war in which the Security Council has found a particular state guilty of breach of peace or of an act of aggression and in which it has called upon the members of the U.N. concerned either to declare war upon the state or to take military action indistinguishable from war."

Thus the abolition of the right to war and the strict restrictions imposed on states to resort to war or use of force, undoubtedly led to the decline of neutrality in the old sense. Though neutrality has undergone a process of change, yet it survives and still remains a part and parcel of the international community.

Rights of a Neutral State

The status of traditional neutrality has undergone considerable changes after the adoption of U.N. Charter. But still the concept of neutrality, and the rights and duties of neutral states are recognised by the international law. Their rights and privileges as well their duties vis a vis the belligerents have been codified in the Hague Convention Nos. V and XIII of 1907 and other instruments, though some of them have become out dated.

The following are the rights of a neutral state against a belligerent state:

1. Inviolability of Neutral Territory

The Hague Conventions guaranteed the right of inviolability of the territory of the neutral states. The belligerents are prohibited from committing any act of hostilities either on the land territory or in the territorial waters of a neutral state. But in the extreme case of self-defence if the belligerent state is responsible for the action, it has to pay reparation to the agrieved neutral state.

But during both the World Wars, this right was violated when Germany violated the territory of neutral Belgium and Luxembourg during the First World War and invaded the neutral territory of Norway, Denmark, Belgium, Luxemburg, and Holland during the Second World War. During the Second World War, Great Britain also occupied the territory of neutral Iceland on ground of self defence.

2. *Immunity from Preparation of Acts of Hostilities*

Belligerents are forbidden to move troops, transport arms, ammunitions and supplies across the territory of a neutral state, and to use the territory as a base for war operations against the other belligerent. If the troops of a belligerent enter into its territory, the neutral government must detain them. But when the prisoners of war who have escaped from their captors enter into the neutral territory, they are not to be detained.

The Conventions allow the belligerent troops to enter into the neutral territory when they are carrying their sick and wounded or when they are driven out of a territory by the enemy.

3. *Right to Make Regulation for Use of its Territory*

The belligerents have a right of innocent passage through the neutral territorial waters, and enter into their parts; yet this right must not be abused by them. Not more than three warships of a belligerent are allowed to enter into the ports of a neutral state at a time for the purpose of refuelling, repair etc., but must leave the port within 24 hours except in cases of severe damages or incriminating weather, failing which the neutral state can intern the ship and its crew.

4. Right to Compensation

When a belligerent by excercise of its right of angary, i.e. requisition any neutral ship or cargo or property which is physically within its jurisdiction, on the ground of urgent necessity and its usefulness in the war, the neutral state is entitled to payment of full compensation from the belligerent.

5. Right to Protection of its Agents and Nationals

The belligerents are duty bound to protect and prevent any harm to the diplomatic and consular agents and the nationals of a neutral state, and prevent harm to the neutral property which are within their own or their occupied territory.

6. Right to Protect its Submarine Cables

According to the Hague Convention, the submarine cables connecting a neutral state with the territory of a belligerent must not be seized or destroyed except under absolute military necessity. In case such cables are seized or destroyed, it must be restored and compensation paid to the neutral state after the conclusion of the peace treaty.

Duties of a Neutral State

The duties of neutral states and their conduct which the belligerents can demand of them as a condition of their neutrality are settled. While the rights of a neutral state becomes the duties of a belligerents, automatically the duties of a neutral state becomes the rights of a belligerents. These duties of a neutral state may broadly be classified as duties of abstention, of prevention, and of acquiescence.

1. Duties of Abstention

These duties of a neutral state are of a negative and passive character by which it abstains from participation in the conflict. The neutral state must not give any direct or indirect assistance to any of the belligerents. It must not supply troops, arms and ammunitions, or war materials of any kind to either belligerent side, nor should provide shelter to armed forces of a belligerent. It should also not give any loans nor stand guarantee for loans to either of the belligerents.

2. Duties of Prevention

The duties of prevention are of a positive and active character. A neutral state is to prevent and take positive steps with in its territory such activities of belligerents as recruitment of troops for belligerent armies, use of its territory by belligerents for preparation or sending out of military or naval operations or military expeditions. A neutral state must also take action to prevent recruitment of its citizens by the army of the belligerent on its territory; but the citizens of a neutral state can leave their country in order to join the army of a belligerent in their individual capacity. A neutral state must prevent a belligerent state from establishing a wireless telegraph stations on its territory. Though the Hague Convention No. XIII allows the belligerent ships to enter into the ports of a neutral state, it must prevent them from staying unduly for more than 24 hours except in cases bad weather or serious damages to the ship. According to the Draft Code of Air Warfare Rules of 1923, a neutral state must prevent the belligerent aircrafts from using its air space and must detain the aircraft, its crew and passengers if it lands on its territory.

3. Duties of Acquiescence

The neutral states must acquiesce or accept certain acts of belligerents such as their right to visit and search the ships in the high sea, their right to seize a neutral ship for carrying contrabands etc.

A neutral state has also to accept the right of Angary of a belligerent of use, and if necessary to destroy, the neutral ships, cargoes, and properties which lies with in the territorial jurisdiction of the belligerent or with in its occupied territory. The right of angary of a belligerent means it has a right to requisition, use, and in certain cases, destroy the means of transports such as ships, aircrafts as well as rolling stocks belonging to a neutral owner which are physically with in its jurisdiction, subject to the following conditions:

(a) the property is urgently required by the belligerent;
(b) the full compensation is paid to the owner.

But these duties of a neutral state are not absolute. A neutral state is bound to perform these duties towards belligerents; but when a stronger belligerent violates its neutrality, it cannot perform its duties towards the other belligerents. So when a weak neutral state is unable to prevent a stronger belligerent from violating its neutrality, then the other belligerent has a right to intervene in the neutral territory.

However, nothing prevents a neutral to be sympathetic towards one of the belligerent; but such sympathy should not take the form of concrete assistance to that belligerent. The laws of neutrality make a distinction between a neutral state and its citizens. So while imposing duties on a neutral state not to take certain actions regarding the belligerents, their individual citizens are made free to take these actions such as their enlistment in the army of a belligerent out side the territory of the neutral state, gifting or giving loans of money to a belligerent or maintaining business relations with one or the other of the belligerents. The neutral states are under no obligations to prevent the persons with in its jurisdiction from expressing opinions or criticisms unfavourable to a belligerent, because it would mean suppression of democratic right to freedom of speech of the citizens.

Unneutral Services

According to Lawrence, the unneutral services are those "acts sometimes performed by neutrals which involve an entry for the time being into the service of a belligerent, and doing for him what is of direct advantage to him in his war." Traditionally, the doctrine of unneutral services relate to duties of neutral citizens in the naval warfare, particularly relating to carriage or transport of persons and things which help one of the belligerents.

Though Hall describes unneutral service as "analogues of contraband", it is different than contraband. In the first place, contraband is a trading activity of carrying cargoes for profit, unneutral service is predominantly a war like activity, of carrying individuals who are in the service of a belligerent and carrying despatches etc. of a belligerent. Secondly, Hyde points out that while proof of enemy destination is required to condemn the enemy contraband, it is the nature of service and actual conduct of the ship which is important to establish unneutral service. Thirdly, there is a difference in penalty as, in case of contraband, the cargo is primarily confiscated and only in the extreme cases, the ship is condemned, in cases of unneutral service primarily the ship is confiscated and only in extreme cases, the cargo is confiscated. Finally, according to Oppenheim, while carrying contraband for a belligerent need not be always direct, in case of unneutral service, carrying the person or despatches is a direct service.

Earlier, the doctrine of unneutral service was mainly related to naval warfare. But in the present day, the aircrafts are now commonly used for transportation of troops, arms and ammunitions etc. and hence carriage by neutral aircrafts can also be included as unneutral service. Today, unneutral service includes transport of enemy armed forces, carriage of despatches to the enemy, and transmission of intelligence to the belligerent, taking direct part in the hostilities, hire the ships or aircrafts to a belligerent, and transmission of intelligence to the belligerent. Thus when a neutral ship or aircraft is engaged in these activities to the advantage of one belligerent while injuring the same interests of the other belligerent, the injured belligerent may stop the ship or aircraft to remove the persons from them and in extreme cases, either capture the ship or aircraft and condemn them, or seize certain portions of their cargoes.

28

BLOCKADE

Meaning and Nature: Blockade is an act of war and if it is effectively carried out as per the rules of warfare, it will deny the freedom of passage to ships or aircrafts of other states. The naval blockade is one of the measures taken by the belligerents to harm the economic interests of the other belligerent. On the one hand, blockade itself is an act of war, on the other hand, Pacific Blockade is one of the methods of settling the international disputes through coersive measures short of war.

According to Oppenheim, "Blockade is the blocking by men-of-war of the approach to the enemy coast, or a part of it, for the purpose of preventing ingress or egress of vessels or aircrafts of all nations." Thus the following are the characteristics of a blockade:

(a) It must be established by war ships, though it may be reinforced by other means such as by aircrafts etc.;
(b) Only the enemy coast or a part of it or the enemy ports are to be blockaded;
(c) It may prevent ingress or egress or both;
(d) It must be applied impartially to ships and aircrafts of all nations;
(e) It is being an act of war, belligerent establishing blockade may deny freedom of passage to the ships and aircrafts of other nations.

The Declaration of Paris, 1856, laid down that blockade, to be binding, should be effective and in order to be effective, the belligerent establishing the blockade must maintain such a force which is "sufficient really to prevent access to the enemy coast." Later, Lord Chief Justice Cockburn in Geipel V. Smith case 1872, said "In the eye of law, a blockade is effective if the enemy's ships are in such numbers and positions as to render running the blockade a matter of danger, although some vessels may succeed in getting through."

Establishment of blockade should be notified to all states as any ship that enters or leaves the blockaded area without the permission of blockading belligerent, commits a violation of blockade and such ships can be captured and their fate decided by the Prize Courts.

The Declaration of London, 1909, laid down that the blockade must not extend beyond the ports and coast line belonging to enemy and access to the neutral ports and coasts must not be prevented by the blockading forces. This type of blockade is known as 'closed blockade'.

But during the last two World Was it wars found that it is no more feasible and possible to follow the traditional rules of closed blockade because of the changing nature of the war, according to which the main aim of one belligerent is to cut off the commerce of the other belligerent in order to cause economic difficulties for him. For this purpose during the First World War, Great Britain enforced 'Long Distance' blockade against Germany in 1915, thousand miles away from the German coast, as a reprisal for the German decision to attack the British and Allied merchant ships in the waters around Great Britain. Further, due to increased range of the artillery guns, laying of mines, attack by submarines, use of torpedo boats and attack from aircrafts, it was impossible to sustain the 'closed blockade'.

The long distance blockade was objected by several states

on the ground that it also blocked the approaches to ports and coast lines of the neutral states and that in many respects it was ineffective. The British Government, however, justified the long distance blockade of Germany on the ground that due to the changed conditions of war, modern blockade could only be effective by covering the sea-borne commerce with the enemy passing through the neutral ports.

The long distance blockade was again enforced in 1939 during the Second World War by England, France, and other countries on the ground that total economic warfare against the enemy was necessary in order to weaken it and destroy its war-making capacity. Thus Medlicott has rightly observed that blockade close to the enemy's coast has "little relevance to a war in which modern artillery, mines, and submarines made such action impossible, and in which the enemy was so placed geographically that he could use adjacent neutral ports as a channel of supplies."

Requirements of a Real and Binding Blockade

The blockade in order to be real and binding must have the following characteristics:

1. A valid blockade must be established properly with the authority of a belligerent government or by its specially authorised naval commanders.
2. As per the Declaration of Paris, 1856 and Declaration of London, 1909, blockade in order to be binding, must be effective. This characteristic was emphasised in the Franciska Case and by Lord Chief Justice Cockburn in Geipel V. Smith Case. The blockade to be effective must be maintained by sufficient force making the ingress or egress of a ship dangerous.
3. As per Declaration of London, the blockade must be properly declared and notified to the neutral ships by the belligerent government or its authorised naval commander. The notification to the neutral states

must contain the date of beginning of blockade, the geographical limit of the coast line under the blockade, and the period during which the neutral ships must come out of the waters of the blockaded area.

4. The blockading force must enforce the blockade impartially against all ships and any relaxation in this impartiality will make the blockade invalid. This principle was established in the Franciska Case in which the British blockade of the port of Riga in Russia was declared as invalid by the Privy Council because they allowed belligerent merchant ships to the exclusion of neutral ships.
5. The blockade must be continuous and if the blockading force is driven out by the superior force of the enemy, the blockade is treated as defective and invalid from the beginning. But temporary withdrawal of blockading force due to fog or bad weather will not be treated as discontinuation.
6. The area of blockade cannot be extended beyond the area which was notified by the forces of blockading state.
7. The blockade being meant for the ports and coast line of the enemy, the neutral states should not suffer any inconvenience and the access to their ports should not be prevented by the blockading forces.

Violation of Blockade

In the case of Betsey, Sir William Scott said, "To constitute a violation of blockade three things must be proved: Firstly, the existence of actual blockade; secondly, the knowledge of the party supposed to have offended; and thirdly, some act of violation either by going in or coming out with cargo laden after commencement of blockade." But practices vary greatly as to what constitutes a violation of blockade. While the Anglo-American practice follow the principle of pressumption and it is sufficient to establish presumptively that those in charge of the neutral ship knew that a blockade has been established, the French practice show that the continuation of blockade should not be pressumed on the part of the neutral ships unless the notification of the blockade was issued to their governments and sufficient time has lapsed since the notification so that the neutral states are aware of the existence of the blockade. A neutral ship when approached a blockaded area, its commander is entitled to get warning from the commander of the blockading force and it is only for subsequent attempts to enter the blockaded area that a neutral ship is liable for capture.

The mere intention to violate the blockade is not sufficient. But when this intention is translated into action such as the attempt to enter into a blockaded port, the ship can be punished. After the capture of a ship which violated the blockade, it is sent to a port of the belligerent for determination of the status of the ship or its cargo, and if found guilty, either the ship or the cargo or both can be confiscated only if it carried contraband of war or ship's owner knew of blockade at the time when cargo was loaded on the ship.

Termination of Blockade

The blockade is terminated when:

(a) the war is terminated;

(b) it is withdrawn by the government establishing it;

(c) it is ineffective;

(d) the blockading force is defeated or driven out by the hostile forces;

(e) the port or the coast line that was blockaded, is occupied by the victorious forces.

29

CONTRABAND

Contrabands of war are those goods which are forbidden by either belligerent to be carried to an enemy destination in order to enable him to conduct the war more vigorously. According to Oppenheim, "Contraband of war is the designation of such goods as are forbidden by either belligerent to be carried to the enemy on the ground that they enable him to carry out the war with great vigour." According to Starke, "Contraband is the designation for such goods as the belligerents consider objectionable because they may assist the enemy in the conduct of war."

The purpose of both blockade and the contraband control is same, namely, to cripple the war-making capacity of the enemy. But while the main objective of blockade is the capture of the ships, it is the cargoes which are involved in the contraband. The Declaration of Paris, 1856, laid down that belligerents may seize enemy contraband which are carried on an enemy ship to an enemy destination. In the era of total war, contraband control is an important weapon in the economic warfare.

Classification of Contrabands: There is no unanimity among the states as to what cargoes are to be considered as contraband. In different times different goods were considered as contraband. Grotius divided all goods into (1) goods useful for war only such as gun powder, arms etc., (2) goods useful for warlike purposes such as soap, clocks etc., (3) goods useful for both war and peace such as ships, money etc. In the Peterhoff case, the U.S. Supreme Court said that though a strictly accurate and satisfactory classification is perhaps impracticable, yet all goods can be divided into three classes, namely, (a) articles which are primarily or ordinarily used for military purposes during the war, (b) articles which are used both for war and peace purposes, and (c) articles which are exclusively used only for peaceful purposes. The Court further said, "Merchandise of the first class, destined to a belligerent country or places occupied by the army or navy of a belligerent, is always contraband; merchandise of the second class is contraband only when actually destined to the military or naval use of belligerent; while the merchandise of the third class is not contraband at all. . . ." The unratified Declaration of London, 1909, divided all goods into absolute, conditional or relative, and free articles. The absolute contraband includes such articles as arms, military clothing, camp equipments etc., which can be used directly in the war. The conditional or relative contraband are those articles which are useful both for war and peace such as food, fuel etc. The list of free articles includes glass, paint, colours, fancy goods, and soap etc. While the absolute contraband can be seized, the conditional or relative contrabands can be seized if destined for enemy armed forces or destined to a port under enemy control. Today it is doubtful if this distinction has any practical value. The articles included in the free list must never be declared as contraband as they can never be used for war.

So far states have not reached general agreement regarding classification of articles into above three categories. The attempt made by the London Declaration could not come into force as it was not ratified. During the last two World Wars, the belligerents declared such goods as absolute or conditional contrabands which were considered as non-contrabands in the earlier period. Starke has pointed out, "In view of the enormous range of equipment required for modern war, of the much more advanced use of scientific weapons and instruments, and of the possible production of ersatz or substitute war materials, it could scarcely be predicted of any article or substance that it did not have a war-like use." Further in the era of total war, in which the civilians are also active participants, the division of articles into absolute, conditional, and free articles is loosing importance, because all of them can be treated as contraband.

Earlier, though states distinguished between absolute, conditional, and free articles, during the Second World War, the practice was to list broad categories of goods which in actual practice covered almost unlimited number of articles as contrabands. Today the distinction between the goods intended for enemy armed forces and enemy civilians have become irrelevant and only consideration to be declared as contraband is that the destination of goods must be the enemy state or enemy occupied territory.

The Laws Relating to Seizure of Contraband

The laws of contraband applies only to transportation and not the sale or bargain of articles. The neutral traders in their own territory are free to sell the arms and other contrabands to the agents of belligerents. But the right to seize the articles of one belligerent is acquired only after their transportation begins from the neutral territory. To seize the articles as contraband, these articles must have a belligerent destination. These articles are liable to be seized the moment the ship leaves the neutral waters, even if they are loaded on a neutral ship.

However, even if the contraband is lawfully seized, in the following cases compensation has to be paid:

(1) When the master of the ship is unaware of the out break of war or ignorant of the list of the articles declared as contraband.

(2) When the master of the ship, though aware of the outbreak of war, did not get an opportunity to unload the contraband before its seizure.

(3) When under the stress of 'military necessity', the medicines, hospital equipments etc., are seized.

But if the ship and the cargo carry 'navicert' i.e., the certificate issued by the diplomatic or consular or other representative of a belligerent state in a neutral country, stating that the cargo carried by the ship is not contraband, or the voyage of the ship is innocent, such a ship or the cargo is not liable to be seized as contraband by that belligerent state. But the neutral must acquire 'ship warrants' from the belligerents by undertaking not to engage in contraband trading in order to get 'navicerts' or naval certificates.

Contraband is liable to seizure and under certain circumstances, the ship carrying the contraband cargo is liable for seizure. According to the unratified Declaration of London, if more than half of the cargo carried is contraband, not only the cargo, but also the ship is liable to be confiscated; and if it is less than half, the contraband cargo may be confiscated and the ship may be released. By law, the seizure of the contraband and the ship are allowed only in the open sea or in the territorial waters of a belligerent; and such seizures in the neutral waters would be a violation of laws of neutrality.

According to the British and continental practices, the contraband cargoes and the ship carrying them seized by a belligerent are sent for adjudication by the Prize Courts established by that state to determine whether the seizures were lawful or not. Though the Prize Courts are not international courts but municipal courts, yet they apply international law to determine the status of the seized contraband cargoes and ships and as per their decisions the cargoes and ships are to be confiscated or sold or released.

Doctrine of Continuous Voyage

When the destination of the goods is clearly to an enemy state, the seizure of the contraband is simple. But to avoid their seizure and interception in the sea, the enemy or the blockaded states may try to get their supplies of goods in indirect ways such as purchase of contrabands through a neutral citizen only to be resold to the enemy. In such case the doctrine of the continuous voyage or continuous transportation is applicable. Explaining the doctrine in the Maria Case, Lord Stowell said, "The continuous voyage consists in treating an adventure which involves the carriage of goods in the first instance to a neutral port and thence to some ulterior and hostile destination as being for certain purposes, only one transportation, with all the consequences which would attach if the neutral port had not interposed."

In other words, the neutral ships which carry the contraband goods with the intention of supplying them to the enemy, break the entire journey into two parts. In the first part, they go to a neutral port from where these contrabands can again be transported to the enemy state either by land or by sea. So if there is proof of intention of the owner or master of the ship or if the documents of the ship indicates continuous journey, the ship along with the cargo can be seized by a belligerent in the first part of the voyage itself.

During the American Civil War, in Peterhoff case, the Supreme Court applied the doctrine to the transportation on land to the enemy destinations also. Though the unratified Declaration of London, 1909, laid down that the doctrine was to apply only to the absolute contrabands and not to the conditional contrabands, during the two World Wars the principle was ignored and the doctrine was applied to large number of cases of conditional contrabands also.

30

INTERNATIONAL ORGANISATION

(a) Historical Background

The concept of international organisation through a body of permanent institutions with the cooperation of states has come into existence only in the second half of 19th century. The evolution of international organisation may be divided into three phases. The first phase was started with Congress of Vienna (1815) and continued upto the outbreak of First World War in which periodic diplomatic conferences were held but no permanent international institutions could be developed. The second phase covers the inter-war period during which permanent international organisations like League of Nations, International Labour Organisation and Permanent Court of Justice were established. The third phase began with the establishment of UNO. Each of these phases has made its unique contribution in the evolution of international organisations.

The League of Nations was established by the Treaty of Versailles with the object to promote international cooperation and to achieve international peace and security through a system of collective security based on pacific settlement of disputes, limitations on the right to war, sanction against the state resorting to war, and collective guarantee of independence of member states. All the decisions of the League were to be taken on the principle of unanimity. Its principal organs were the Assembly, the Council, and the Secretariat assisted by the Economic and Financial Organisation, the Organisation for Communications and Transits, the Health Organisation, the Permanent Mandates Commission, the Permanent Court of International Justice.

Though the League failed in its main objective and could not prevent the outbreak of the Second World War, still its experience provided direct .precedence for the United Nations system.

The outbreak of Second World War sounded the death knell of the League of Nations, yet the international community still felt the need of international organisation of states with the primary function of maintenance of peace. To give shape to this universal desire, the Allied Powers took initiative even during period of war.

The idea of creating an effective international organisation was first mooted out in the Atlantic Charter, 1941, signed by Mr. Roosevelt, President of USA and Mr. Churchill, Prime Minister of UK, which enunciated certain principles such as the right to self-determination, equal access of all nations to raw materials, freedom of seas, disarmament etc. On January 1, 1942, twenty six states including USA proclaimed United Nations Declaration, incorporating the ideas envisaged in the Atlantic Charter. On 30th October, 1943 the foreign ministers of USA, UK, USSR and China adopted Moscow Declaration in which they accepted the necessity of an international organisational based on the principle of sovereign equality of all peace loving states with the objective of maintaining international peace and security. The representatives of these four states met at Dumarton Oaks on October 7, 1944, and prepared the proposal for the structure of United Nations with a body called Security Council in which the Big Five states-USA, USSR, UK, France and China were to be permanent members. In 1945, Roosevelt, Stalin and Churchill met in Yalta to consider the Dumbarkton Oak proposals. In this conference it was decided to convene an international conference of all peace loving states for the purpose of creating the new international organisation. A committee of Jurists representing 44 states also met at Washington and drafted statute for the proposed International Court of Justice, which was to be an intergral part of the future UNO. Finally, 60 states in a conference met from 25th April to 26th June, 1945, at Sanfransisco to discuss the Dumbarkton Oak proposal as well as the draft statute of International Court of Justice. After thorough discussion, the present UN Charter, along with the Statute of International Court of Justice was signed and after being ratified, the UNO came into existence on October 24, 1945. By April, 1946, the General Assembly, the International Court of Justice, the Security Council and the Secretariat started functioning.

The period of 1944-46 also witnessed increased international cooperation in different specialised fields. Not only the existing organisations like I.L.O, I.T.U and UPU underwent constitutional changes to meet the needs of post war world, but also a number of new organisations like, International Monetary Fund, the International Bank for Reconstruction and Development, International Civil Aviation Organisation, UNESCO, F.A.O. and WHO were created. The most remarkable features of post-war development of international organisations are universalism, regionalism and functionalism.

(b) The United Nations

Aims and Objectives: The UNO is governed by its Charter which is the result of a multilateral treaty signed by its members. It not only deals with the constitution of the UN, but also describes rights and duties of member states.

The preamble lays down the following aims of UNO:

(1) To save the future generations from the scourge of war;

(2) To ensure rights and dignity to all human beings;
(3) To ensure equal rights to men and women and to all states large or small;
(4) To ensure justice, performance of treaty obligations and respect of international law;
(5) To promote social progress, better standard of life and good neighbourliness;
(6) To maintain international peace and security;
(7) To ensure that force is not used except in common interest;
(8) To ensure social and economic development of all people.

Accordingly, Art. 1 of the Charter clearly enunciates the objectives by stating that UN is to maintain international peace and security, develop friendly relations among nations, foster international cooperation in social, economic, cultural and humanitarian matters, develop respect for human rights and freedom; take necessary steps to achieve these objectives.

Article 2 lays down the following six basic principles to be observed both by the UN and it's members:

(1) Basis of UN shall be sovereign equality of its members;
(2) UN shall not interfere in the matters which are within the domestic jurisdiction of member states;
(3) The member states should fulfill their obligations under the charter;
(4) The member states should settle their disputes by peaceful means;
(5) Member states should not threaten or use force against territorial integrity or political independence of another member state;
(6) All member states are to assist the UN when it takes preventive or enforcement actions against a state and

(7) Member states are to deny assistance to a state against whom such actions are being taken.

Membership: The UN is an inter-governmental organisation in which sovereign independent states can only be members. According to Art. 4, membership of UN is open to "all peace loving states which accept the obligations contained in the Charter, and in the judgement of the organisation, are able and willing to carry out these obligations." There are two types of members, namely, those 51 states who participated in Sanfransisco Conference and signed and ratified the charter are described as "original" members, and those who were admitted later according to Art. 4. However; there is no discrimination in rights and obligations between original and admitted members.

According to the Advisory Opinion of the International Court of Justice, Art. 4 lays down the following five conditions, that a member should:

(a) be a state,
(b) be peace-loving,
(c) accept the obligation of the Charter,
(d) be able to carry out these obligations, and
(e) be willing to do so.

As per Art. 4 a state can be admitted when it is first recommended by a majority of nine members, including all Five Permanent Members of Security Council and later approved by the General Assembly by 2/3 majority of votes. The International Court of Justice in its Advisory Opinion said that in the absence of a favourable recommendation by the Security Council, the General Assembly has no power to admit a new member on its own decision. On the other hand, the General Assembly has the power to reject the recommendation of the Security Counfil for membership of a state. In other words, a state to be admitted in UN must require the approval of Security Council including all its permanent members and 2/3 majority of General Assembly. However, the requirement of consent of all Five Permanent Members for admission of a new state, defeated the principle of universality during the cold War period because of the use of Veto by Great Powers in the admission of some states. But the situation has considerably changed in recent times and now there are 179 members in the UNO.

According to Art. 5 and 6, the General Assembly can take a decision to suspend or expel a member on the recommendation of the Security Council. Though the grounds of suspension are mentioned in Art. 5, the grounds of expulsion are not enumerated in Art. 6, thereby allowing considerable discretion to the General Assembly and Security Council in the matter.

As regards the withdrawal of membership, though there is no provision for it in the Charter, the Sanfransisco Conference adopted a declaration which stated that a member can withdraw "because of exceptional circumstances". But the term "exceptional circumstance" is imprecise and the declaration has not provided for a competent body to decide whether a particular circumstance is "exceptional" or not.

(c) The Organs of UNO

The Charter has accepted the principle of decentralisation of powers and functions and on the basis of this principle distributed them among six principal organs, namely, the General Assembly, the Security Council, the Trusteeship Council, the Secretariat, and the International Court of Justice. In addition, the Charter authorises the General Assembly and Security Council to establish subsidiary organs which are deemed necessary for the performance of their functions.

(i) **The General Assembly:** The General Assembly is the only principal organ of the UNO consisting of all members. At present there are 179 members. Each member state is having one vote though it can send upto five delegates.

The General Assembly regularly meets once a year. But special sessions can also be convened by the Secretary General either on the request of Security Council or on the request of majority of member states or at the request of one member concurred by a majority of member states.

The General Assembly elects a President, 21 Vice Presidents, Chairman of its Seven Main Committees at the beginning of each annual session.

It is mainly a deliberative body with powers of discussion, investigation, review, supervision, recommendation and criticism about the work of the UN as a whole including its other organs and specialised agencies. Though primarily a recommending body without having binding effect, the General Assembly can also take final decision over certain matters like, budget and admission or suspension or explusion of a member etc. While decisions on certain "important" matters like election of non-permanent members of Security Council or matters enumerated in Art. 18 are taken by 2/3 majority, all other decisions are taken by simple majority.

The function of the General Assembly are laid down in Art. 10 to 17 of the Charter.

The General Assembly has the power:

(a) to discuss and recommend matters relating to international peace and security;
(b) to direct and supervise the international social and economic cooperation;
(c) to supervise the international trusteeship system;
(d) to consider the reports and informations on non-self governing territories;
(e) to approve the budget and to exercise exclusive control over finances of UNO;

(f) to admit, expel, and suspend member states;

(g) to adopt amendments to the Charter;

(h) to elect 10 non-permanent members of Security Council, 54 members of Economic and Social Council, 15 judges of International Court of Justice etc.

(i) to receive reports on the working of the UN and consider them;

(j) to elect Secretary General of UN;

(k) to adopt international conventions.

In addition to the above powers the Charter grants powers to General Assembly:

(i) to consider general principles of cooperation in the maintenance of peace and security, disarmament and arms regulation and make recommendations to the member states or the Security Council;

(ii) to discuss any specific question relating to maintenance of peace and security brought before it either by a member state or by Security Council or a non-member and make recommendation on it;

(iii) to recommend peaceful solutions to any situation which is likely to harm the general welfare or friendly relations among nations;

(iv) to call the attention of Security Council to any situation which is likely to endanger international peace and security;

But there is one restriction on these power of recommendation: While the General Assembly may discuss them, it cannot make any recommendation on them to the Security Council, if the matter is under active consideration of the Security Council. This limitation, however, did not prevent the General Assembly from taking a leading role in matters relating to international peace and security, such as in regard to Palestine, Korea, Suez, Congo, Kuwait and Middle East.

The General Assembly which has been given the power to encourage the progressive development of International Law and codification, made a positive contribution by helping in the conclusion of a number of conventions in which the International Laws have been codified.

The study of powers and functions of the General Assembly would give an impression that it is equivalent to a Parliament of Nations with powers of deliberation, recommendation and supervision only, having no effective powers. The primary responsibility of maintaining peace and security has been entrusted to the Security Council and the General Assembly can recommend measures only when such matters are referred to it by the Security Council. During the initial years the five permanent powers who were Allies during the War, worked unitedly in the Security Council. But soon the permanent members were divided into two groups of Power Blocks headed by the USA and USSR. The Cold War that began between the Two Great Powers had its effect on Security Council.

The frequent use of "veto" by the Big Powers in Security Council specially upto 1960, brought the primary task of maintenance of international peace and security to standstill. This difficulty forced the General Assembly to expand the scope of its power by making general as well as specific recommendations on issues of peace and security, though such recommendations could not compel compliance. There was, of course, no unanimity of opinion between the two Power blocs regarding the increased scope of powers of General Assembly. The Soviet Union insisted on the strict adherence of the provisions of Charter and argued that the division of powers between the Security Council and General Assembly and the power of Security Council regarding the enforcement of actions in the matter of maintenance of peace and security be strictly followed. On the other hand, the Western Powers led by the U.S.A., and supported by a large number of states from Asia, Africa, and Latin America, demanded on active role of General Assembly in the maintenance of peace and security, by arguing that the division of powers between the two organs is not absolute. They also pointed out that the activities of the General Assembly showed a high degree of maturity in that it never made any recommendation when majority of Security Council was opposed to any involvement of the UN. In pursuance of this opinion the General Assembly passed a resolution called "Uniting for Peace" on 3rd November, 1950 in which its powers are interpreted as follows:

"If the Security Council, because of the lack of unanimity of the permanent members, fails to excercise its primary responsibility for the maintenance of international peace and security in any case where there appears to be a threat to peace, breach of peace or act of aggression, the General Assembly shall consider the matter immediately with a view to making appropriate recommendations to Members for Collective measures, including in case of a breach of peace or act of aggression the use of armed force when necessary, to maintain or restore international peace and security. If not in the session at the time, the General Assembly may meet in an emergency special session within 24 hours of the request thereof, such emergency special session shall be called if requested by the Security Council on the vote of any seven members, or by a majority of members of the United Nations."

The "Uniting for Peace" resolution is a landmark in the evolution of UNO which considerably changed the relationship between the General Assembly and Security Council in the field maintenance of peace and security. This resolution also enabled the General Assembly to step in when the Security Council is unable to take any action due to differences among the five permanent members.

The study of the practice of the General Assembly shows that it never went to the full length of its powers, including the Uniting for Peace resolution. Instead of recommending use of force, it recommended non-military measures such diplomatic measures and economic measures like embargo, sanctions etc. Even though during the Suez crisis in 1956, the General Assembly created United Nations Emergency Force (UNEF) as a subsidiary organ, composed of military forces supplied voluntarily by the member states, the UNEF did not and does not take any enforcement action against anybody as its main function is of a peace-keeping in nature.

Apart from dealing with the problems of international peace and security, the General Assembly also dealt successfully with certain political questions such as Apartheid in South Africa, Civil Wars in Greece, Cango and Palestine questions and in the erstwhile Yugoslavia. The General Assembly also took initiative in the codification of international law as a result of which important conventions on Genocide, Diplomatic Relations, Consular Relations, Law of Treaties and Law of Sea etc. could be concluded.

Security Council

One of the primary purpose of the UN being maintenance of international peace and security and settlement of dispute by peaceful means, the Charter created Security Council to achieve the purpose. The Security Council by peaceful means and in accordance with the principles of justice and international law tries to adjust or settles international "disputes" or "situations" which might lead to breach of peace. The practices of UN however, show that main attention is given by Security Council to the maintenance or restoration of peace than to the settlement of disputes.

The Security Council is a continuously functioning body, originally consisted of eleven members, but since 1965 of fifteen members. Of these fifteen members China, France, Soviet Union, U.K. and USA are permanent members, while ten non-permanent members are elected by the General Assembly for a period of two years keeping in view the contribution of member states to maintenance of peace and security. In order to have equitable geographical distribution, 5 members from Afro-Asian nations, one from Eastern Europe, Two from Latin America and two from Western countries are elected. In addition, any member state or non member state who is a party to a dispute or who is invited by the Security Council may also participate in the discussion without right to vote. The presidency of the Security Council is rotated among member states according to their alphabetical order for a term of two months. The Security Council has three standing Committees, namely, the Committee of Experts, the Committee on the Admission of New Members, and the Committee on Council Meetings Away from Headquarters.

Voting Procedure: Each member of the Council has one vote. Decisions on procedural matters such as time and place of Council meetings, adoption of rules of procedure, creation of subsidiary organs, etc., are to be made by affirmative vote of nine members and decisions on all other substantive matters are to be made by an affirmative vote of nine members, including the concurring votes of five permanent members. Thus unanimity of Big Powers is a prerequisite of all decisions on substantive matters. But if a permanent member casts a negative vote on a substantive matter, the decision is blocked or "vetoed". The five permanent powers enjoy the power of veto only over substantive, but not over procedural matters.

Further, the decision whether a particular matter falls within the category of procedural matter or not, also requires nine affirmative votes including the concurring vote of five permanent members, and in this case, any one of them can also cast a negative vote to veto it. Thus every permanent member can veto on this matter twice, first, by casting a negative vote against calling the matter as "procedural" after which the matter as becomes "substantive", and second, by casting another negative vote against this "substantive" matter. This double negative voting has come to be known as "Double

Veto". According to Andrew Martin and John B. S. Edwards "In borderline cases, the preliminary question, whether a matter is procedural in itself is subject to veto. In fact, that rules turn the veto into what has been rightly called "double veto": first a negative vote is cast to prevent the Council from treating question as procedural, and a vote is cast for the second time to defeat the substance of the motion." The Charter prescribes only one limitation on veto power in chapter VI and Art. 52 which states that when a permanent or non-permanent member is a party to a dispute which is referred to regional settlement, it must abstain from voting. But a customery practice has also developed according to which when a permanent member abstain from voting, it is not considered as casting a negative vote or veto and if the required number of affirmative vote is cast, the decision is deemed to have taken by the Security Council not withstanding the abstention. The legality of the practice was upheld by the International Court of Justice in the Advisory Opinion on the Continued Presence of South Africa in South West Africa 1971.

The theory behind the right of veto is that since Great Powers have undertaken the responsibility of maintaining peace and security, no permanent member should be compelled to follow a course of action which it disagrees.

At the Sanfransisco Conference, it was hoped that the Great Powers would not use their veto power "wilfully" to obstruct the operation of the Security Council. But unfortunately that hope was belied and the use of veto had paralysed the operation of the Security Council. Kelsen has pointed out that the veto power of Five permanent members has placed them as "Privileged Powers" trying to establish their legal hegemony which is the halmark of an autoratic regime. Further he points out that it contradicts the basic principle of the Sovereign equality of states enunciated in the Charter.

But Starke has pointed out "even if there were no veto it is probable that some alternative methods of obstructing the Security Council's work would have been resorted to, leading to equal abuses and absurdities, or that, as occurred in the League of Nations certain powers might have quitted the organisation." W.M. Reisman justifying the right of veto has said "in a curious way it (the veto) may have preserve the United Nations by allowing or forcing it to yield to reality." The "Uniting for Peace" resolution of 1950 according to which the General Assembly can take up an issue which is likely to threaten the international peace and security and which the Security Council has failed to resolve as a result of a veto, has helped the United Nation to neutralise some effects of veto.

Powers and Functions

Art. 25 of the Charter makes the Security Council the principal organ for the maintenance of international peace and security. It also exercises several other powers concerning the structure and functioning of the UN and shares some powers with the General Assembly. To take prompt and effective action, it acts as the executive body of the UN with Great Powers as it core members. All members of the UN agree to abide by and carry out its decisions. The Security Council enjoys not only the express powers granted to it by the Charter, but also implied powers as are deemed necessary and requisite for fulfillment of its functions.

The powers of Security Council are summarised by Starke as follows:

(a) Pacific settlement of International Disputes;
(b) Preventive and enforcement action to maintain peace and security;
(c) Regional agencies and regional agreements;
(d) Control and supervision of trust territories classified as "strategic areas";

(e) The admission, suspension or expulsion of members;
(f) Election of 15 judges of International Court of Justice in conjunction with General Assembly;
(g) Amendment to Charter.

(a) In disputes which are "likely to endanger the maintenance of international peace and security", the Security Council according to Art. 33 may call on the parties to settle the dispute by negotiation, inquiry, mediation, by regional agencies or regional agreements or other peaceful means. If they fail to reach an agreement, they are obliged under Art. 37 to refer the dispute to Security Council which shall then decide either to recommend "appropriate procedures or methods" of settlement or actual terms of settlement.

The Security Council can also investigate into any "dispute" or "situation" which is likely to endanger peace and security, either on its own or when it is bought to its notice by member states or General Assembly or Secretary General or a non-member state which is a party to the dispute. Though the Charter differentiates between a "dispute" and "situation", it has not defined them. However, while a "dispute" exists when a state makes a definite allegation of an alleged or threatened breach of law against another state which deny it, a "situation" may arise due to combination of certain facts leading to a controversy which does not possess a marked degree of specificity either in the parties involved or their claims. A "dispute" may arise from a "situation" and which inturn might give rise to a new "situation", or a "situation" without giving rise to a "dispute" may create a threat to international peace and security. The Security Council has the power to investigate any "dispute" or "situation" whose continuance might lead to friction or dispute or danger to international peace and security. The Security Counfil may call on parties to settle their disputes by peaceful means prescribed in Art. 33 or recommend such settlement as it considers appropriate. Usually, all legal disputes are referred to International Court of Justice.

(b) But if the dispute or situation is of serious nature resulting "threat to peace, breach of the peace, or act of aggression", the Security Council according to Art. 39, has the power to recommend such measures as are necessary to maintain or restore peace and its decisions are binding on all members of UN. It is to be noted that while recommending measures for settlement of disputes or situations under Art. 37 or 39, the Security Council must excercise its powers "by peaceful means, and in conformity with international law", no such restriction exists on its enforcement powers relating to suppression of threats to peace, breaches of peace, and acts of aggression.

The Security Council can decide any of the enforcement actions: either it can decide for non-military action calling upon member states to cut off fully or partially all means of communication, economic, and diplomatic relations; or military action by air, sea and land forces which may also involve blockade. The Security Council may also decide whether such action shall be taken by all or some member states only, such decisions are binding on the member states, but if a state faces any special economic problem arising out of the decided action, it has a right to consult the Security Council.

The Charter in chapter VII also provides for a Military Staff Committee composed of the Chief of Staffs of five permanent members, to advise and assist the Security Council on the military aspects of enforcement action. Further, Art. 43 provides that Security Council can enter into agreement with member states regarding supply of armed forces and other assistance for enforcement action. However, this provision has not till today implemented, as a result of which the Security Council is unable to act in a decisive manner. So Starke has remarked "the Security Council has yet to excercise the full range of its powers in relation to preventive or enforcement action." But it has not prevented the Security Council in authorising enforcement measures as in case of Korean conflict or in the Congo situation, in order to maintain or restore international peace and security.

(c) The Charter under Arts. 52, 53 and 54 permits the formation of "regional arrangements" and creation of appropriate "agencies" in order to strengthen the system of collective security. These regional agencies encourage pacific settlement of local disputes and also to use appropriate enforcement actions. Since the sole responsibility for peace and security is vested on the Security Council, all enforcement actions taken or to be taken by such agencies or arrangements must have prior approval of Security Council.

(d) The trusteeship system created by UNO is now of historical importance only. The trust territories which are described as "strategic" are placed under Security Council. The Security Council has not only to approve the agreement with the trustee state but also to supervise its administration if necessary, with the assistance of trusteeship Council relating to political, economic, social and educational matters in the strategic areas. Today there is only the Pacific Islands which has the status of strategic trust territory.

(e) The Security Council has to make recommendations to the General Assembly in the matter of membership of a state in the UN. It has also to recommend to General Assembly in the matters of suspension or expulsion of a member state.

(f) The Security Council takes part along with the General Assembly in the appointment of the Secretary General of UN and in the election of the Judges of International Court of Justice.

(g) In the amendment of Charter as per Art. 108 approval of five permanent members is essential along with 2/3 members of General Assembly.

(3) Economic and Social Council (ECOSOC)

The preamble of the Charter envisages equality, dignity, and rights of human beings, promotion of social progress, and "better standards of life in larger freedom". The Charter in order to achieve the economic and social advancement of all people, created the Economic and Social Council as a permanent organ of UN with a view to secure international prosperity, stability and justice.

The Council originally had 18 members but now composed of 54 members elected by members of General Assembly for a term of three years and retiring members are eligible for re-election. The representatives of the member states and the "specialised agencies" can participate in the discussion without right to vote. The decisions of the Council are taken by majority of votes.

The functions of ECOSOC are:

(a) to discuss international economic and social issues and formulate recommendations to member states and to other organs and agencies of UN;
(b) to initiate surveys, studies, and reports on international social, economic, educational, cultural, health and other matters and to make recommendations to General Assembly, specialised agencies and member states;
(c) to recommend for promotion of respect of human rights and freedom;
(d) to prepare draft conventions on matters within its scope of powers to General Assembly;
(e) to convene international conferences to discuss social and economic issues;
(f) to coordinate the activities of the "specialised agencies" of the UN;
(g) to collect reports from the specialised agencies and

submit them to the General Assembly with its observations.

The Council has established four regional economic commissions concerned with special problems for Europe, Asia and Far East, Africa and Latin America. It has also played an important role in the organisation of programme of technical assistance to the underdeveloped nations.

The Council can also establish "functional commissions" to deal with particular subjects such as Human Rights, Transport and Communications, Narcotic Drugs, Population, and status of Women. Nothing prevents the Council to establish any number of adhoc or functional commissions to deal with especial subjects within its competance.

(4) The Trusteeship Council

The Trusteeship Council is of historical interest today because, of the eleven territories placed under the system, now only one territory continues under it. Today, only the Trust Territory of the Pacific Islands, which has the status of "strategic" trust territory continues under the system of which the USA is the trustee. By 1981, all trust territories except the strategic trust territory of Pacific Island had either attained independence or were united with a neighbouring state. The trusteeship Council has consistently maintained that the people of Pacific Islands have the right of self-determination. So the day is not far off when these islands will either merge together or merge with some other state or become independent states and with that the Trusteeship system will wound up.

(5) Secretariat

For smooth running of UN, for execution of its decision, and for administering its policies and programmes, the Charter created a Secretariat headed by a Secretary General assisted by such staff as the UN may require. The international Charter of the Secretariat is safeguarded by Art. 100 and 101. They are to take oath of loyalty to organisation, not to take instructions from their own states in performance of their duties.

The Secretary General who is the chief administrative officer of UN and its organs, is appointed for a term of five years by the General Assembly on the recommendation supported by nine affirmative votes including the concurring vote of five permanent members of the Security Council. He attends all meetings of not only General Assembly and Security Council, but also of Economic and Social Council and Trusteeship Council. He has to draw the attention of Security Council to matters which threaten the international peace and security. He has to submit annual report to the General Assembly on the working of the UN organisation as a whole. The Secretary General can summon special sessions of General Assembly on the request of Security Council or of a majority members of the UN. The Secretary General receives reports from the administering states of non-self governing territories and after their analysis by his secretariat, submit them to General Assembly for its consideration.

According to Art. 102 of the Charter, the Secretary General acts as the registering authority of all treaties and international agreements and it is his duty to publish them in the United Nations Treaty Series. The Secretary General has been assigned the control of various peace keeping forces created by the UN at different times.

The Secretary General and Assistant Secretary Generals enjoy full diplomatic immunities, while other officials of the Secretariat are "immune from legal process is respect of words spoken or written and all acts performed by them in their official capacity." Their salaries are exempted from taxation.

Since 1954, other organs of UN have entrusted him with diplomatic and operational responsibilities for maintenance or restoration of peace, such as in 1954, on request of General

Assembly the Secretary General helped in the release of U.S.A. airmen detained by China, in 1959, his Special Representative mediated in the dispute between Thailand and Cambodia, in 1964 he was entrusted with the task of maintaining peace and order and restoring normal condition in Cyprus etc.

The role of Secretary General depends upon the personality of the incumbant. An activist Secretary General like Dag Hammarskojld expanded the scope of his role by maintaining that "it is in keeping with the philosophy of the Charter that the Secretary General, also should be expected to act without any guidance from the Assembly or the Security Council should this appear to him necessary towards helping to fill any vacuum that may appear in the systems which the Charter and traditional diplomacy provide for safeguarding of peace and security."

But several Secretary General performed to function strictly within the ambits of the express provisions of the Charter.

International Court of Justice

The need for the establishment of a Permanent Court to solve international disputes was felt in the First Hague Conference. It was in the Second Hague Peace Conference, the United States proposed for the establishment of such a Court. Though the Conference prepared the draft, due to difference of opinion between the Great Powers and Smaller Powers regarding the procedure of appointment of judges, the draft could not be accepted.

The Paris Conference 1919, proposed that League Council should formulate proposals for the establishment of a Permanent Court of International Justice and submit them to members. So a Statute was prepared in which the judges of the Court were to be elected both by the League Council and Assembly, was acceptable to both Great or Smaller Powers. The draft was approved by both League Council and Assembly and the Permanent Court of International Justice (PCIJ) was established in 1921, which continued to function upto the outbreak of Second World War in 1940.

After the War, a Committee of Jurists at Washington prepared a draft Statute for the establishment of International Court of Justice (ICJ) which was accepted by the Sanfransisco Conference. It also accepted the suggestion that the International Court of Justice should be treated as a Principal organ of the UN and its Statute as an integral part of the UN Charter. So in 1946 the Permanent Court of International Justice was formally dissolved in the last session of the League Assembly and the new International Court of Justice started functioning on 18 April, 1946 with its headquarters at the Hague. The function of the International Court of Justice was conceived primarily to decide legal disputes between state parties when they agree to submit their dispute to it. The International Court of Justice was not given the power of judicial review over the actions taken by other international organs. Thus the absence of compulsory jurisdiction over states and lack of power of judicial review makes it a weaker Court than the municipal constitutional courts.

The Art. 92 of the UN Charter describes the International Court of Justice as its principal judicial organ. So all members of the UN are ipso facto parties to the Statute of International Court of Justice. The member states are under an obligation to comply with the decision of International Court of Justice in the cases to which they are parties.

Organisation: The Court consists of 15 judges who are elected; regardless of their nationality, from among persons of high moral character who possess the qualifications required for the appointment to the highest judicial office of their own states, or, who are juris consult of repute in international law. But no two judges shall be elected from the same state.

The list of persons to be elected as the judges is prepared by the national groups in the Permanent Court of Arbitration on the request of Secretary General of UN. No national group shall nominate more than four persons. The Secretary General then prepare the list of nominees in alphabetical order from which judges are to be elected by the General Assembly and Security Council, each voting independently. To be elected absolute majority is required in both General Assembly and Security Council, and these two organisations keep in mind that the judges elected are representatives of "main forms of civilisation" and "principal legal systems of the World". Under a sort of "gentlemen's agreement", the judges are elected on regional basis and as per present practice 3 from Africa, 3 from Asia, 2 from Latin America, 2 from Eastern Europe and 5 from Western Europe and other countries are elected. The casual vacancies due to death or resignation are also filled in the same manner.

One third, i.e. 5 judges are elected, once in every three years. Thus once elected a judge enjoys a tenure of 9 years and is also eligible for reelection. The seat of the Court is at the Hague, though it can also sit else where if it considers necessary. The quorum of the Court is nine judges. The judges elect a President and a Vice-president from among themselves, to preside over the Court for a period of three years. The salary and allowances of judges are determined by the General Assembly. Each judge of the Court receives an annual salary. While the President is paid a special annual allowance, the Vice-president is paid special allowance only for the days he acts as president. The judges enjoy diplomatic privileges and immunities.

The decisions regarding the disputes before the Court are taken by majority of votes of judges and in case there is a tie, the President of the Court exercises his casting vote. Though the judgement of the Court is "final and without appeal", yet a state party may appeal for revision of judgement under certain circumstances. The Court's decision has no binding force except between parties and in respect of that particular case only. Art. 38 (1) of the Statute directs the Court to apply international law to disputes derived from international conventions, international customs, general principles of law, and subject to Art. 59, judicial decisions and teachings of the most highly qualified publicists.

Jurisdiction: The access to the Court is open to states which are parties to the Statute and Charter, as well as to the non-members who are admitted to UN under Art. 92 (2) of the Charter. The states which are not parties to the Statute can have access to the Court if they fulfil the conditions laid down by the Security Council, i.e. the state must deposit a declaration with the Registrar of the Court accepting the jurisdiction of the Court, undertaking to comply with the decisions of the Court, and contributing towards expenses of the Court.

The Court enjoys two types of jurisdictions, namely (1) Contentious, and (2) Advisory.

1. Contentious Jurisdiction: In all contentious cases the Court can exercise its jurisdiction only with the Consent of the state-parties to the dispute. The state parties to disputes who voluntarily refer their contentious disputes to the Court convey their consent through notification in bilateral agreement known as 'compromise". But since the 1980s, the usual method of notifying their joint consent is through a 'Special Agreement', instead of a 'compromise'. A unilateral reference of a dispute to the Court by one state party without a prior special Agreement can also be made under the "Principle of Prorogatum", provided the other state party or parties convey their assent to voluntary submission to the jurisdiction of Court either after the case is referred or subsequently. However, if the consent of the other state party or parties is not forthcoming either after the case is referred or subsequently, the Court cannot excercise jurisdiction over such a case.

The Court also excercises compulsory or obligatory jurisdiction over following types of cases:

(1) (a) Where the state parties to a treaty have agreed that the Court shall have jurisdiction over the disputes arising under the treaty;

(b) Where a treaty which is in force has a provision also come under compulsory jurisdiction of the International Court of Justice.

(2) The Statute in Art. 3 (2), known as "Optional Clause" provides "the state parties to the present Statute may at any time declare that they recognise as compulsory ipso facto and without special agreement, in relation to any other state accepting the same obligation", the jurisdiction of the Court shall extend over the legal disputes: relating to (a) interpretation of a treaty (b) any question of international law (c) the existence of any fact which, if established, would constitute a breach of an international obligations; (d) the nature and extent of reparation to be made for the breach of an international obligation. Such a declaration under 'Optional Clause' by states may be made either unconditionally or on condition of reciprocity on the party of several or certain states, or for a specified time only. But the too many reservations which are "merely escape clauses or consciously designed loopholes" prompted Starke to say "such a system of 'optional ' compulsory jurisdiction verges on absurdity."

(3) The disputes regarding application or interpretation of trusteeship agreement between a trustee and another member of UN are to be compulsorily referred to the Court as per the provision of the trusteeship agreement.

(4) The statutes of certain Specialised Agencies of the UN contain provisions to refer their disputes with

other specialised agencies to the Court. Such disputes with agreement of the concerned Specialised Agencies must be referred to Court.

The Statute does not provide any method for enforcement of the decisions of the Court in the contentious cases, which is a major weakness of International Court of Justice. However, under Art. 94 of the Charter, each member of UN undertakes to comply with the decision of the Court in a case to which it is a party. If a state party to a dispute does not fulfil its obligations as per the decision of the Court, the other state party has a right to approach the Security Council which may decide how the decisions can be made effective.

Advisory Opinion: According to Art. 96 of the Charter the General Assembly and the Security Council may request the advisory opinion of the Court on any legal question. Other organs of the UN and the Specialised Agencies may also, if authorised by the General Assembly, request for advisory opinion on legal questions relating to their activities. The General Assembly has already authorised the Economic and Social Council, the Trusteeship Council and several Specialised Agencies to request the Court for advisory opinion. An advisory opinion of the Court does not have the binding force of a judgement as in contentious case. But states may, by treaty or agreement undertake in advance to be bound by advisory opinion on certain questions.

The approach of the Court to request for advisory opinions is explained in the Peace Treaty case (First Phase), 1950, in the following words:

"The consent of states, parties to a dispute, is the basis of Court's jurisdiction in contentious cases. The situation is different in regard to advisory proceedings where the request for an opinion relates to a legal question actually pending between states. The Court's reply is only of an advisory character: as such, it has no binding force. It follows that no state, whether a Member of UN or not, can prevent the giving of an advisory opinion which the UN considered to be desirable in order to obtain enlightenment as to the course of action it should take. The Court's opinion is given not to states, but to the organ which is entitled to request it; the reply of the Court, itself an 'organ of the UN', represents its participation in the activities of the organisation, and in principle, should not be refused".

Ordinarily the Court cannot refuse to render advisory opinion on a legal question referred to it. But the Court has the discretion not to excercise its advisory jurisdiction when:

(a) the main point of the legal question referred relates to a controversy between certain states, and any one of these states is not before the Court. In Eastern Carellia case the Permanent Court of International Justice declined to render advisory opinion, when Russia, one of the parties to the dispute, refused to take part.

(b) the question referred involves other than legal aspects, or is embarrassing.

Though the advisory opinion of the Court do not have the binding force, yet the agencies which sought such opinion have invariably treated the opinions with respect and as authoritative statements of law. Oppenheim has rightly said, "The advisory jurisdiction has infact proved to be much fertile and more important than was originally contemplated. The number of advisory opinions given by the Court almost equals that given by way of judgements".

The International Court of Justice, and its predecessor the Permanent Court of International Justice have provided solutions to more than sixty contentious cases which have been quite satisfactory to the parties. Over more than hundred contentious and advisory cases, the two courts have classified the law on many points and helped in the progressive development of the law. Though due to a very limited jurisdiction, the states had submitted very few cases, that too, less serious cases, yet in many cases the Court has contributed to lessening of tensions in the areas of dispute. Since the establishment of the UN, the Court has been called upon to tender advisory opinion on legal aspects of issues of great political consequences and it was expected that it would lead to the settlement of disputes. But this expectation from the Court is yet to be fulfilled.